CAPTAIN AMERICA

★ AMERICA ★

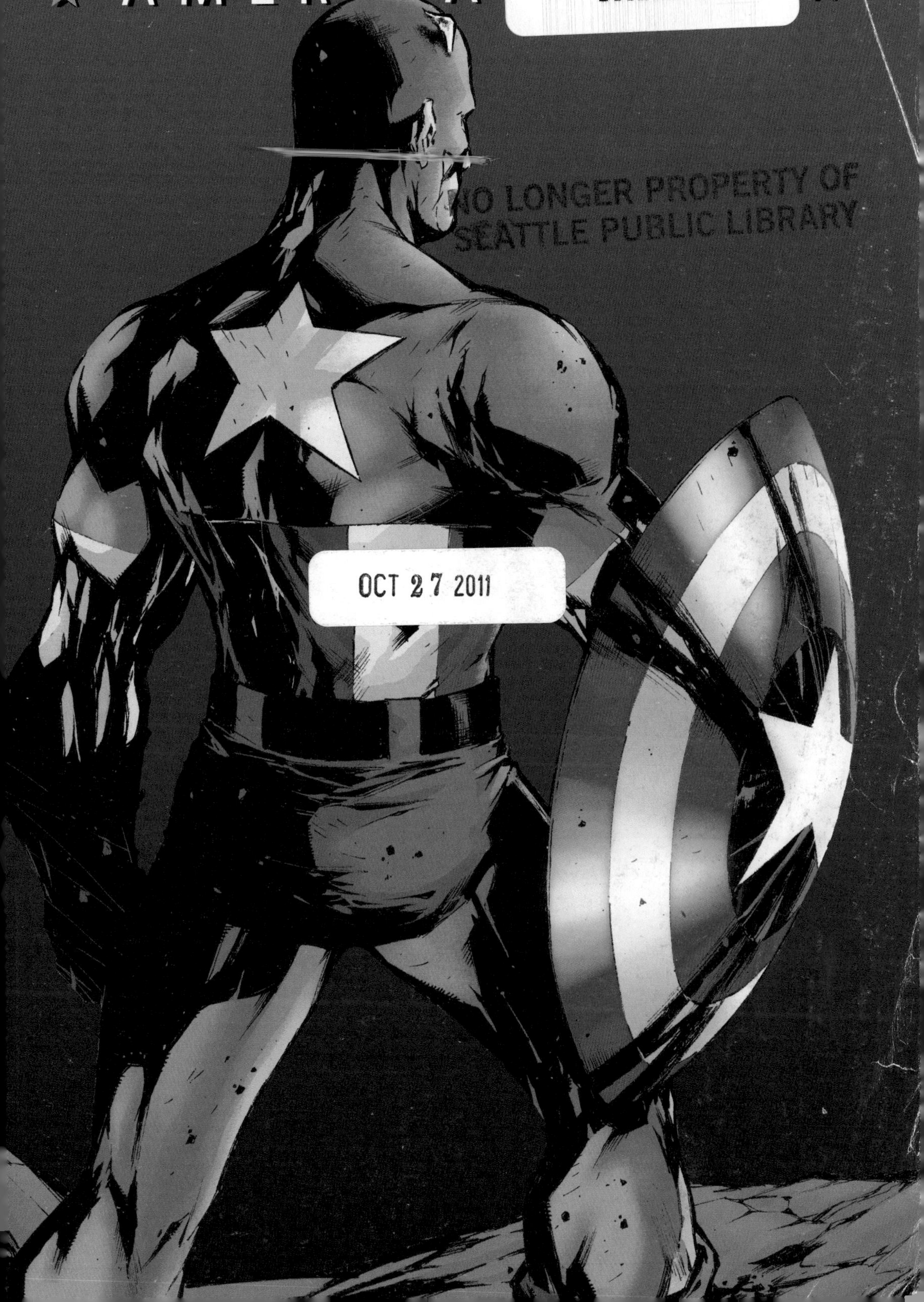

CAPTAIN AMERICA
★ AMERICA FIRST ★

"OPERATION: ZERO POINT"

WRITERS: DANIEL & CHARLES KNAUF

ARTIST: MITCH BREITWEISER

COLORIST: ELIZABETH BREITWEISER

LETTERER: ARTMONKEYS STUDIOS

"PRISONERS OF DUTY"

WRITERS: KYLE HIGGINS & ALEC SIEGEL

ARTIST: AGUSTIN PADILLA

COLOR ARTIST: GUILIA BRUSCO

LETTERER: JARED K. FLETCHER

"AMERICA FIRST!"

WRITER & ARTIST: HOWARD CHAYKIN

COLORIST: EDGAR DELGADO

LETTERER: DAVE LANPHEAR

EXECUTIVE EDITOR: TOM BREVOORT

EDITORS: JEANINE SCHAEFER, AUBREY SITTERSON & LAUREN SANKOVITCH

COVER ARTISTS: MITCH BREITWEISER & ELIZABETH BREITWEISER,
MIRCO PIERFEDERICI, AND HOWARD CHAYKIN & EDGAR DELGADO

CAPTAIN AMERICA CREATED BY JOE SIMON & JACK KIRBY

COLLECTION EDITOR: MARK D. BEAZLEY • **EDITORIAL ASSISTANTS:** JAMES EMMETT & JOE HOCHSTEIN
ASSISTANT EDITORS: NELSON RIBEIRO & ALEX STARBUCK • **EDITOR, SPECIAL PROJECTS:** JENNIFER GRÜNWALD
SENIOR EDITOR, SPECIAL PROJECTS: JEFF YOUNGQUIST
SENIOR VICE PRESIDENT OF SALES: DAVID GABRIEL
PRODUCTION: JERRY KALINOWSKI • **BOOK DESIGNER:** SPRING HOTELING

EDITOR IN CHIEF: JOE QUESADA • **PUBLISHER:** DAN BUCKLEY
EXECUTIVE PRODUCER: ALAN FINE

In the dark days of the early 1940s,

STEVE ROGERS,

a struggling young artist from the
LOWER EAST SIDE OF MANHATTAN,
found himself horrified by the war raging overseas.
Desperate to help, he was rejected by the

U.S. ARMY

as unfit for service when he tried to enlist.

Undeterred, convinced this was where he needed to be, he was
selected to participate in a covert military project called

OPERATION: REBIRTH.

There, he was chosen by scientist
ABRAHAM ERSKINE
as the first human test subject, and overnight was transformed into

AMERICA'S FIRST SUPER-SOLDIER.

Enhanced to the peak of human perfection with superior strength,
reflexes and speed, Steve Rogers now fights to protect the people and the
country he loves from the forces that would destroy them as

CAPTAIN AMERICA.

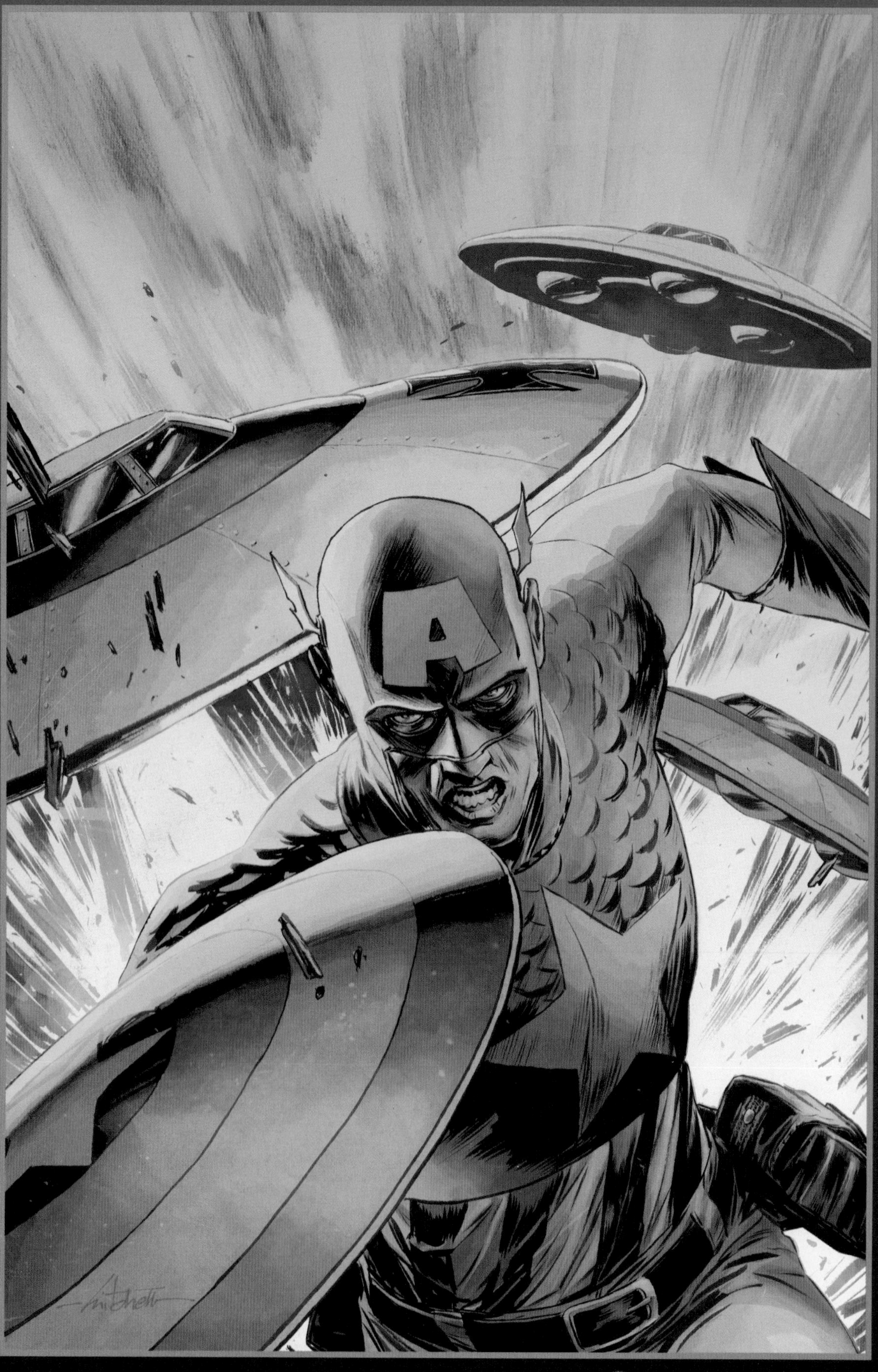

OPERATION: ZERO POINT

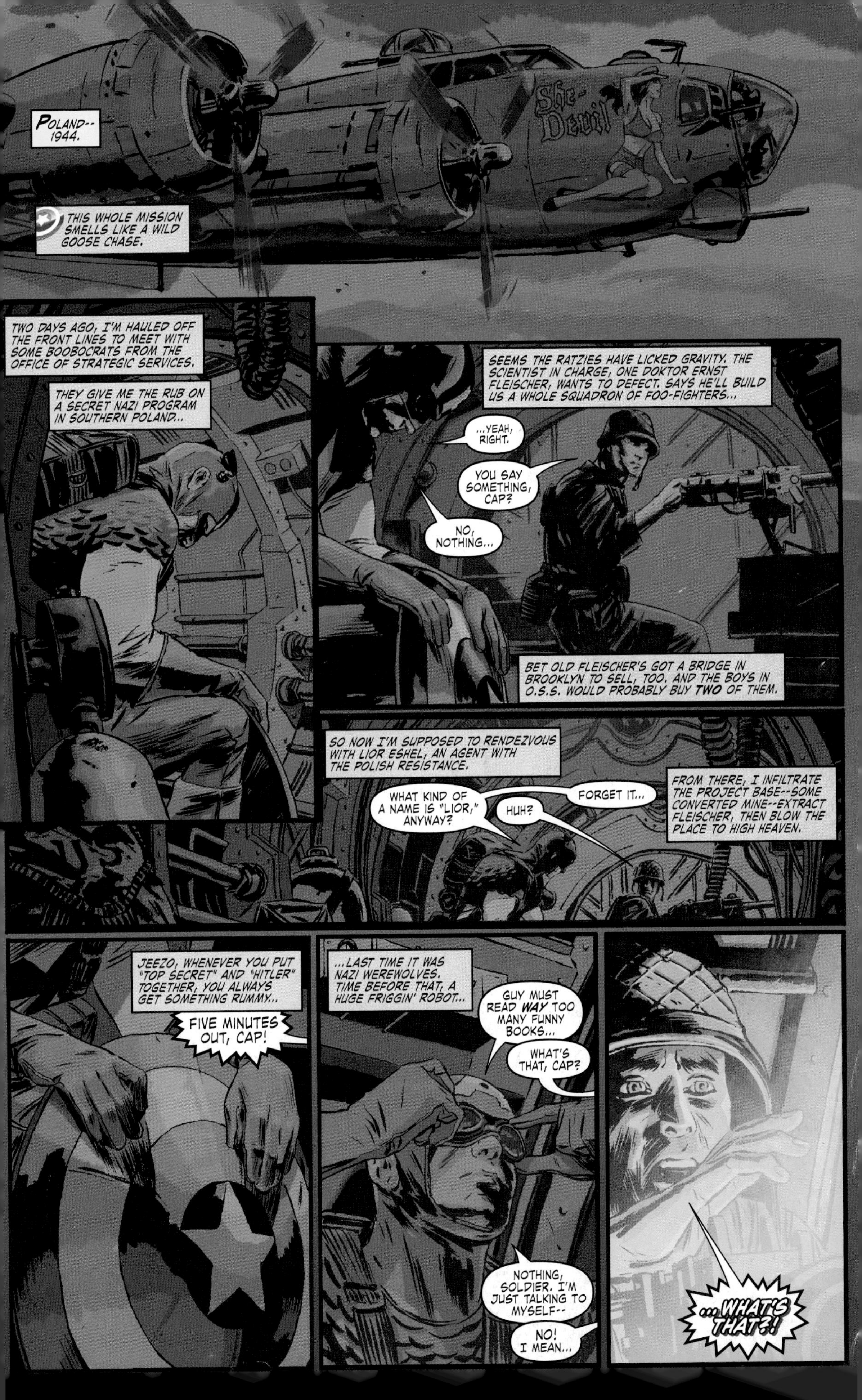
POLAND--
1944.
THIS WHOLE MISSION SMELLS LIKE A WILD GOOSE CHASE.
TWO DAYS AGO, I'M HAULED OFF THE FRONT LINES TO MEET WITH SOME BOOBOCRATS FROM THE OFFICE OF STRATEGIC SERVICES.
THEY GIVE ME THE RUB ON A SECRET NAZI PROGRAM IN SOUTHERN POLAND...
SEEMS THE RATZIES HAVE LICKED GRAVITY. THE SCIENTIST IN CHARGE, ONE DOKTOR ERNST FLEISCHER, WANTS TO DEFECT. SAYS HE'LL BUILD US A WHOLE SQUADRON OF FOO-FIGHTERS...
...YEAH, RIGHT.
YOU SAY SOMETHING, CAP?
NO, NOTHING...
BET OLD FLEISCHER'S GOT A BRIDGE IN BROOKLYN TO SELL, TOO. AND THE BOYS IN O.S.S. WOULD PROBABLY BUY TWO OF THEM.
SO NOW I'M SUPPOSED TO RENDEZVOUS WITH LIOR ESHEL, AN AGENT WITH THE POLISH RESISTANCE.
WHAT KIND OF A NAME IS "LIOR," ANYWAY?
HUH?
FORGET IT...
FROM THERE, I INFILTRATE THE PROJECT BASE--SOME CONVERTED MINE--EXTRACT FLEISCHER, THEN BLOW THE PLACE TO HIGH HEAVEN.
JEEZO, WHENEVER YOU PUT "TOP SECRET" AND "HITLER" TOGETHER, YOU ALWAYS GET SOMETHING RUMMY...
FIVE MINUTES OUT, CAP!
...LAST TIME IT WAS NAZI WEREWOLVES. TIME BEFORE THAT, A HUGE FRIGGIN' ROBOT...
GUY MUST READ WAY TOO MANY FUNNY BOOKS...
WHAT'S THAT, CAP?
NOTHING, SOLDIER. I'M JUST TALKING TO MYSELF--
NO! I MEAN...
...WHAT'S THAT?!

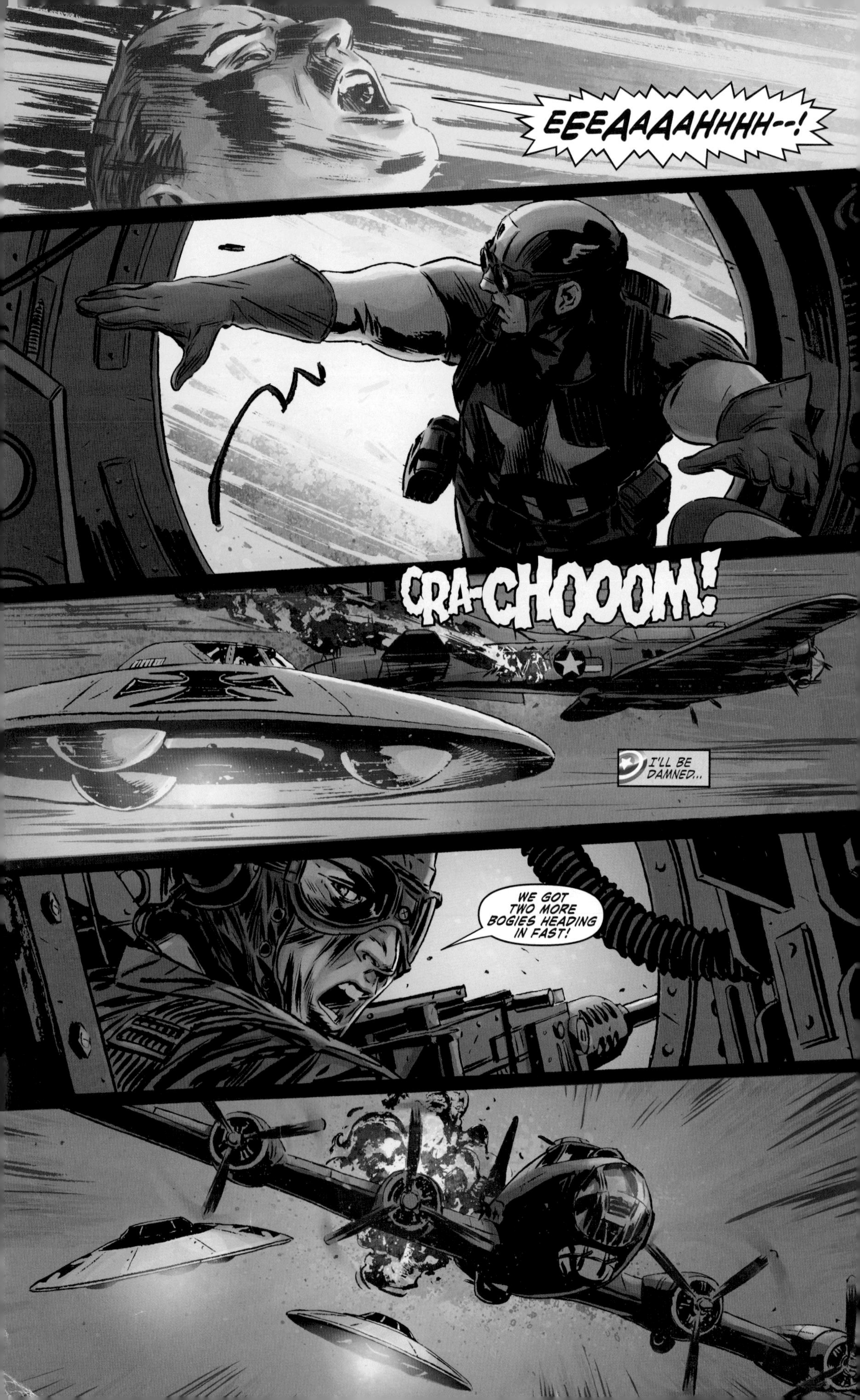
EEEAAAAHHHH--!
CRA-CHOOOM!
I'LL BE DAMNED...
WE GOT TWO MORE BOGIES HEADING IN FAST!

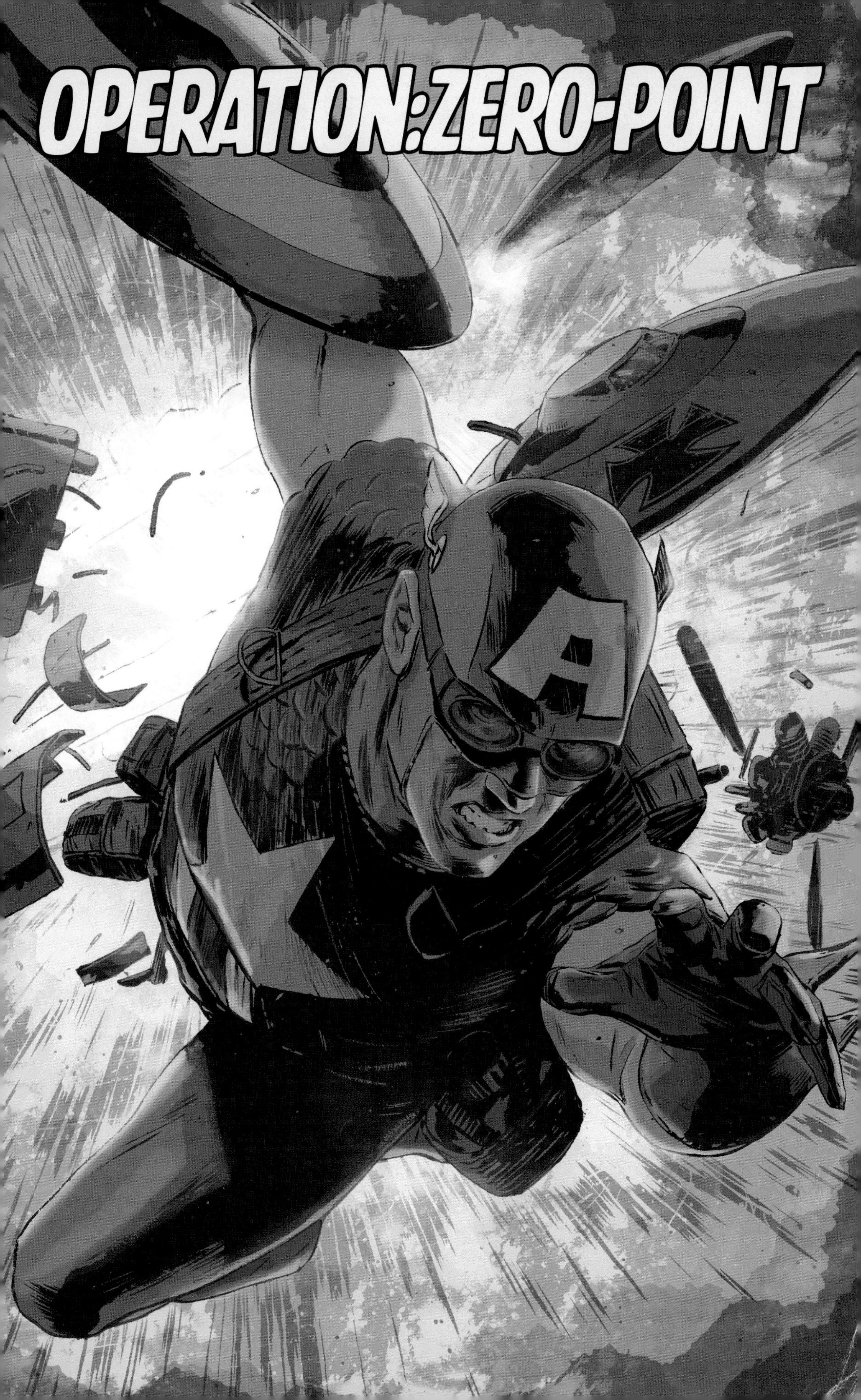
OPERATION:ZERO-POINT

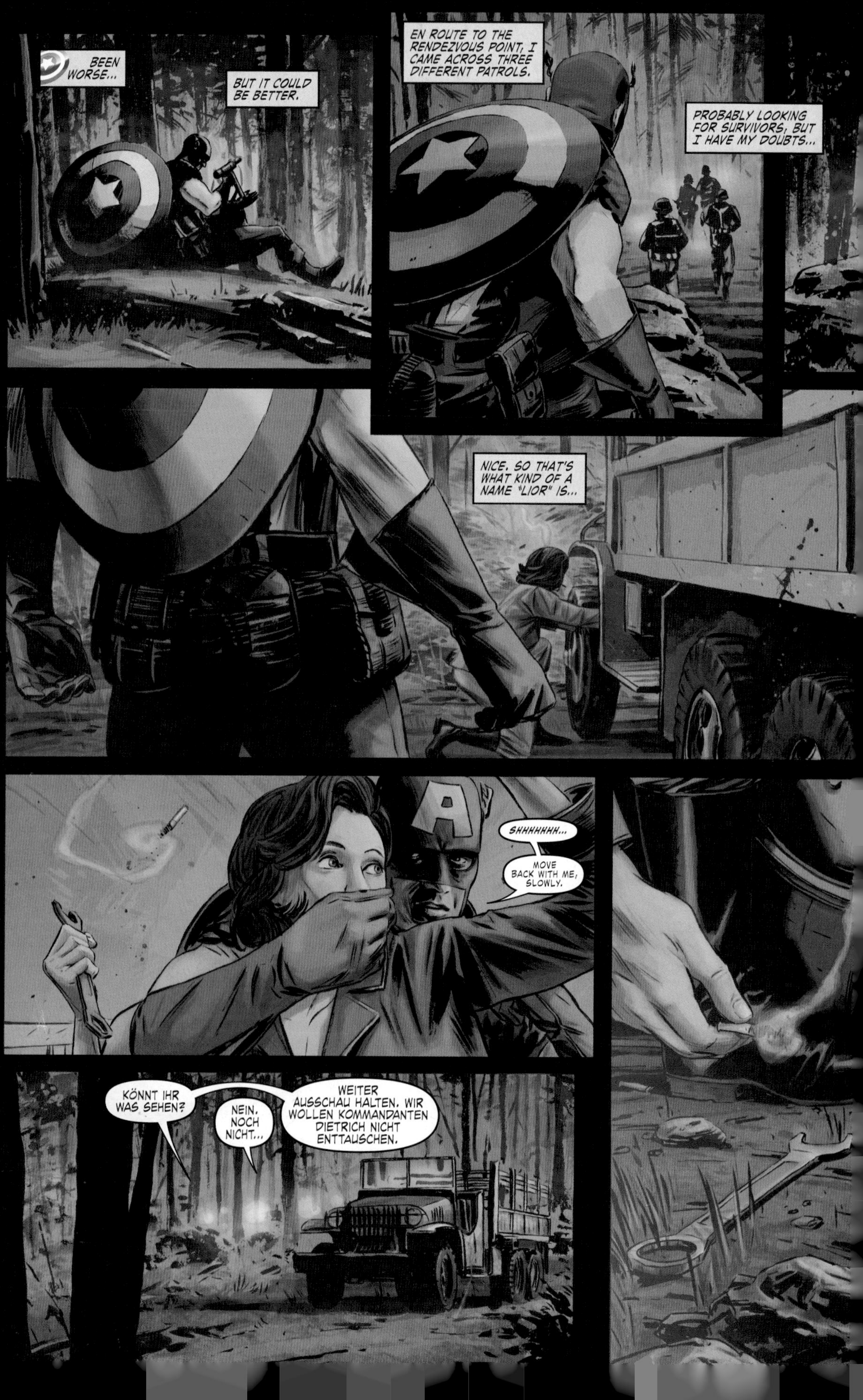
BEEN WORSE...
BUT IT COULD BE BETTER.
EN ROUTE TO THE RENDEZVOUS POINT, I CAME ACROSS THREE DIFFERENT PATROLS.
PROBABLY LOOKING FOR SURVIVORS, BUT I HAVE MY DOUBTS...
NICE. SO THAT'S WHAT KIND OF A NAME "LIOR" IS...
SHHHHHHH...
MOVE BACK WITH ME, SLOWLY.
KÖNNT IHR WAS SEHEN?
NEIN. NOCH NICHT...
WEITER AUSSCHAU HALTEN. WIR WOLLEN KOMMANDANTEN DIETRICH NICHT ENTTAUSCHEN.

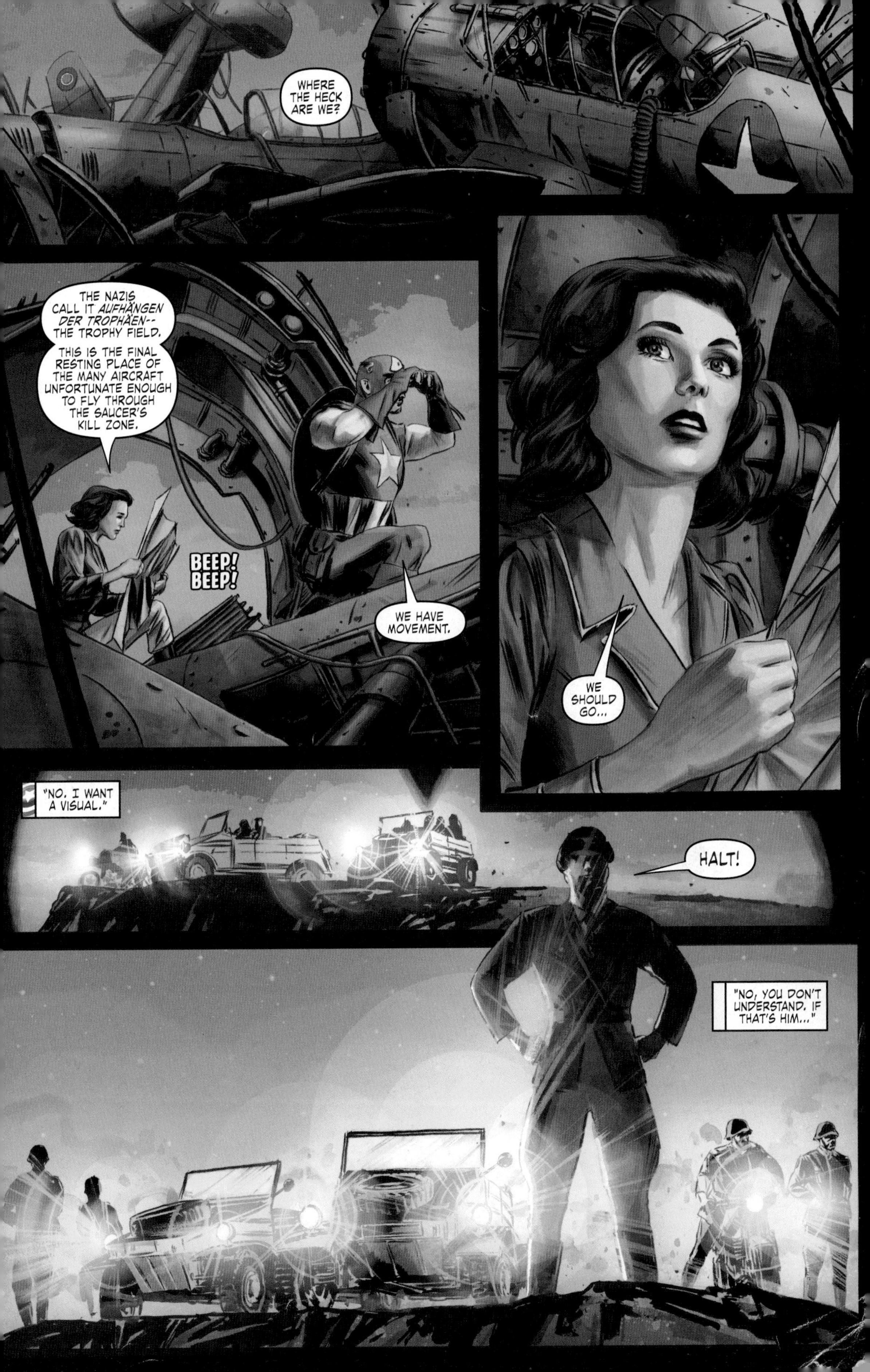
WHERE THE HECK ARE WE?
THE NAZIS CALL IT *AUFHÄNGEN DER TROPHÄEN*-- THE TROPHY FIELD.
THIS IS THE FINAL RESTING PLACE OF THE MANY AIRCRAFT UNFORTUNATE ENOUGH TO FLY THROUGH THE SAUCER'S KILL ZONE.
BEEP! BEEP!
WE HAVE MOVEMENT.
WE SHOULD GO...
"NO. I WANT A VISUAL."
HALT!
"NO, YOU DON'T UNDERSTAND. IF THAT'S HIM..."

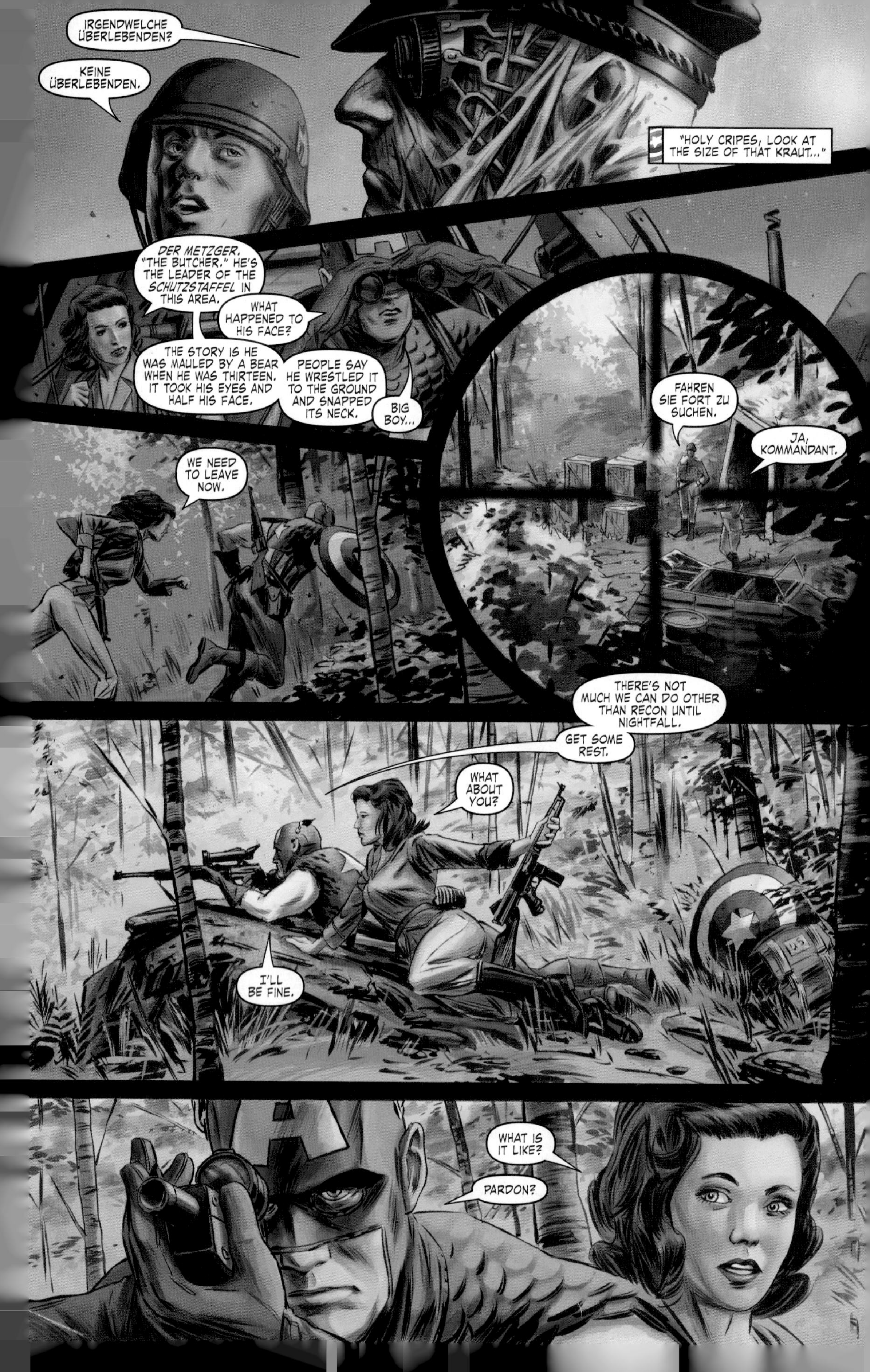
IRGENDWELCHE ÜBERLEBENDEN?
KEINE ÜBERLEBENDEN.
"HOLY CRIPES, LOOK AT THE SIZE OF THAT KRAUT..."
DER METZGER. "THE BUTCHER." HE'S THE LEADER OF THE *SCHUTZSTAFFEL* IN THIS AREA.
WHAT HAPPENED TO HIS FACE?
THE STORY IS HE WAS MAULED BY A BEAR WHEN HE WAS THIRTEEN. IT TOOK HIS EYES AND HALF HIS FACE.
PEOPLE SAY HE WRESTLED IT TO THE GROUND AND SNAPPED ITS NECK.
BIG BOY...
FAHREN SIE FORT ZU SUCHEN.
JA, KOMMANDANT.
WE NEED TO LEAVE NOW.
THERE'S NOT MUCH WE CAN DO OTHER THAN RECON UNTIL NIGHTFALL.
GET SOME REST.
WHAT ABOUT YOU?
I'LL BE FINE.
WHAT IS IT LIKE?
PARDON?

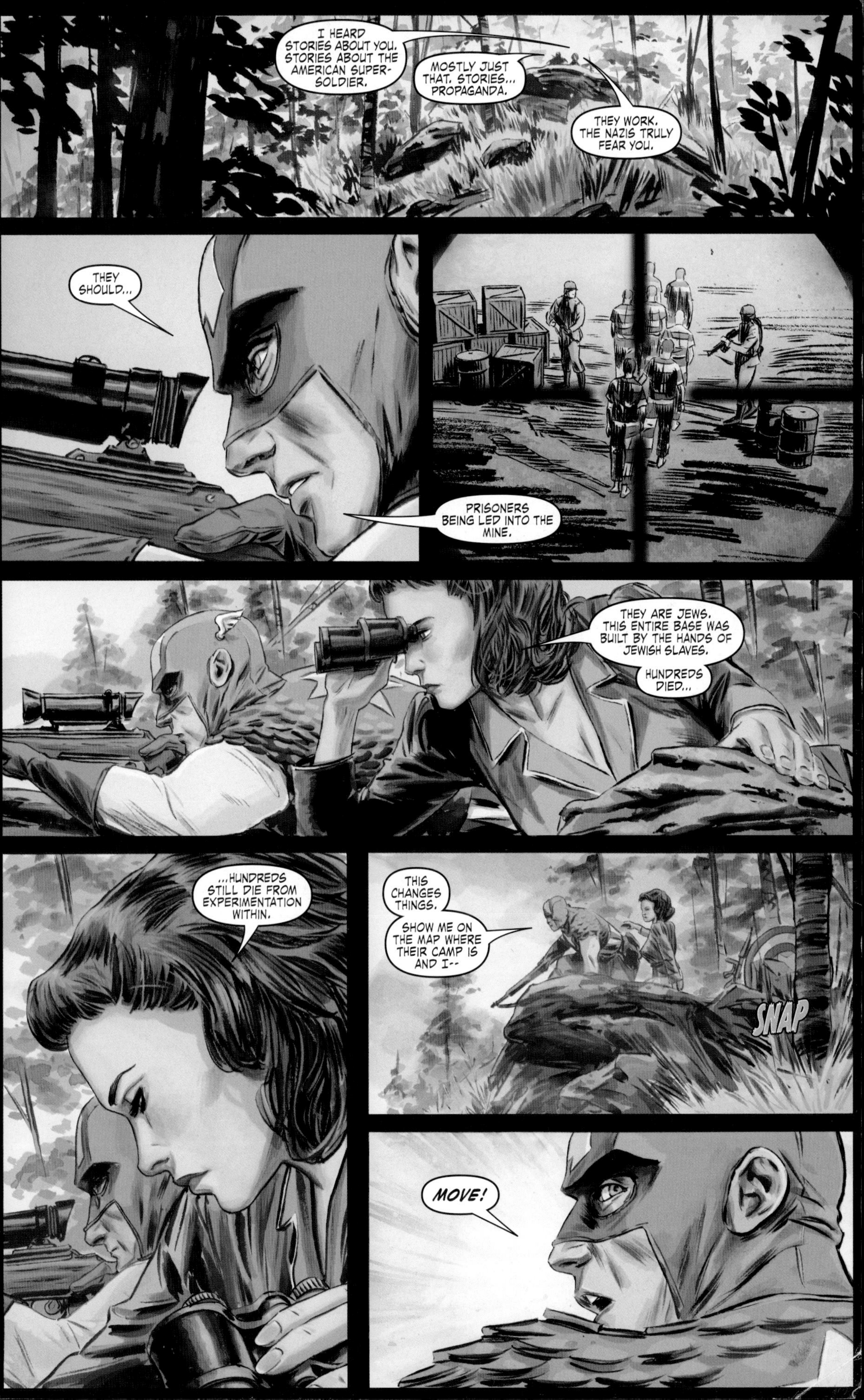

I HEARD STORIES ABOUT YOU. STORIES ABOUT THE AMERICAN SUPER-SOLDIER.
MOSTLY JUST THAT. STORIES... PROPAGANDA.
THEY WORK. THE NAZIS TRULY FEAR YOU.
THEY SHOULD...
PRISONERS BEING LED INTO THE MINE.
THEY ARE JEWS. THIS ENTIRE BASE WAS BUILT BY THE HANDS OF JEWISH SLAVES.
HUNDREDS DIED...
...HUNDREDS STILL DIE FROM EXPERIMENTATION WITHIN.
THIS CHANGES THINGS.
SHOW ME ON THE MAP WHERE THEIR CAMP IS AND I--
SNAP
MOVE!

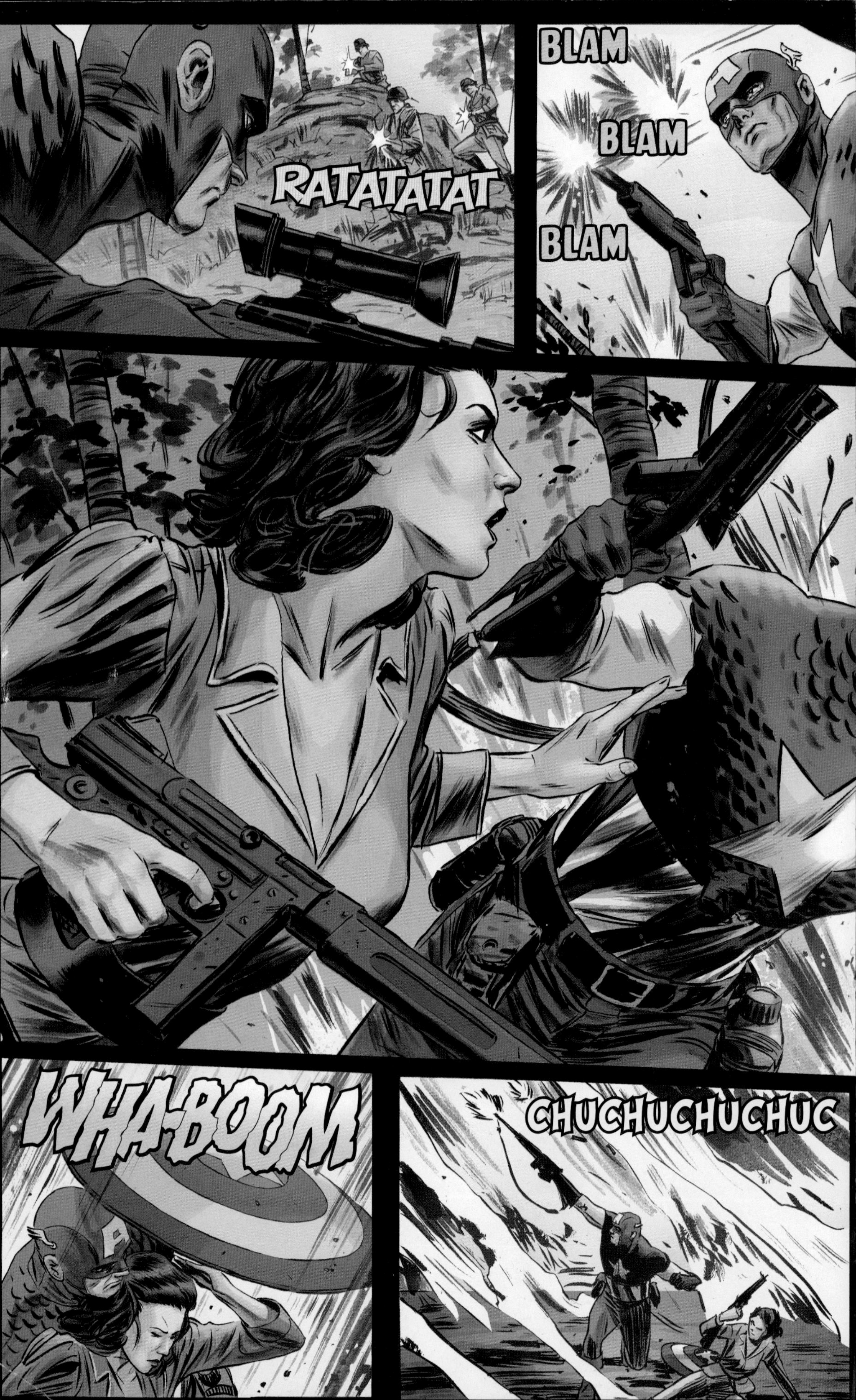
RATATATAT
BLAM
BLAM
BLAM
WHA-BOOM
CHUCHUCHUCHUC

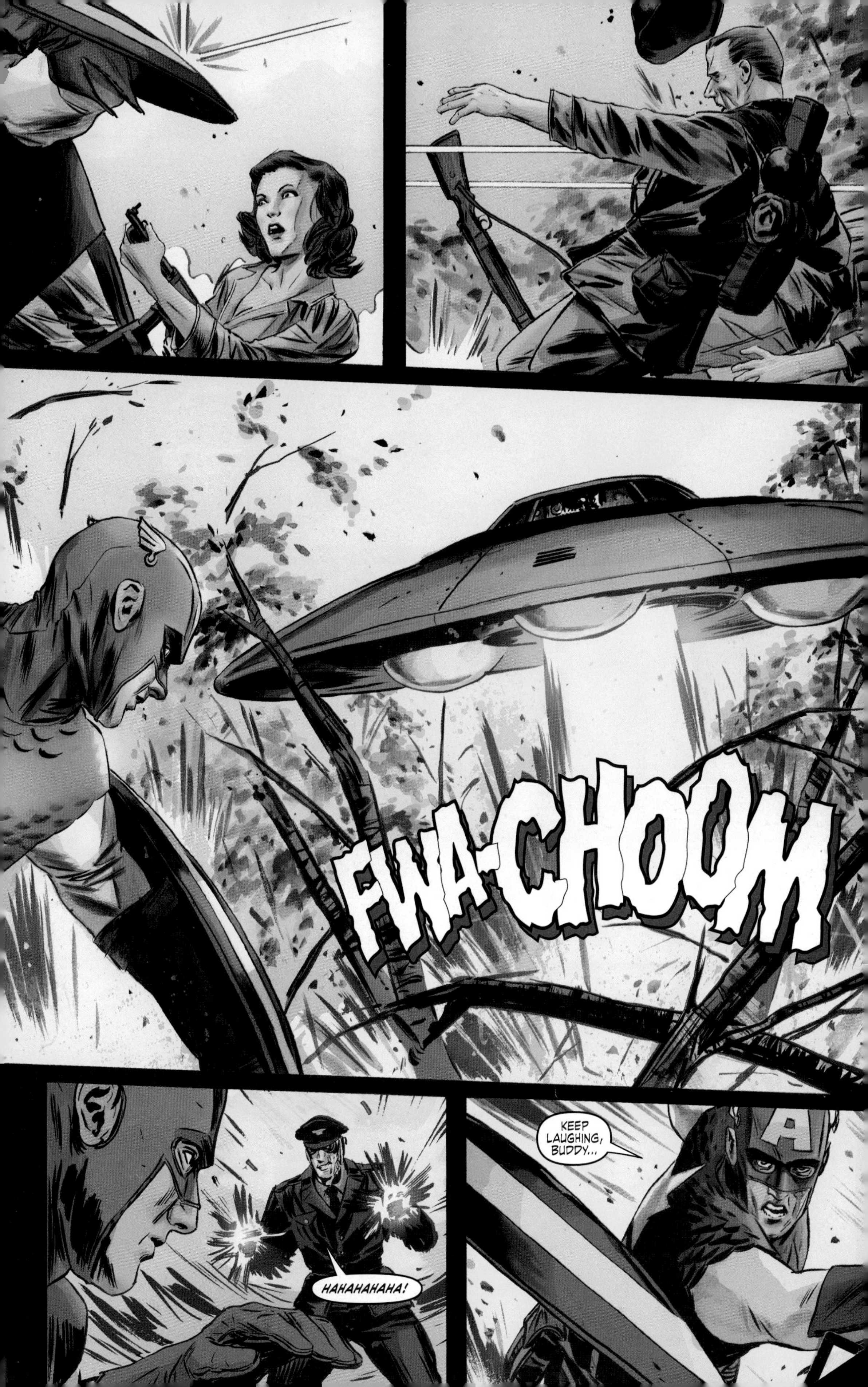
FWA-CHOOM
HAHAHAHAHA!
KEEP LAUGHING, BUDDY...

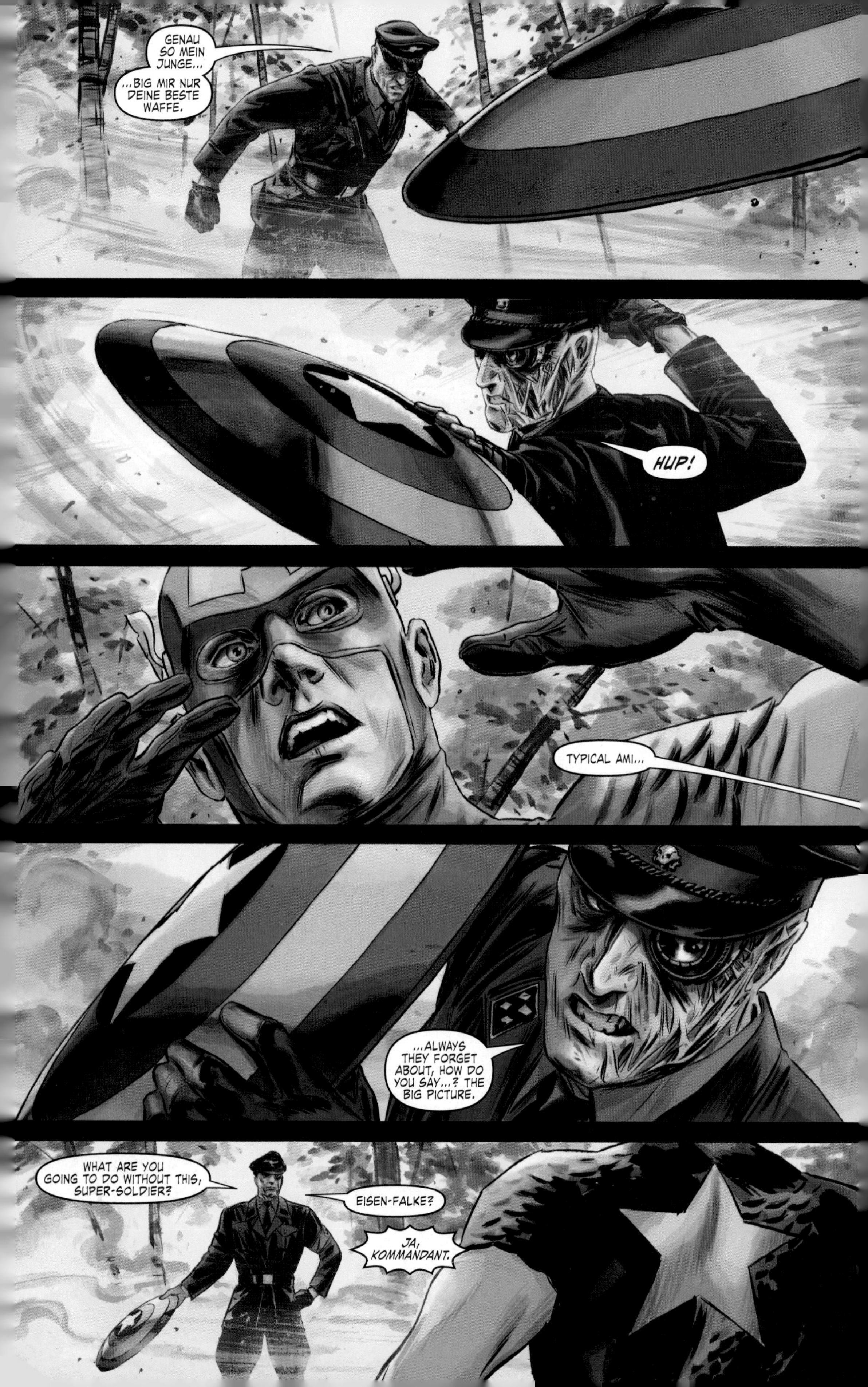
GENAU SO MEIN JUNGE...
...BIG MIR NUR DEINE BESTE WAFFE.
HUP!
TYPICAL AMI...
...ALWAYS THEY FORGET ABOUT, HOW DO YOU SAY...? THE BIG PICTURE.
WHAT ARE YOU GOING TO DO WITHOUT THIS, SUPER-SOLDIER?
EISEN-FALKE?
JA, KOMMANDANT.

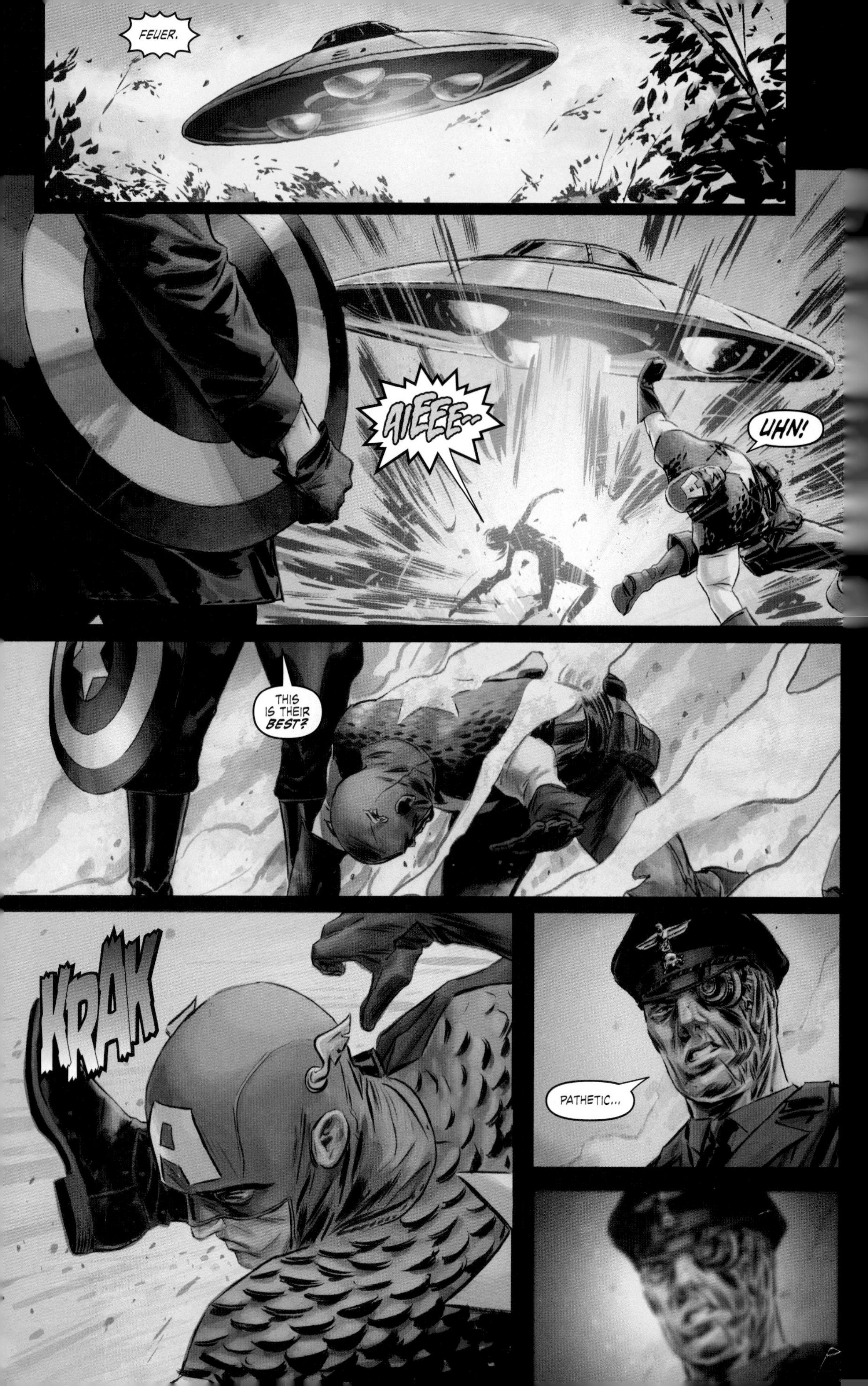
FEUER.
AIEEE--
UHN!
THIS IS THEIR BEST?
KRAK
PATHETIC...

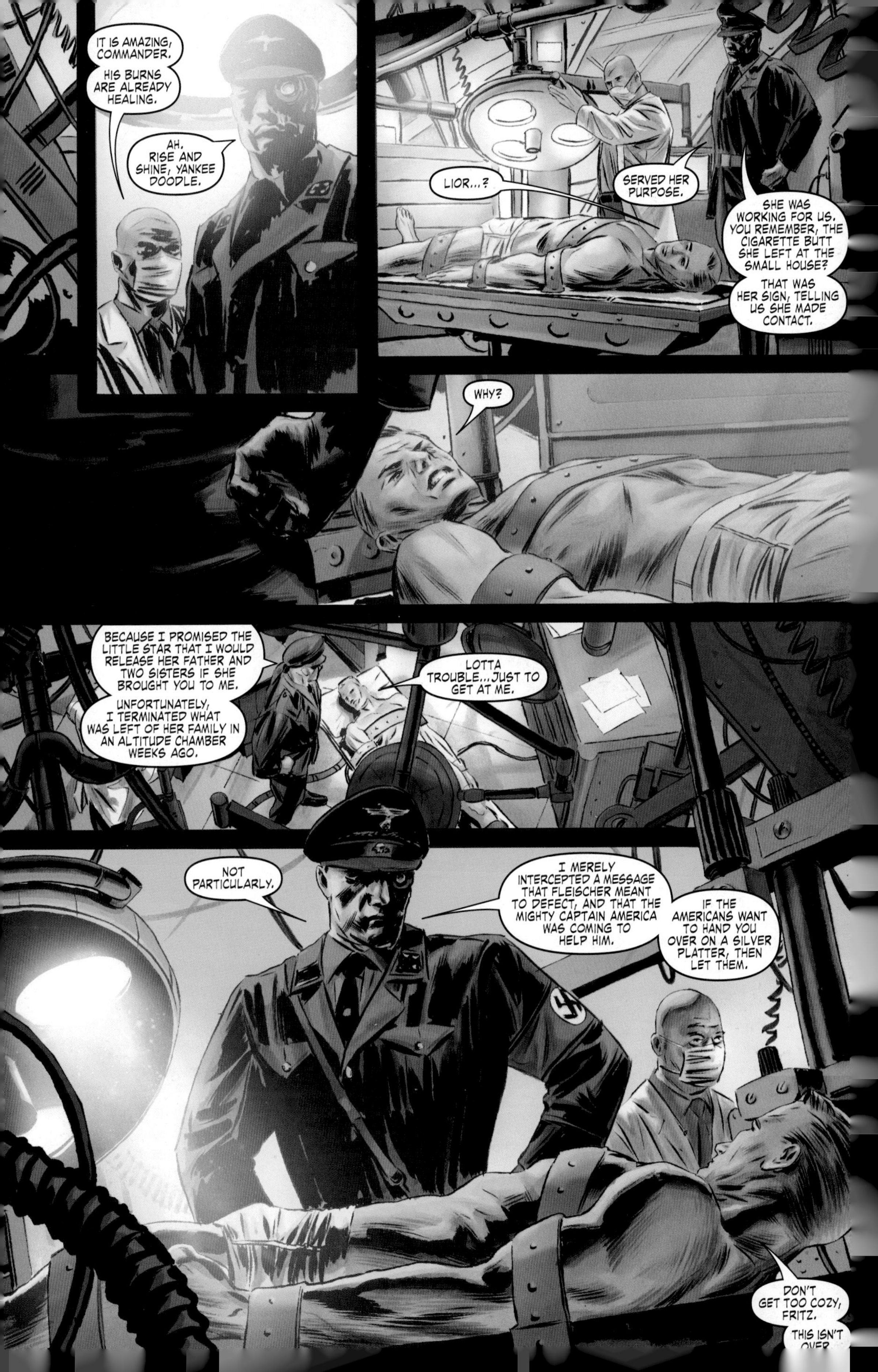
IT IS AMAZING, COMMANDER.
HIS BURNS ARE ALREADY HEALING.
AH. RISE AND SHINE, YANKEE DOODLE.
LIOR...?
SERVED HER PURPOSE.
SHE WAS WORKING FOR US. YOU REMEMBER, THE CIGARETTE BUTT SHE LEFT AT THE SMALL HOUSE?
THAT WAS HER SIGN, TELLING US SHE MADE CONTACT.
WHY?
BECAUSE I PROMISED THE LITTLE STAR THAT I WOULD RELEASE HER FATHER AND TWO SISTERS IF SHE BROUGHT YOU TO ME.
UNFORTUNATELY, I TERMINATED WHAT WAS LEFT OF HER FAMILY IN AN ALTITUDE CHAMBER WEEKS AGO.
LOTTA TROUBLE...JUST TO GET AT ME.
NOT PARTICULARLY.
I MERELY INTERCEPTED A MESSAGE THAT FLEISCHER MEANT TO DEFECT, AND THAT THE MIGHTY CAPTAIN AMERICA WAS COMING TO HELP HIM.
IF THE AMERICANS WANT TO HAND YOU OVER ON A SILVER PLATTER, THEN LET THEM.
DON'T GET TOO COZY, FRITZ.
THIS ISN'T

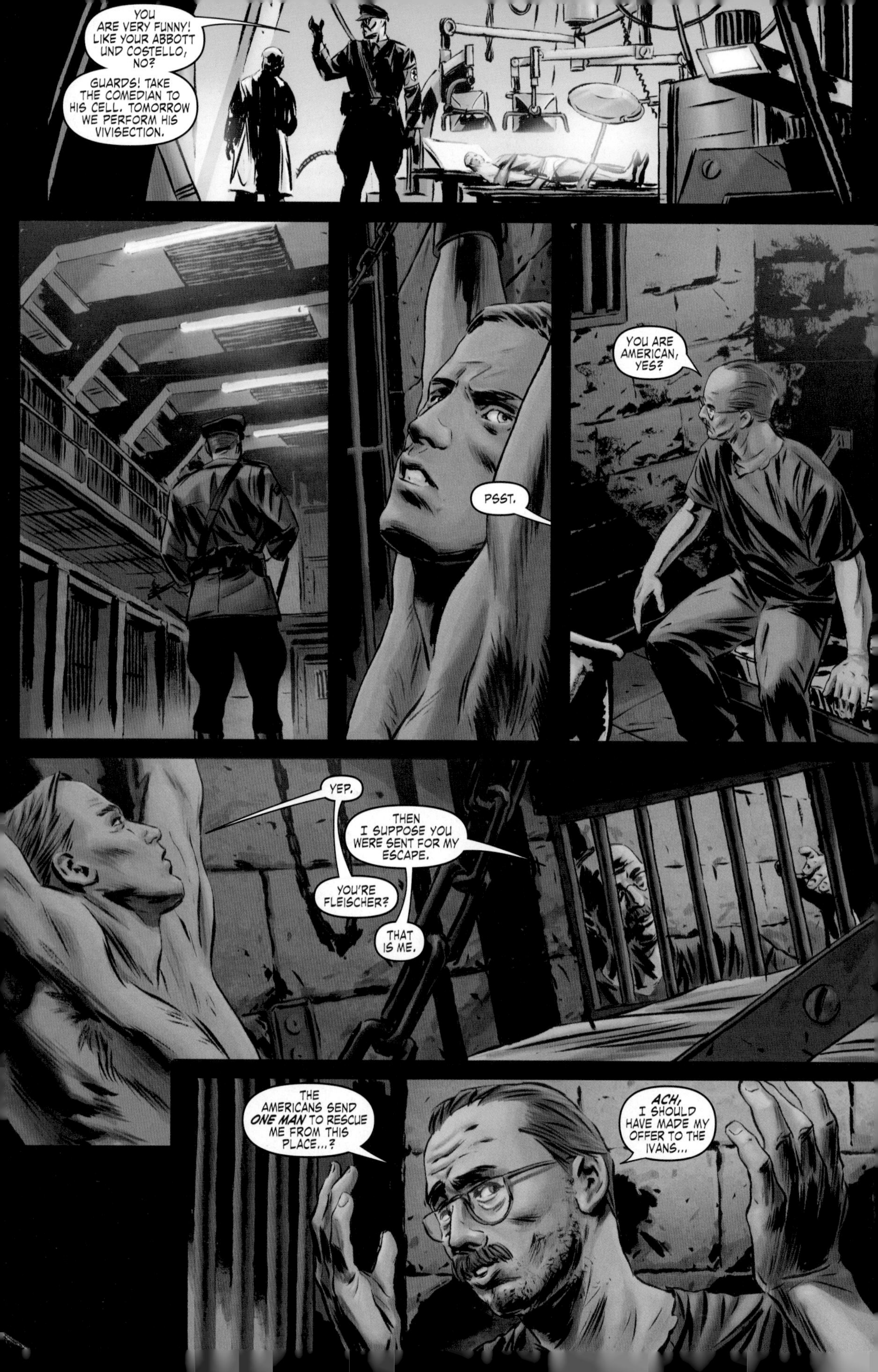
YOU ARE VERY FUNNY! LIKE YOUR ABBOTT UND COSTELLO, NO?
GUARDS! TAKE THE COMEDIAN TO HIS CELL. TOMORROW WE PERFORM HIS VIVISECTION.
PSST.
YOU ARE AMERICAN, YES?
YEP.
THEN I SUPPOSE YOU WERE SENT FOR MY ESCAPE.
YOU'RE FLEISCHER?
THAT IS ME.
THE AMERICANS SEND ONE MAN TO RESCUE ME FROM THIS PLACE...?
ACH, I SHOULD HAVE MADE MY OFFER TO THE IVANS...

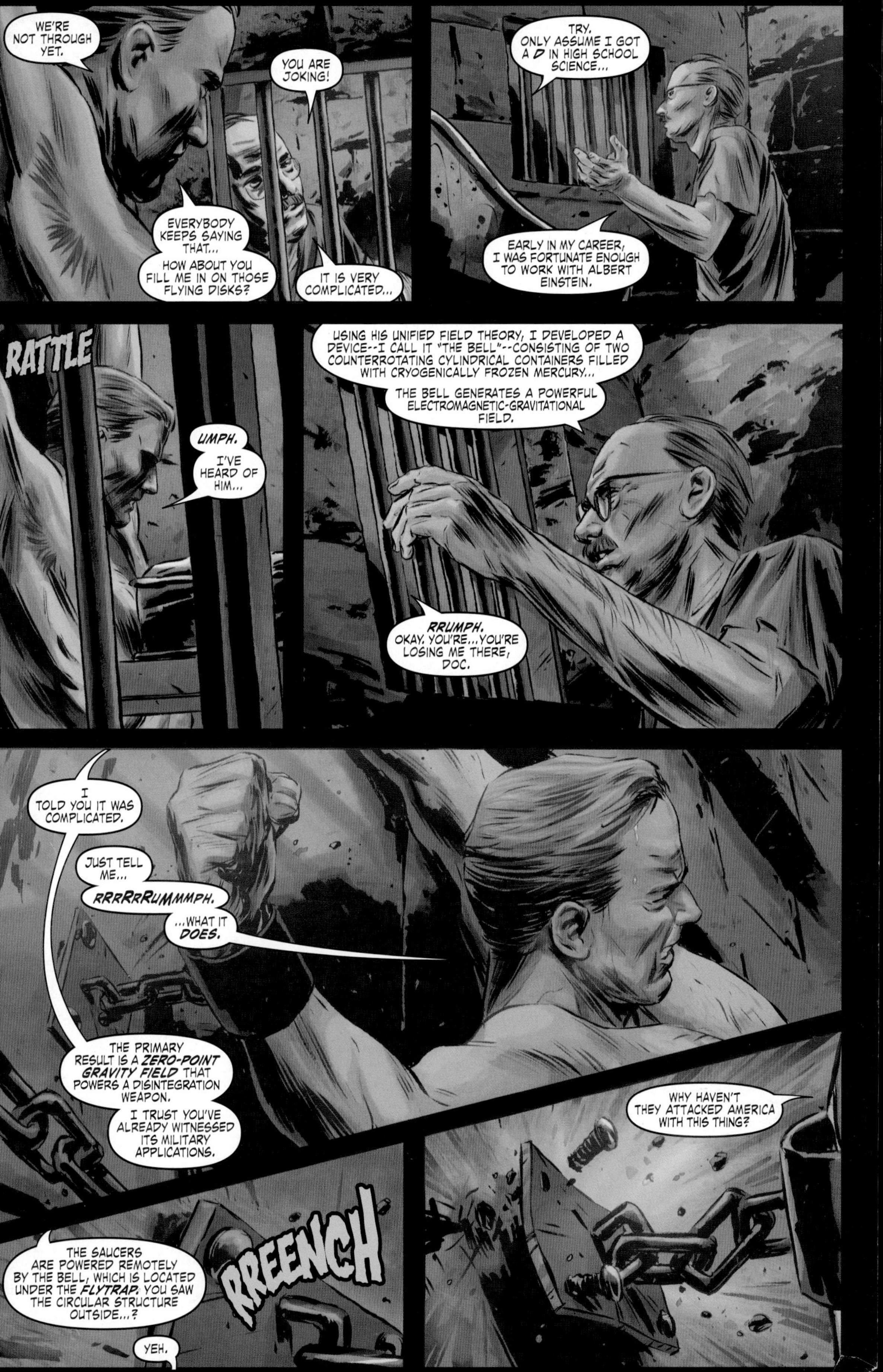

WE'RE NOT THROUGH YET.
YOU ARE JOKING!
EVERYBODY KEEPS SAYING THAT...
HOW ABOUT YOU FILL ME IN ON THOSE FLYING DISKS?
IT IS VERY COMPLICATED...
TRY. ONLY ASSUME I GOT A D IN HIGH SCHOOL SCIENCE...
EARLY IN MY CAREER, I WAS FORTUNATE ENOUGH TO WORK WITH ALBERT EINSTEIN.
RATTLE
UMPH.
I'VE HEARD OF HIM...
USING HIS UNIFIED FIELD THEORY, I DEVELOPED A DEVICE--I CALL IT "THE BELL"--CONSISTING OF TWO COUNTERROTATING CYLINDRICAL CONTAINERS FILLED WITH CRYOGENICALLY FROZEN MERCURY...
THE BELL GENERATES A POWERFUL ELECTROMAGNETIC-GRAVITATIONAL FIELD.
RRUMPH.
OKAY. YOU'RE...YOU'RE LOSING ME THERE, DOC.
I TOLD YOU IT WAS COMPLICATED.
JUST TELL ME...
RRRRRRUMMMPH.
...WHAT IT DOES.
THE PRIMARY RESULT IS A ZERO-POINT GRAVITY FIELD THAT POWERS A DISINTEGRATION WEAPON.
I TRUST YOU'VE ALREADY WITNESSED ITS MILITARY APPLICATIONS.
WHY HAVEN'T THEY ATTACKED AMERICA WITH THIS THING?
THE SAUCERS ARE POWERED REMOTELY BY THE BELL, WHICH IS LOCATED UNDER THE FLYTRAP. YOU SAW THE CIRCULAR STRUCTURE OUTSIDE...?
RREENCH
YEH.

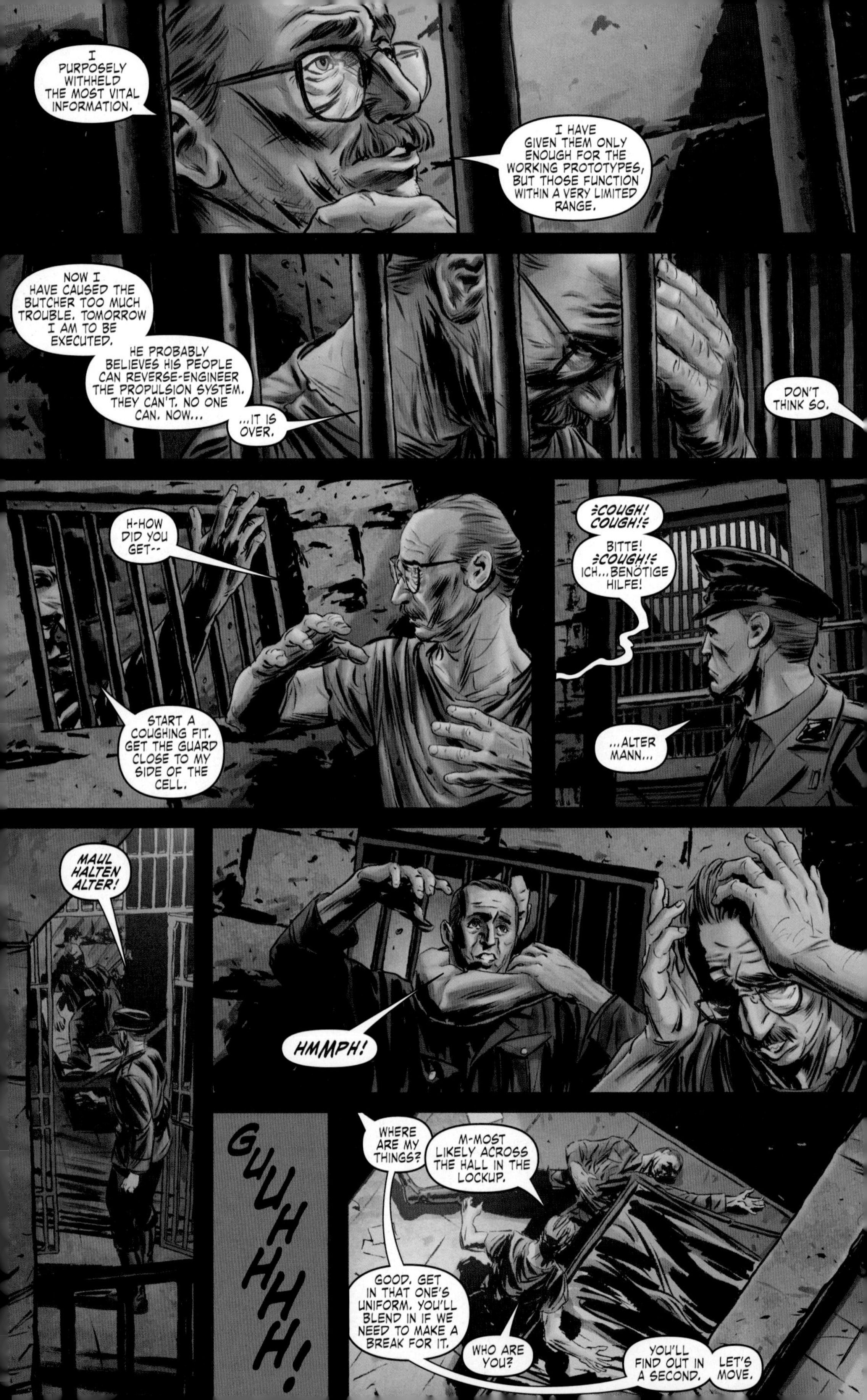
I PURPOSELY WITHHELD THE MOST VITAL INFORMATION.
I HAVE GIVEN THEM ONLY ENOUGH FOR THE WORKING PROTOTYPES, BUT THOSE FUNCTION WITHIN A VERY LIMITED RANGE.
NOW I HAVE CAUSED THE BUTCHER TOO MUCH TROUBLE. TOMORROW I AM TO BE EXECUTED.
HE PROBABLY BELIEVES HIS PEOPLE CAN REVERSE-ENGINEER THE PROPULSION SYSTEM. THEY CAN'T. NO ONE CAN. NOW...
...IT IS OVER.
DON'T THINK SO.
H-HOW DID YOU GET--
START A COUGHING FIT. GET THE GUARD CLOSE TO MY SIDE OF THE CELL.
COUGH! COUGH!
BITTE! COUGH! ICH...BENÖTIGE HILFE!
...ALTER MANN...
MAUL HALTEN ALTER!
HMMPH!
GUUHHHH!
WHERE ARE MY THINGS?
M-MOST LIKELY ACROSS THE HALL IN THE LOCKUP.
GOOD. GET IN THAT ONE'S UNIFORM. YOU'LL BLEND IN IF WE NEED TO MAKE A BREAK FOR IT.
WHO ARE YOU?
YOU'LL FIND OUT IN A SECOND.
LET'S MOVE.

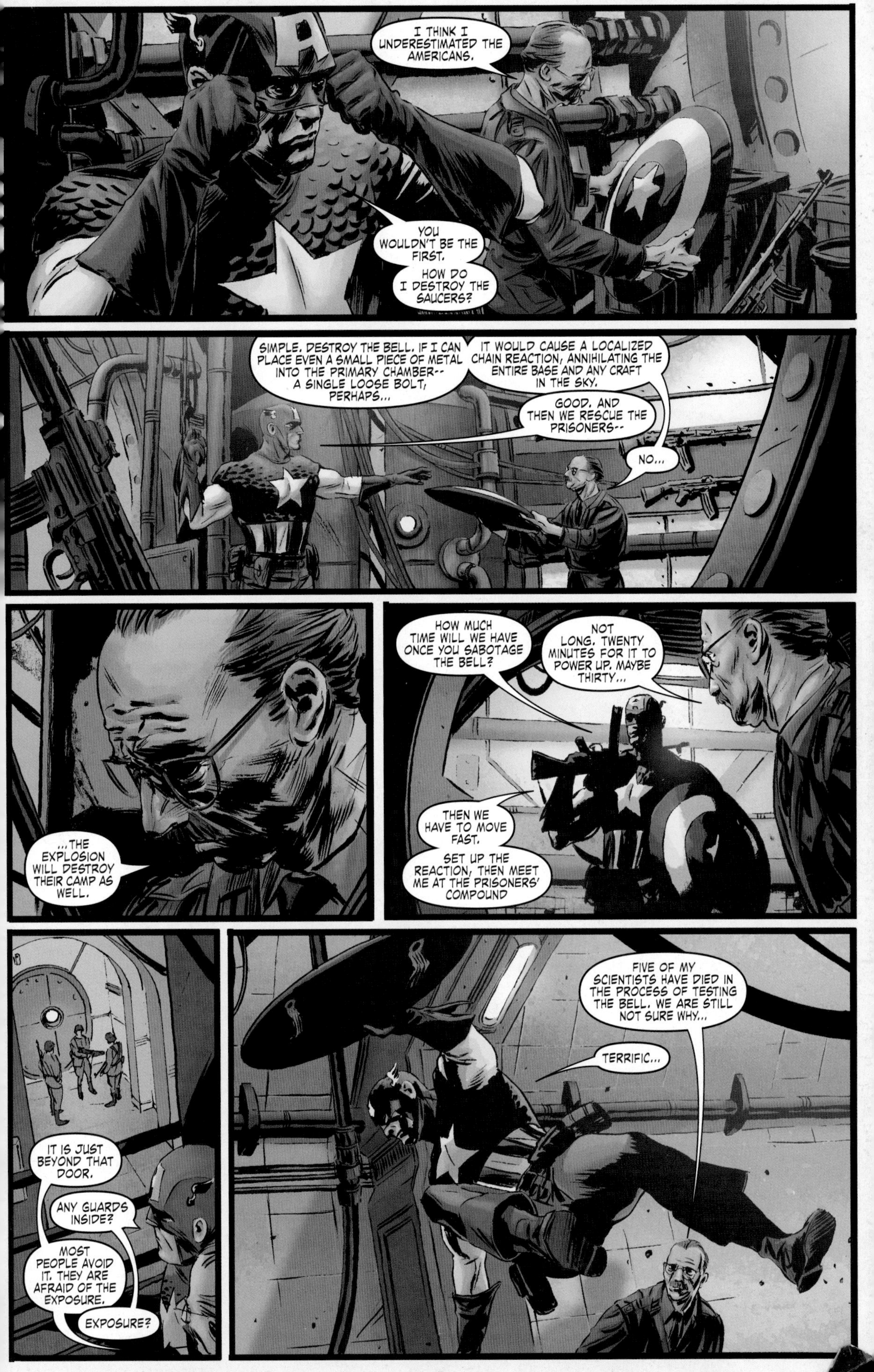
I THINK I UNDERESTIMATED THE AMERICANS.
YOU WOULDN'T BE THE FIRST.
HOW DO I DESTROY THE SAUCERS?
SIMPLE. DESTROY THE BELL. IF I CAN PLACE EVEN A SMALL PIECE OF METAL INTO THE PRIMARY CHAMBER-- A SINGLE LOOSE BOLT, PERHAPS...
IT WOULD CAUSE A LOCALIZED CHAIN REACTION, ANNIHILATING THE ENTIRE BASE AND ANY CRAFT IN THE SKY.
GOOD. AND THEN WE RESCUE THE PRISONERS--
NO...
...THE EXPLOSION WILL DESTROY THEIR CAMP AS WELL.
HOW MUCH TIME WILL WE HAVE ONCE YOU SABOTAGE THE BELL?
NOT LONG. TWENTY MINUTES FOR IT TO POWER UP. MAYBE THIRTY...
THEN WE HAVE TO MOVE FAST.
SET UP THE REACTION, THEN MEET ME AT THE PRISONERS' COMPOUND
IT IS JUST BEYOND THAT DOOR.
ANY GUARDS INSIDE?
MOST PEOPLE AVOID IT. THEY ARE AFRAID OF THE EXPOSURE.
EXPOSURE?
FIVE OF MY SCIENTISTS HAVE DIED IN THE PROCESS OF TESTING THE BELL. WE ARE STILL NOT SURE WHY...
TERRIFIC...

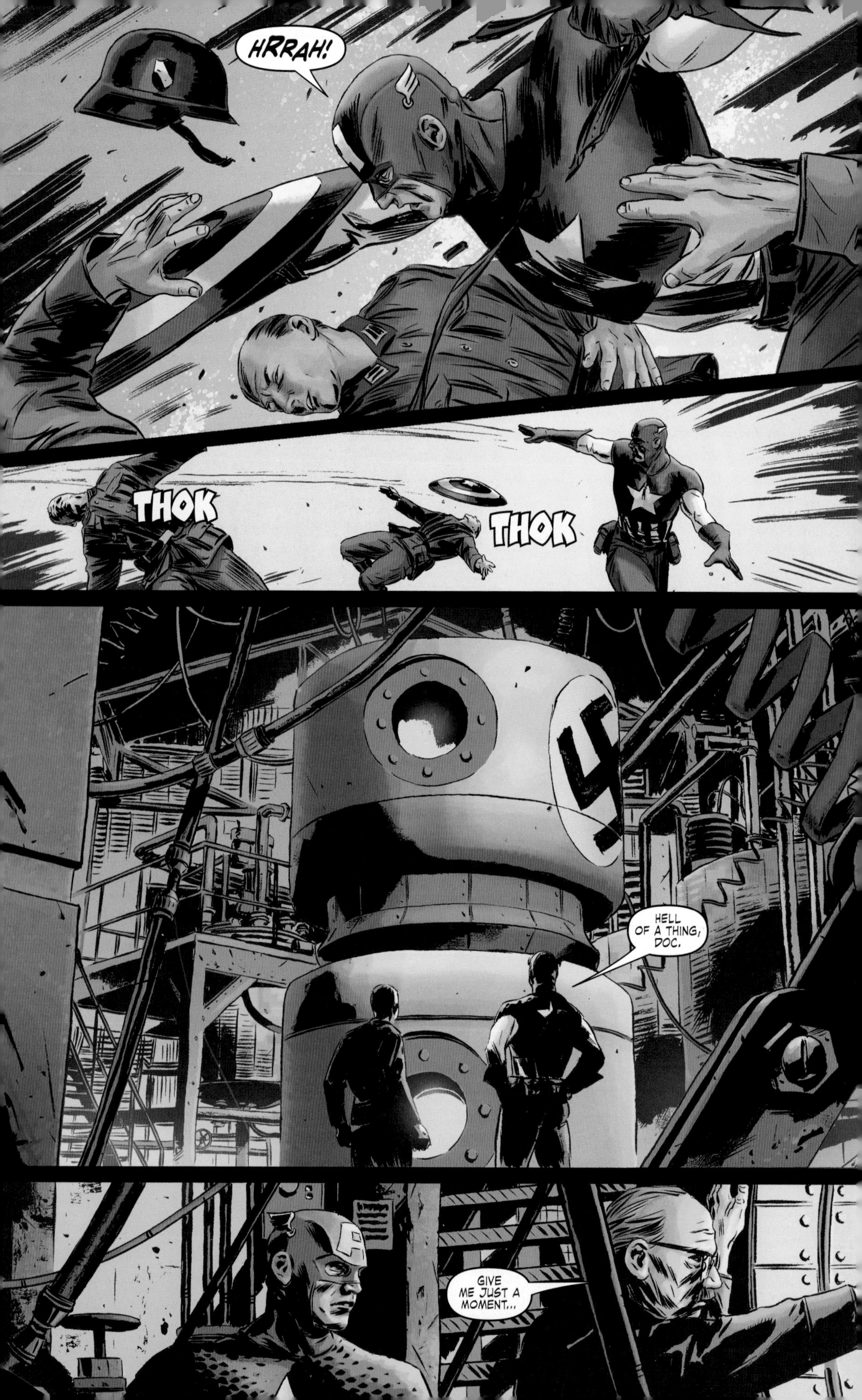
HRRAH!
THOK
THOK
HELL OF A THING, DOC.
GIVE ME JUST A MOMENT...

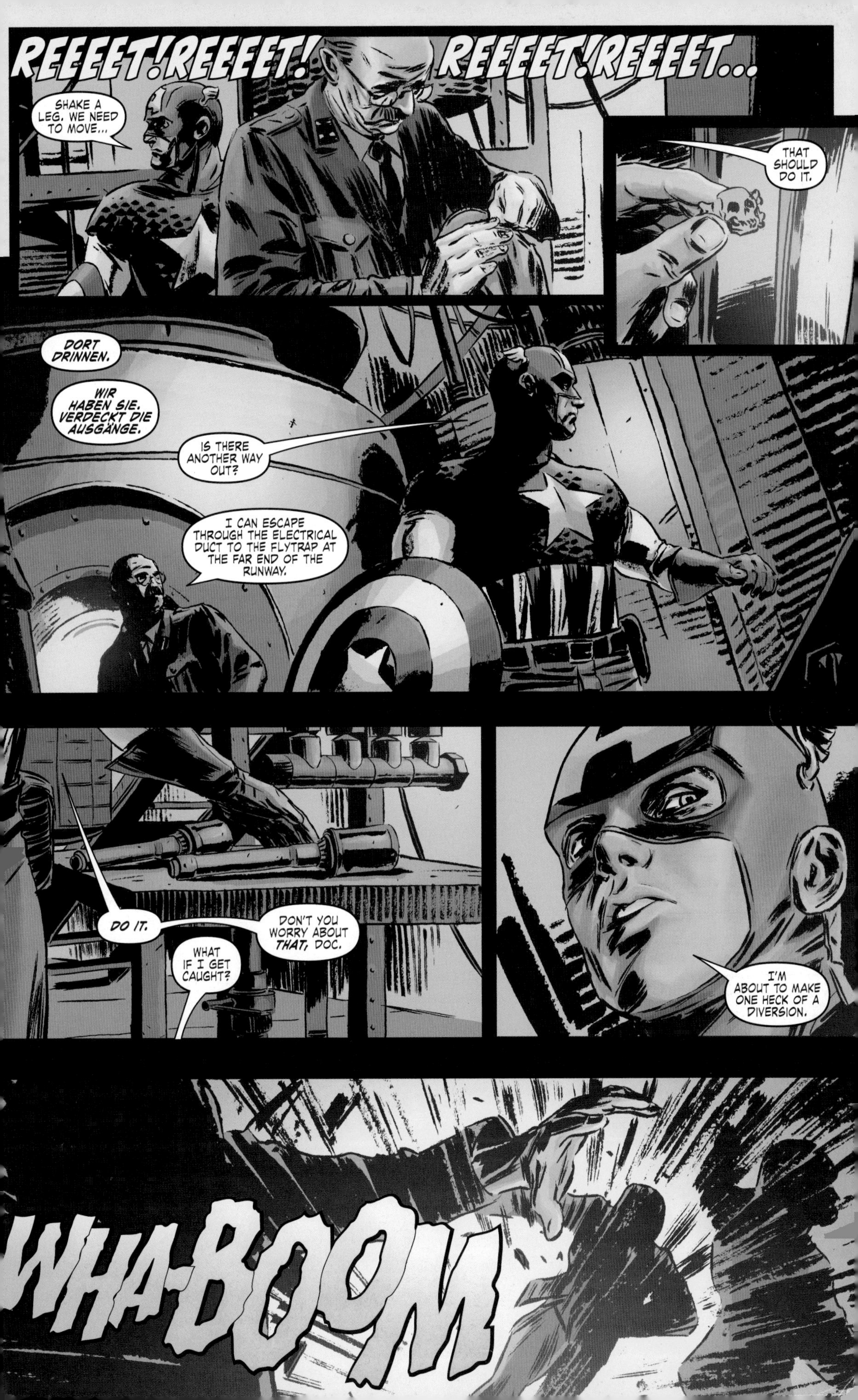
REEEET! REEEET! REEEET! REEEET...
SHAKE A LEG. WE NEED TO MOVE...
THAT SHOULD DO IT.
DORT DRINNEN.
WIR HABEN SIE. VERDECKT DIE AUSGÄNGE.
IS THERE ANOTHER WAY OUT?
I CAN ESCAPE THROUGH THE ELECTRICAL DUCT TO THE FLYTRAP AT THE FAR END OF THE RUNWAY.
DO IT.
WHAT IF I GET CAUGHT?
DON'T YOU WORRY ABOUT THAT, DOC.
I'M ABOUT TO MAKE ONE HECK OF A DIVERSION.
WHA-BOOM

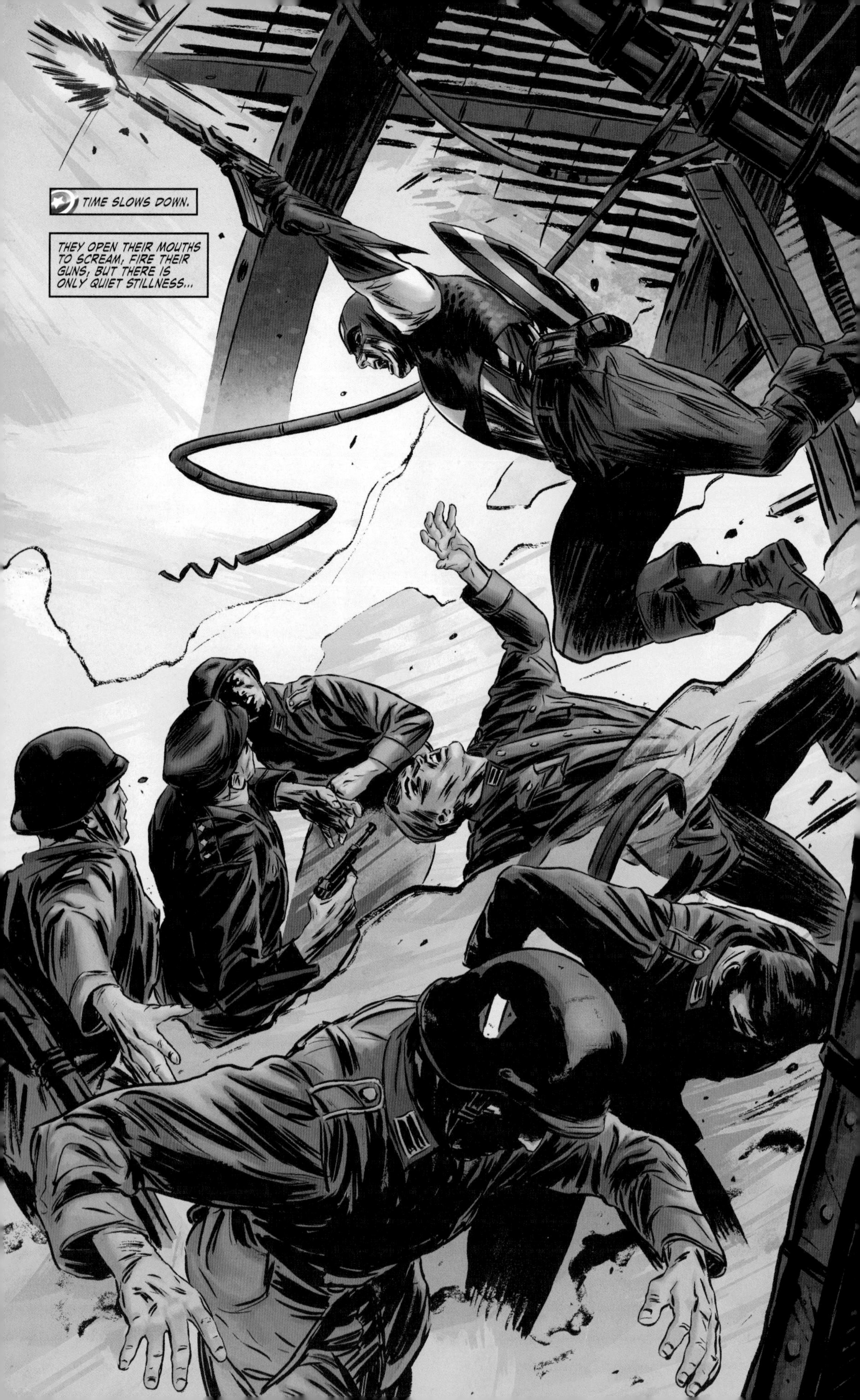
TIME SLOWS DOWN.
THEY OPEN THEIR MOUTHS TO SCREAM, FIRE THEIR GUNS, BUT THERE IS ONLY QUIET STILLNESS...

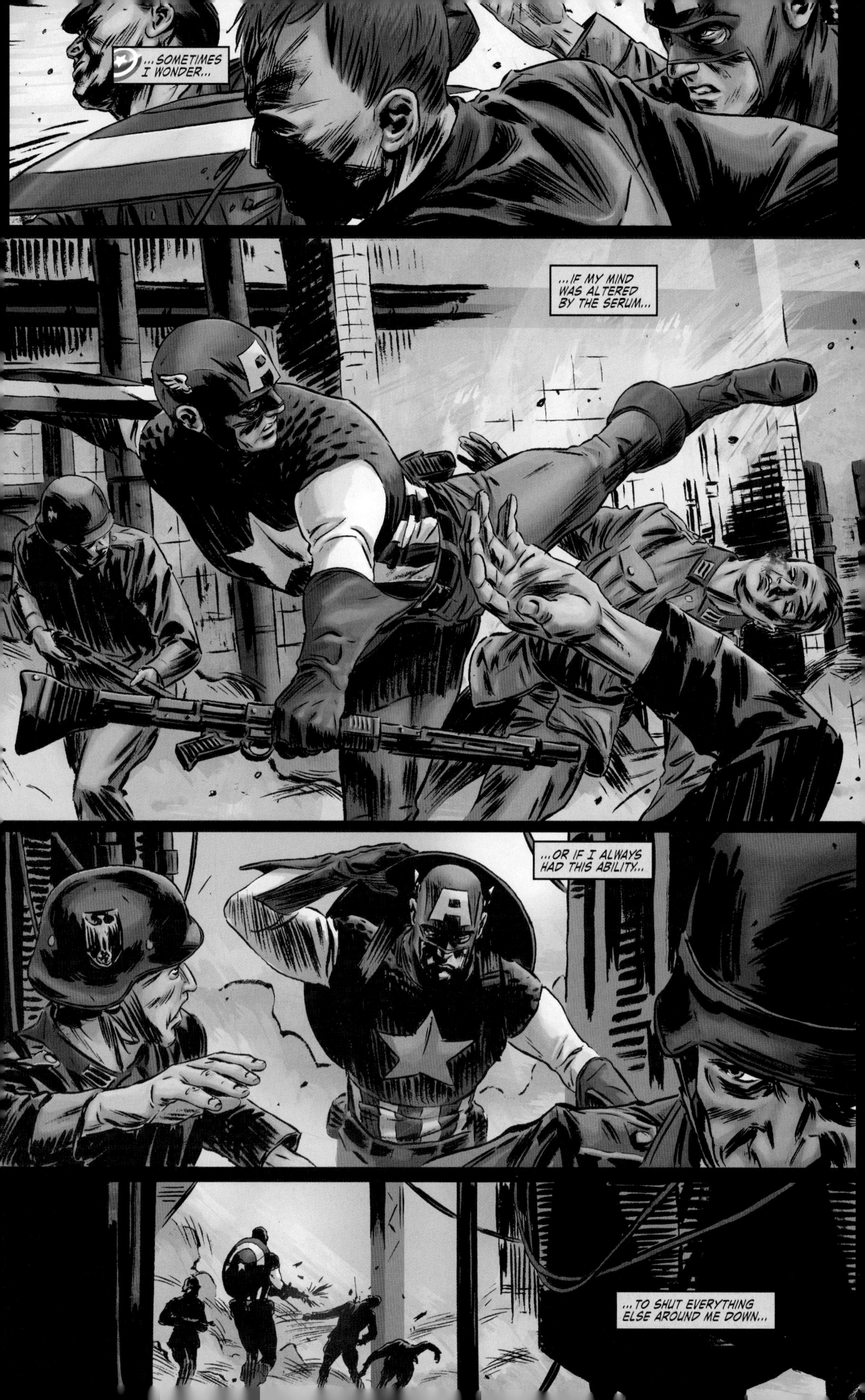
...SOMETIMES I WONDER...
...IF MY MIND WAS ALTERED BY THE SERUM...
...OR IF I ALWAYS HAD THIS ABILITY...
...TO SHUT EVERYTHING ELSE AROUND ME DOWN...

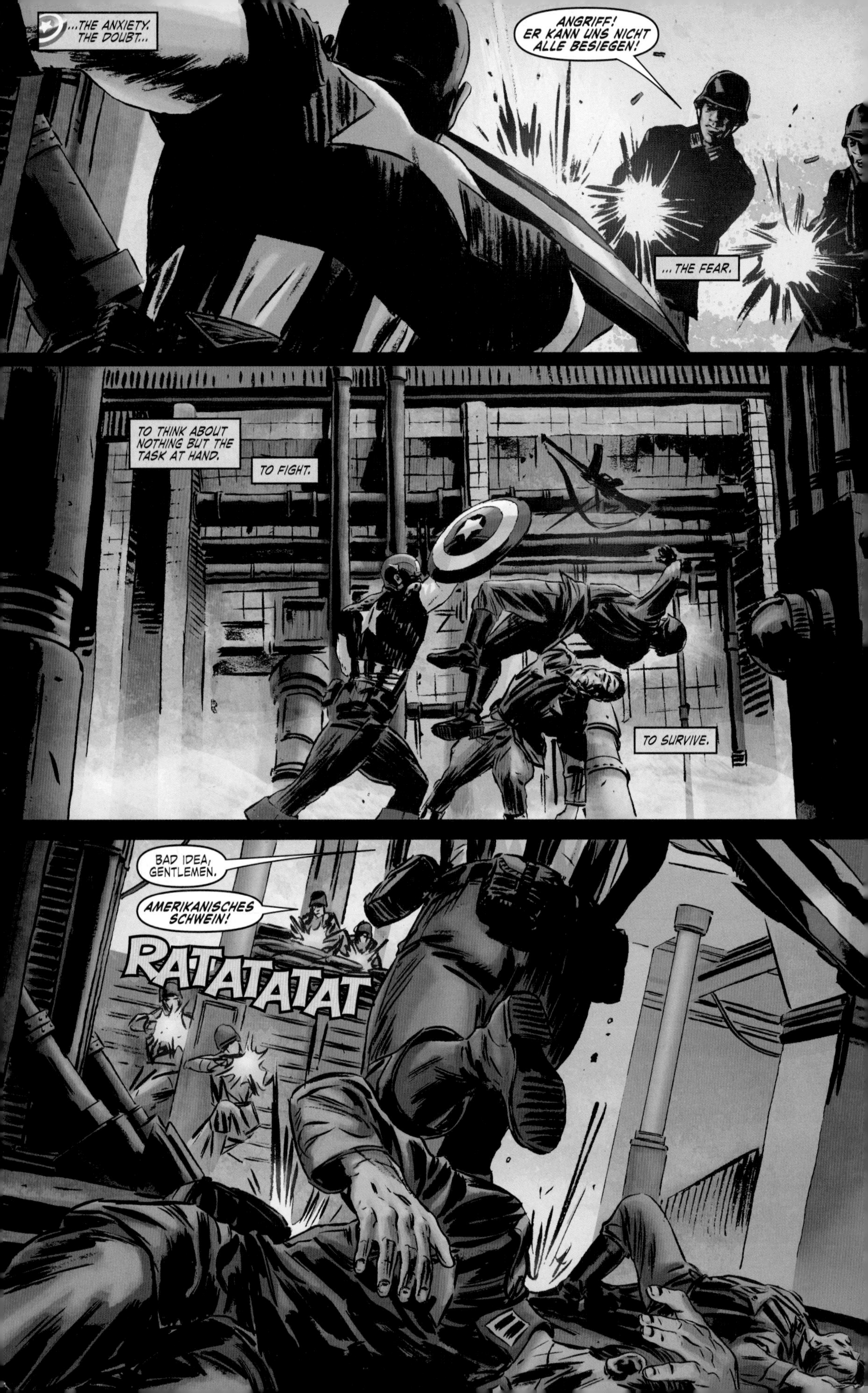
...THE ANXIETY. THE DOUBT...
ANGRIFF! ER KANN UNS NICHT ALLE BESIEGEN!
...THE FEAR.
TO THINK ABOUT NOTHING BUT THE TASK AT HAND.
TO FIGHT.
TO SURVIVE.
BAD IDEA, GENTLEMEN.
AMERIKANISCHES SCHWEIN!
RATATATAT

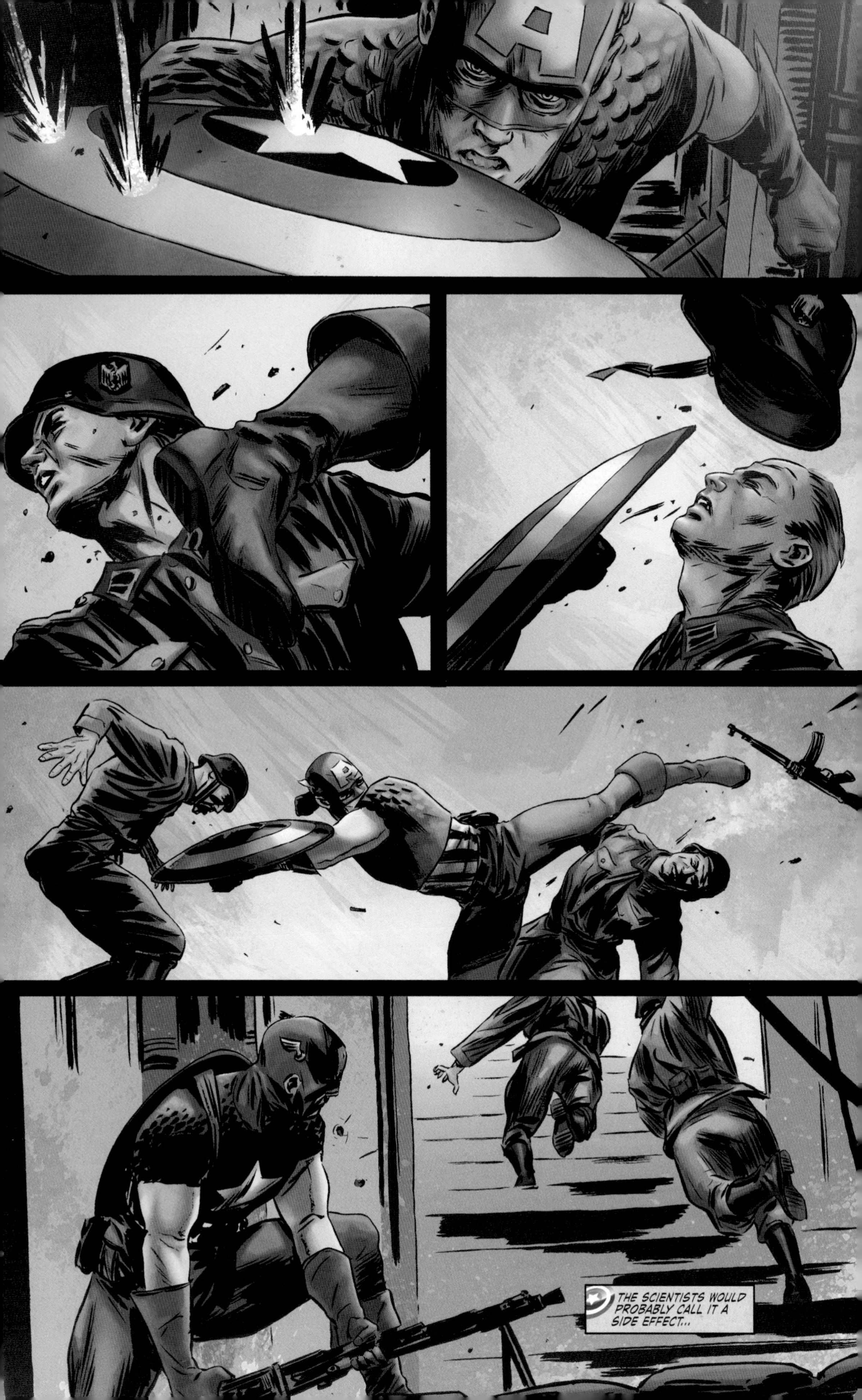
THE SCIENTISTS WOULD PROBABLY CALL IT A SIDE EFFECT...

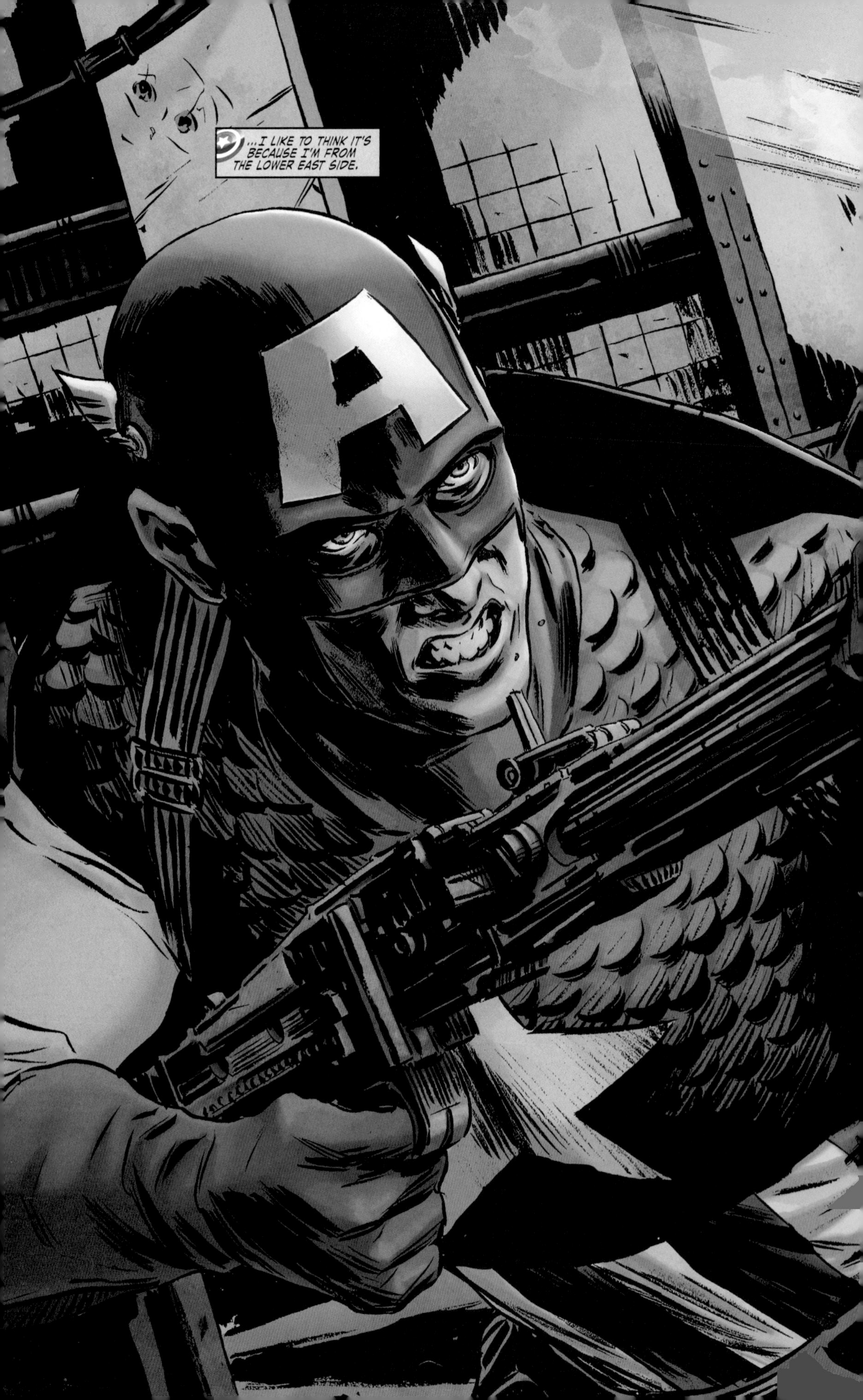
...I LIKE TO THINK IT'S BECAUSE I'M FROM THE LOWER EAST SIDE.

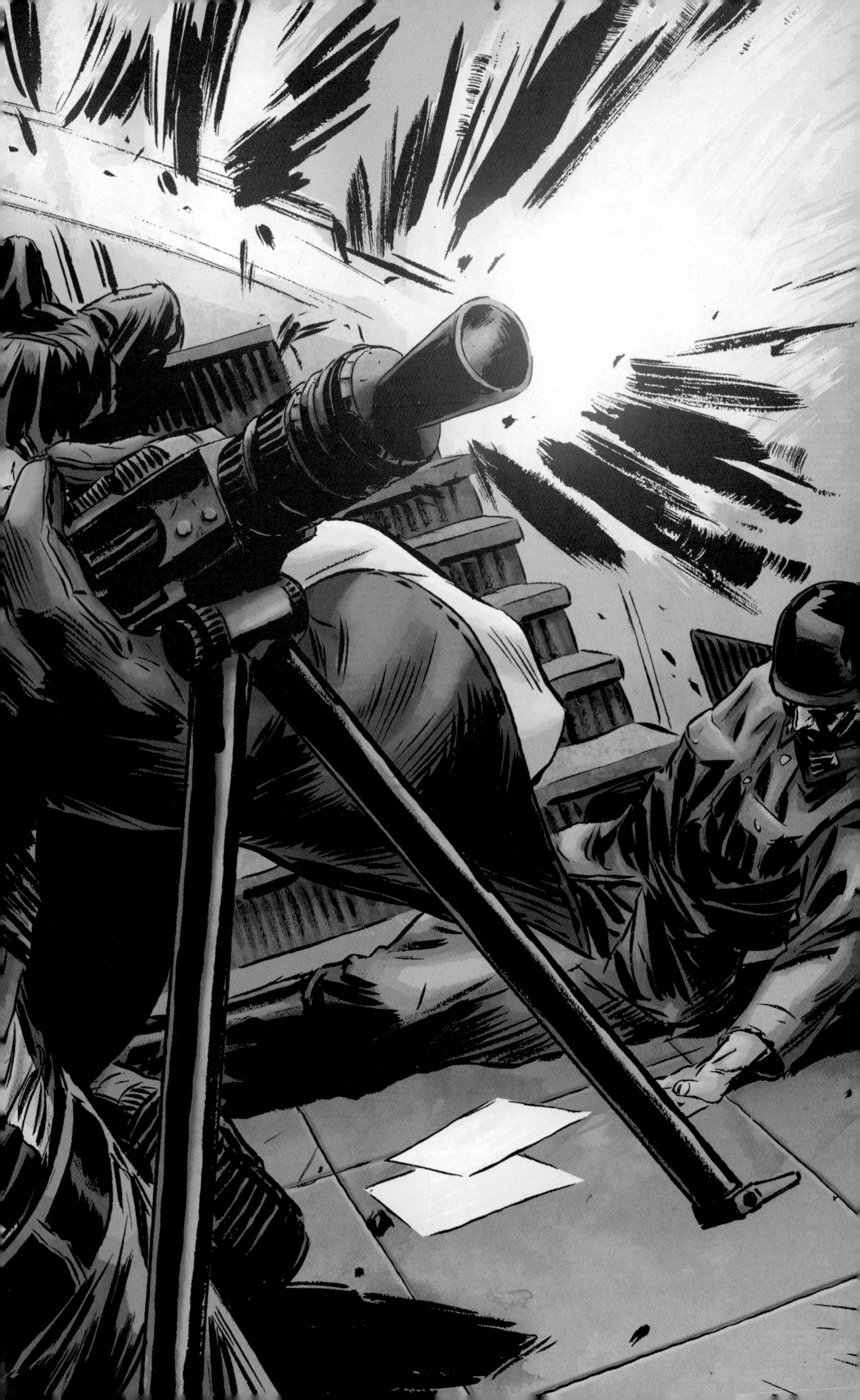

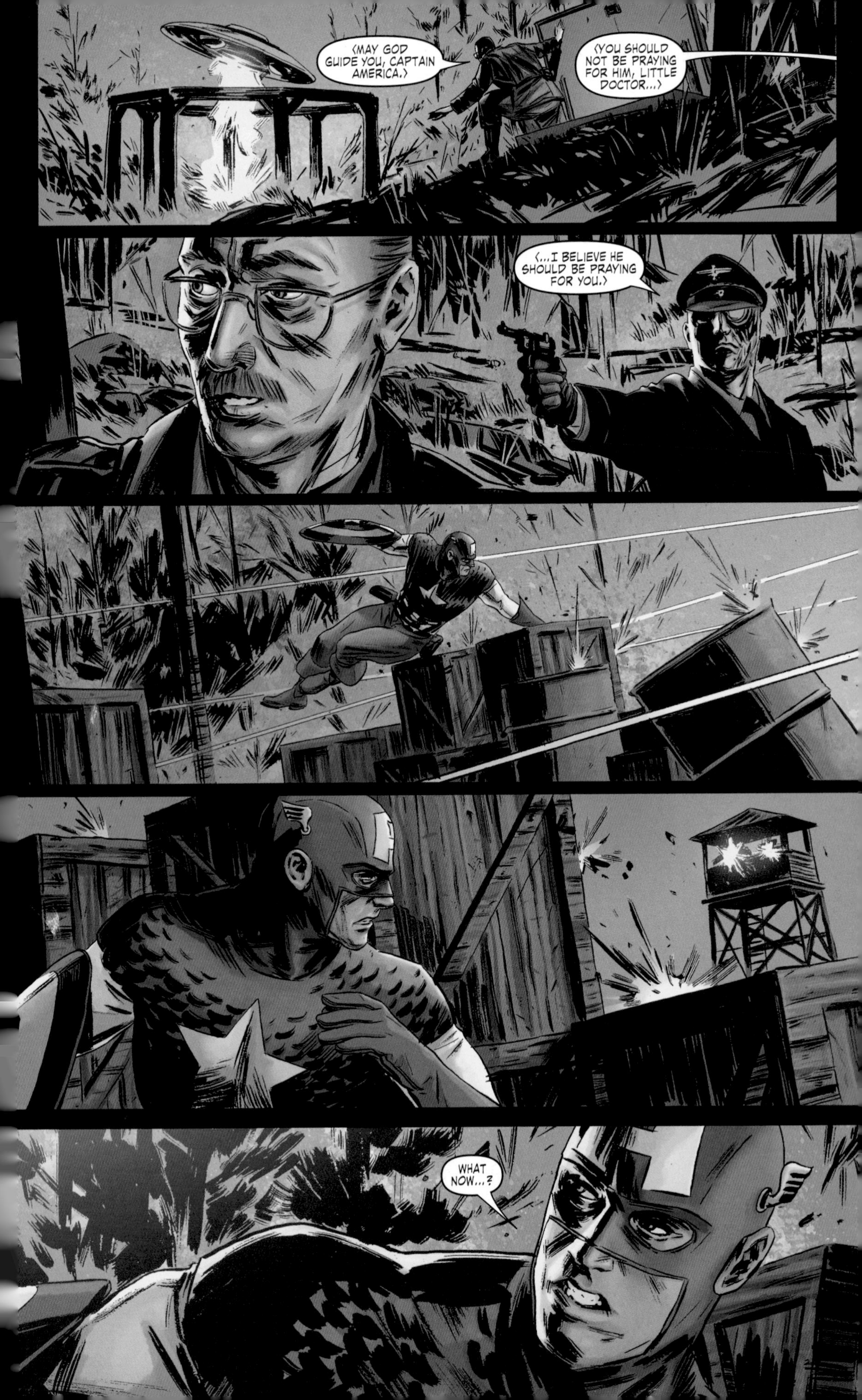
‹MAY GOD GUIDE YOU, CAPTAIN AMERICA.›
‹YOU SHOULD NOT BE PRAYING FOR HIM, LITTLE DOCTOR...›
‹...I BELIEVE HE SHOULD BE PRAYING FOR YOU.›
WHAT NOW...?

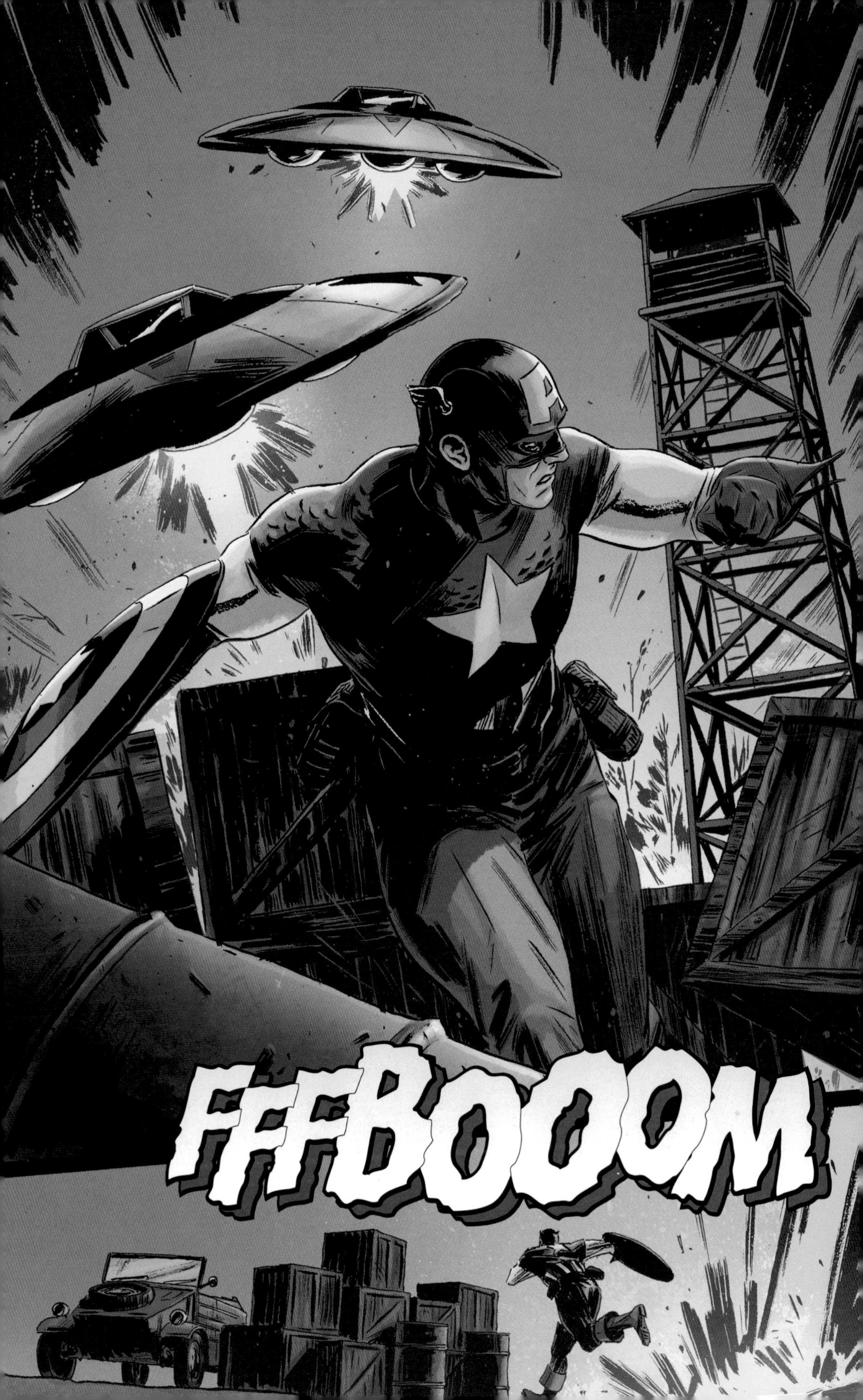
FFFBOOOM

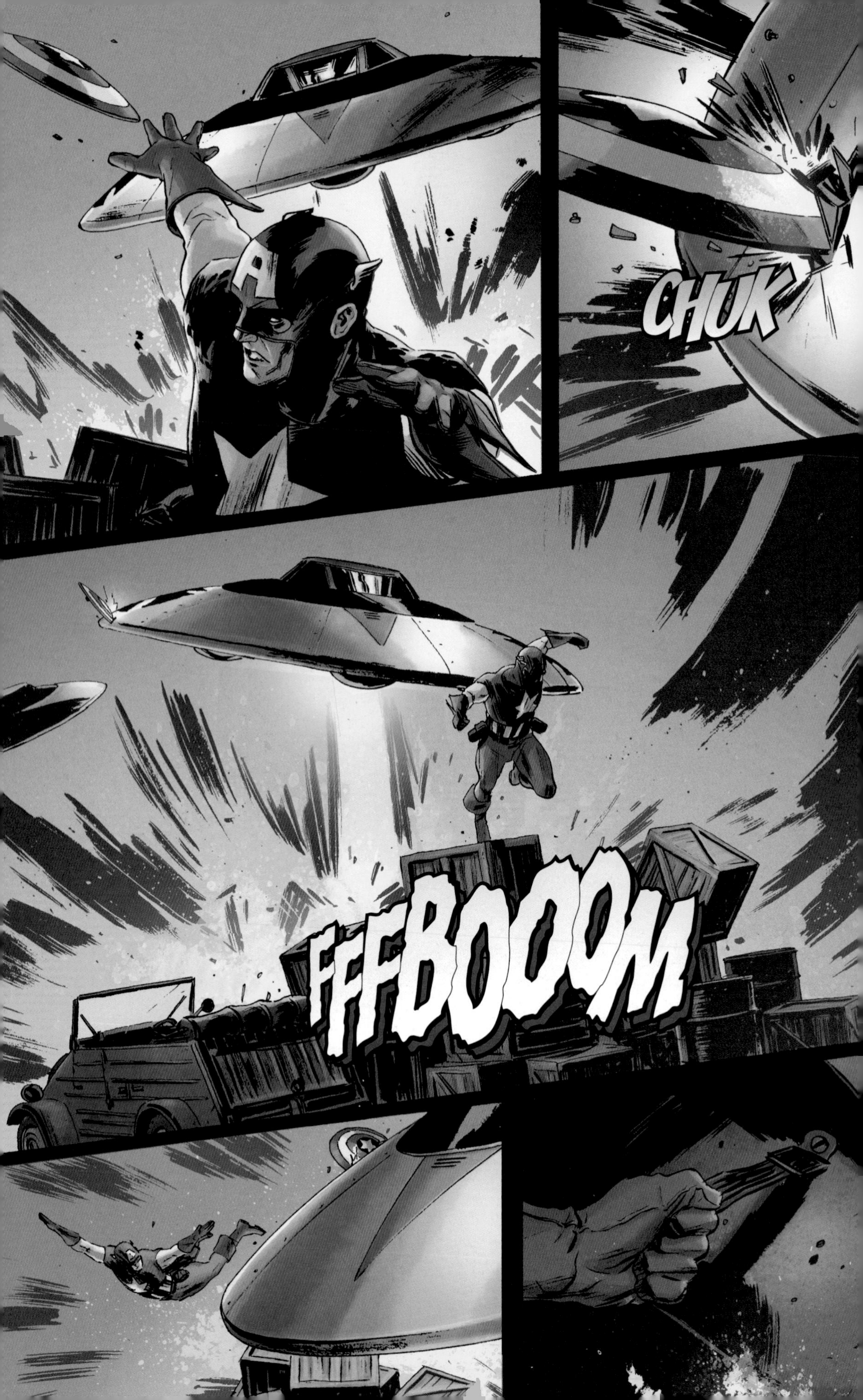
CHUK
FFFBOOOM

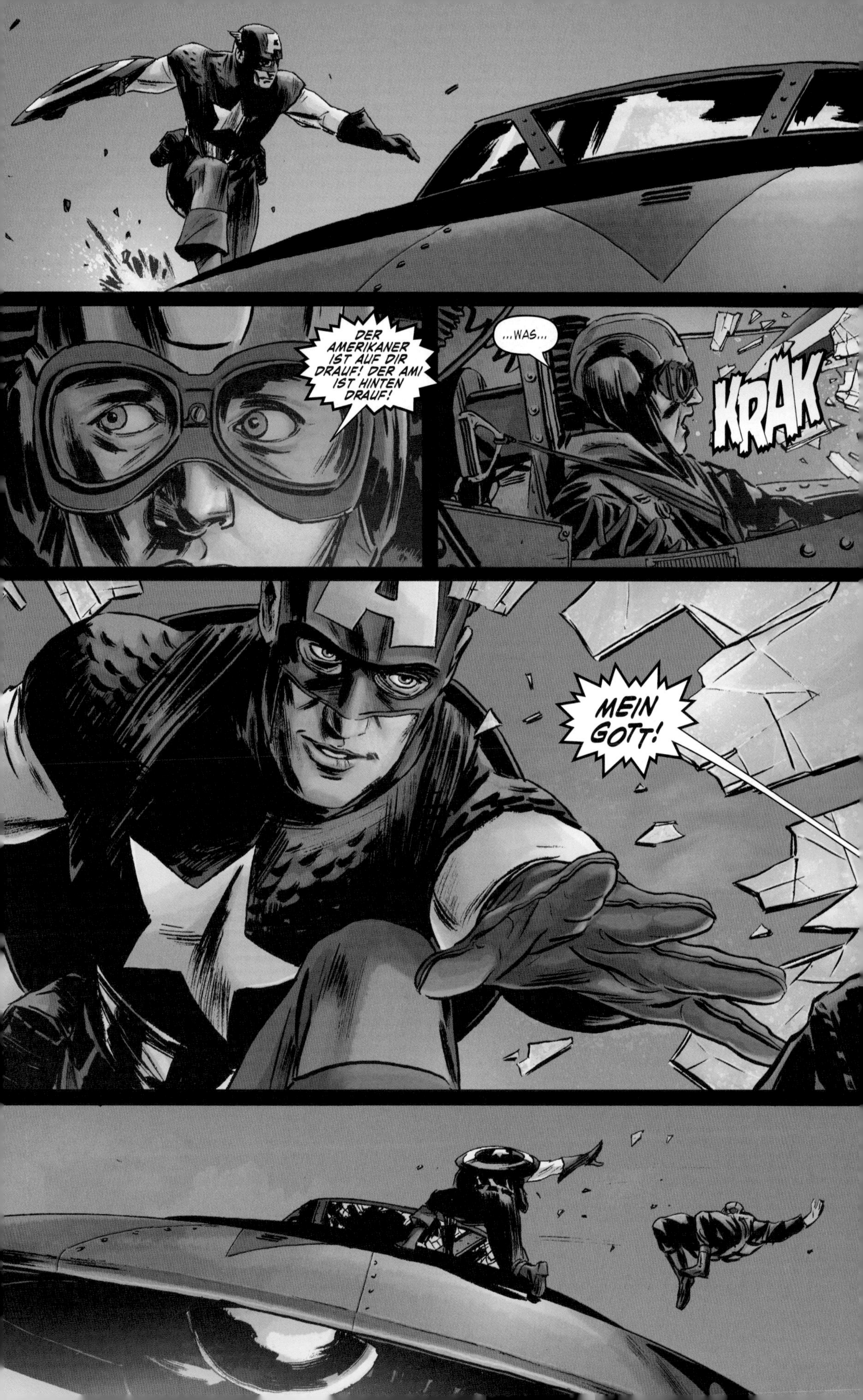
DER AMERIKANER IST AUF DIR DRAUF! DER AMI IST HINTEN DRAUF!
...WAS...
KRAK
MEIN GOTT!

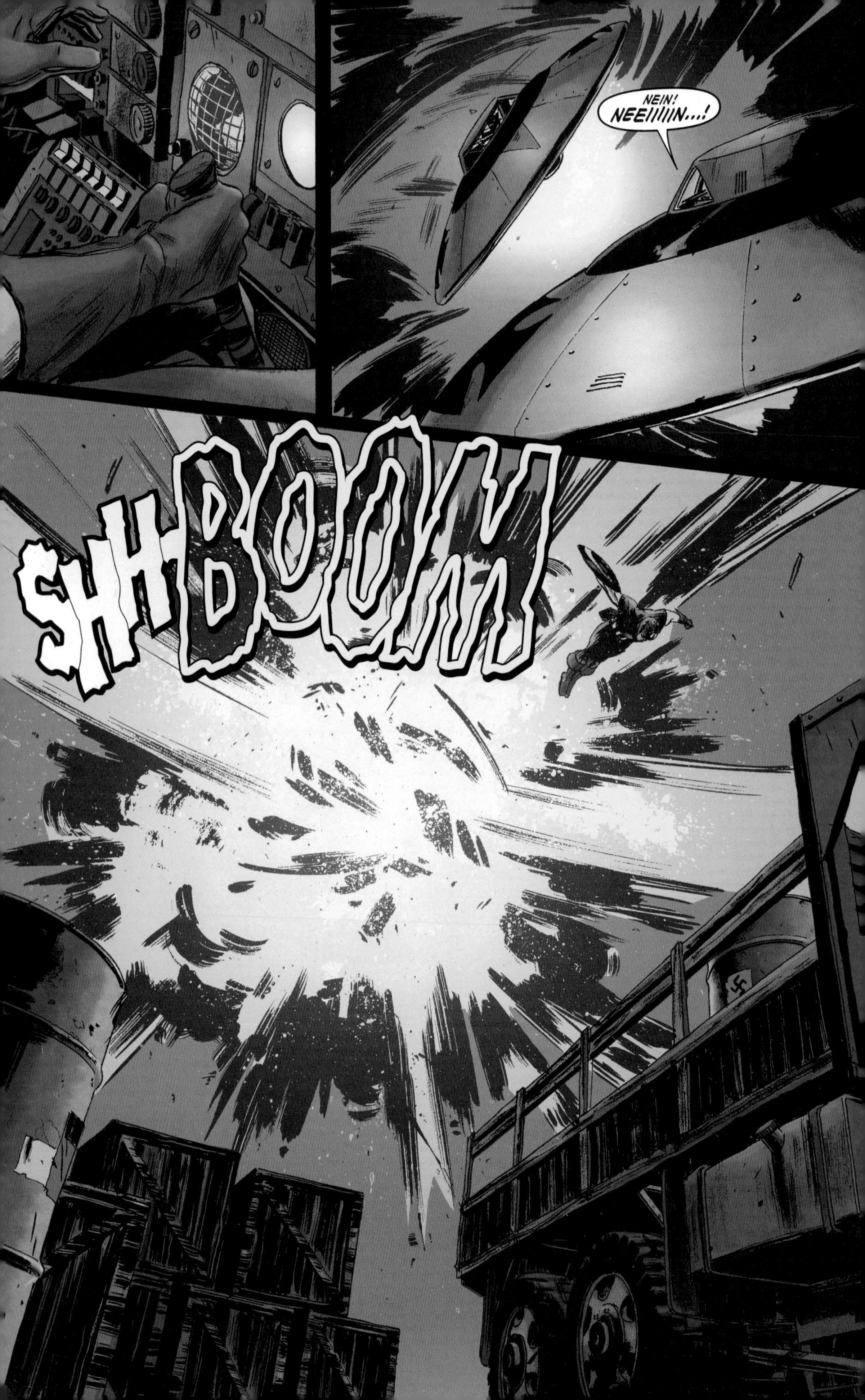
NEIN! NEEIIIIIN...!
SHHBOOM

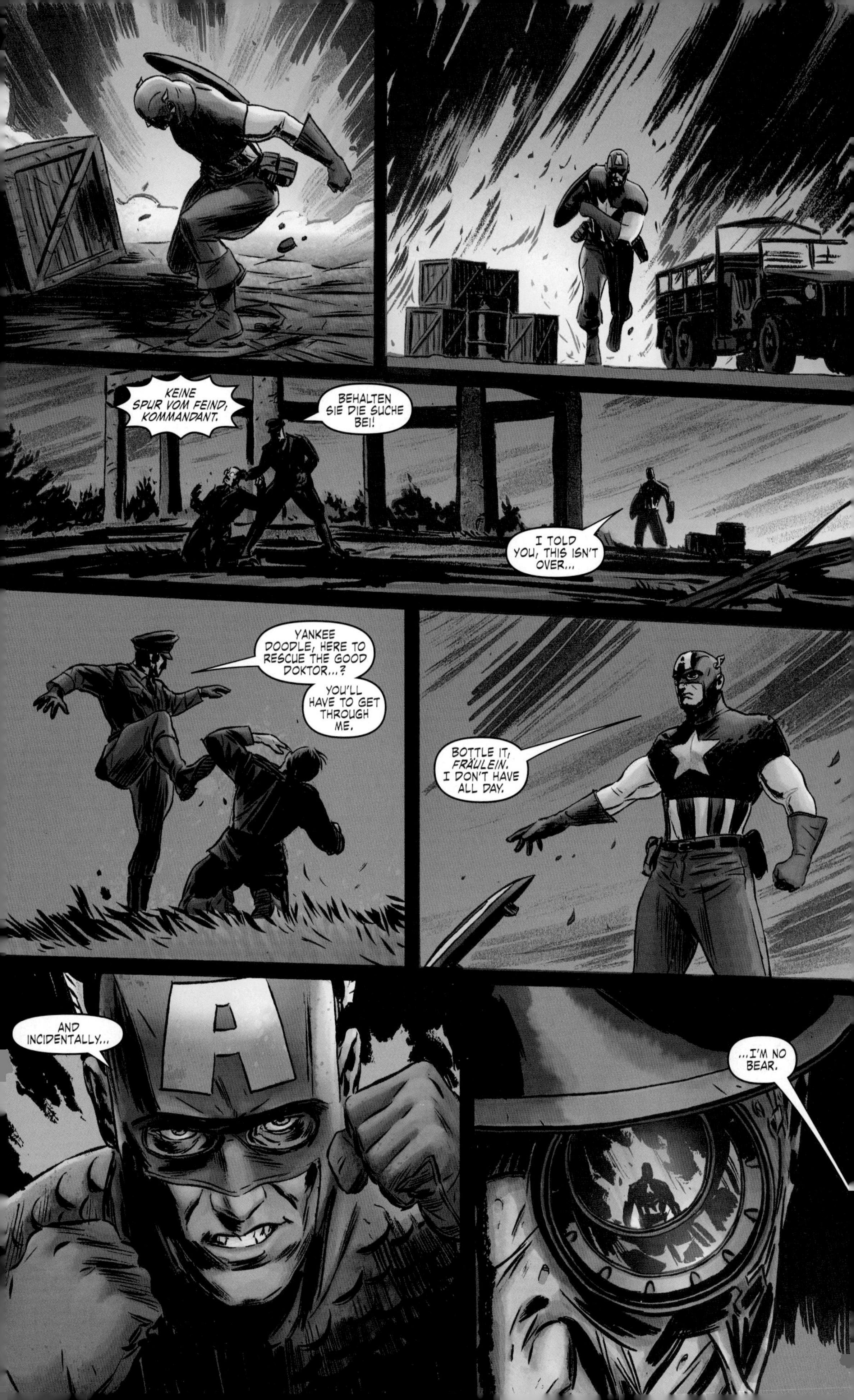
KEINE SPUR VOM FEIND, KOMMANDANT.
BEHALTEN SIE DIE SUCHE BEI!
I TOLD YOU, THIS ISN'T OVER...
YANKEE DOODLE, HERE TO RESCUE THE GOOD DOKTOR...?
YOU'LL HAVE TO GET THROUGH ME.
BOTTLE IT, *FRÄULEIN*. I DON'T HAVE ALL DAY.
AND INCIDENTALLY...
...I'M NO BEAR.

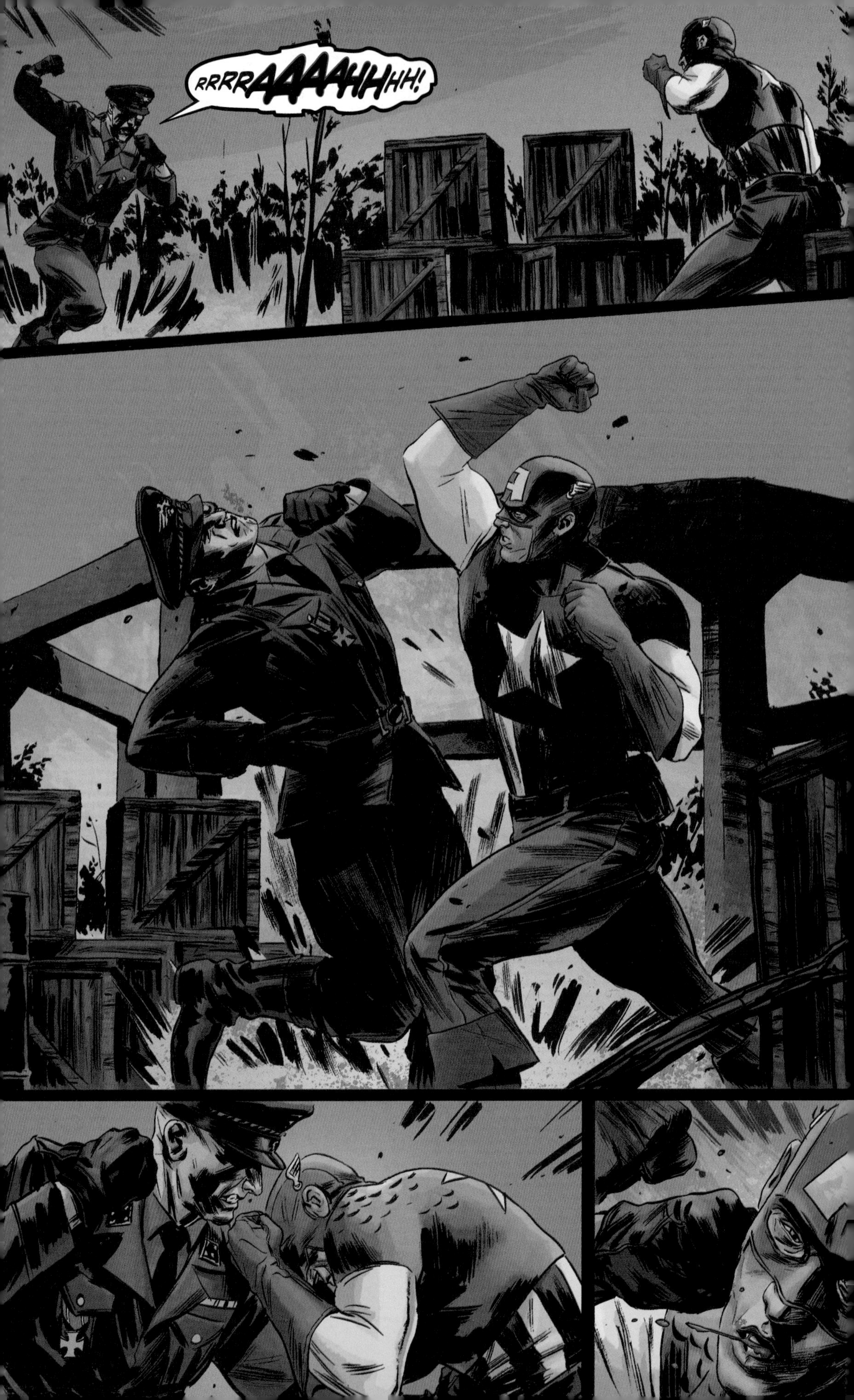
RRRRAAAAHHHH!

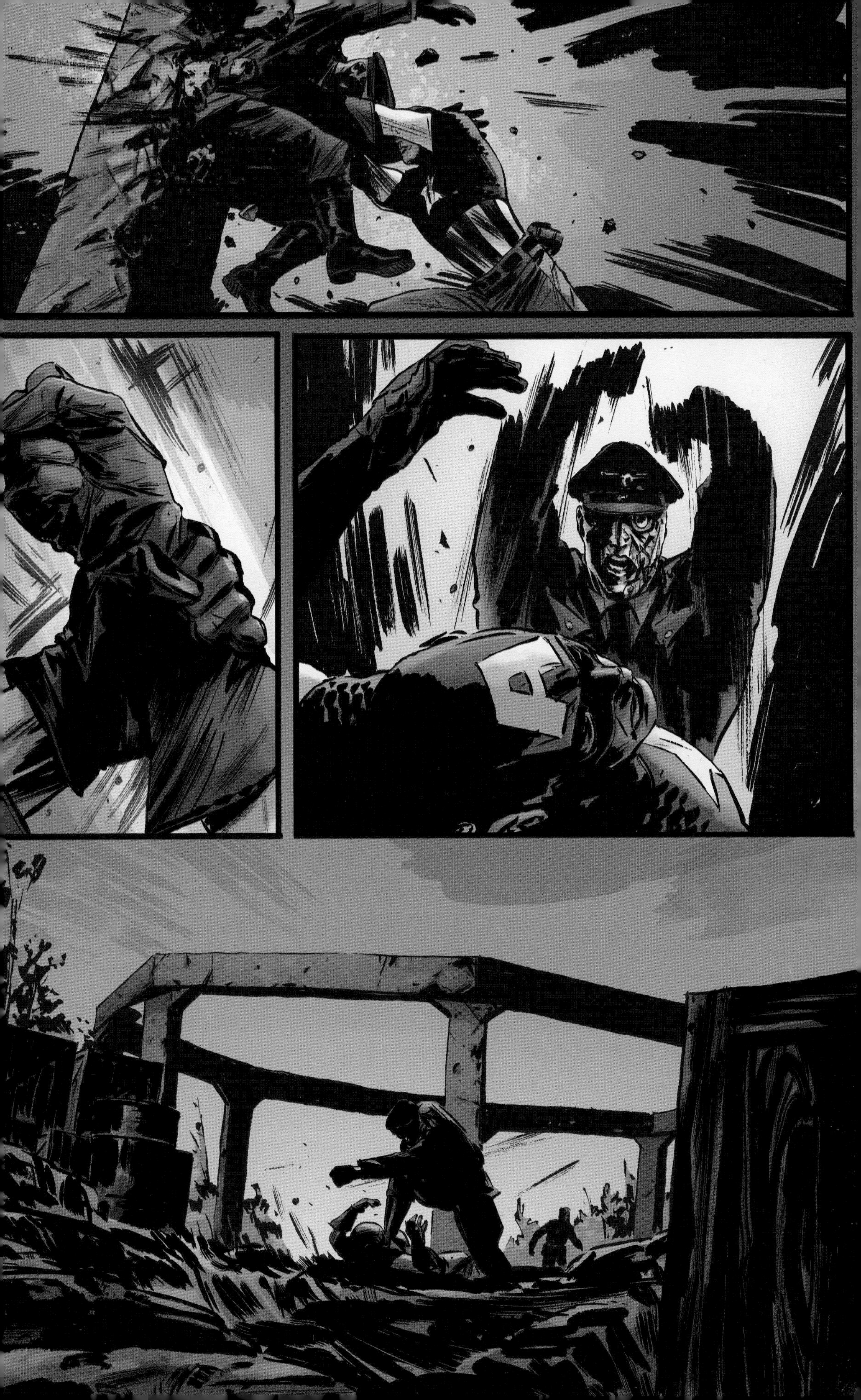

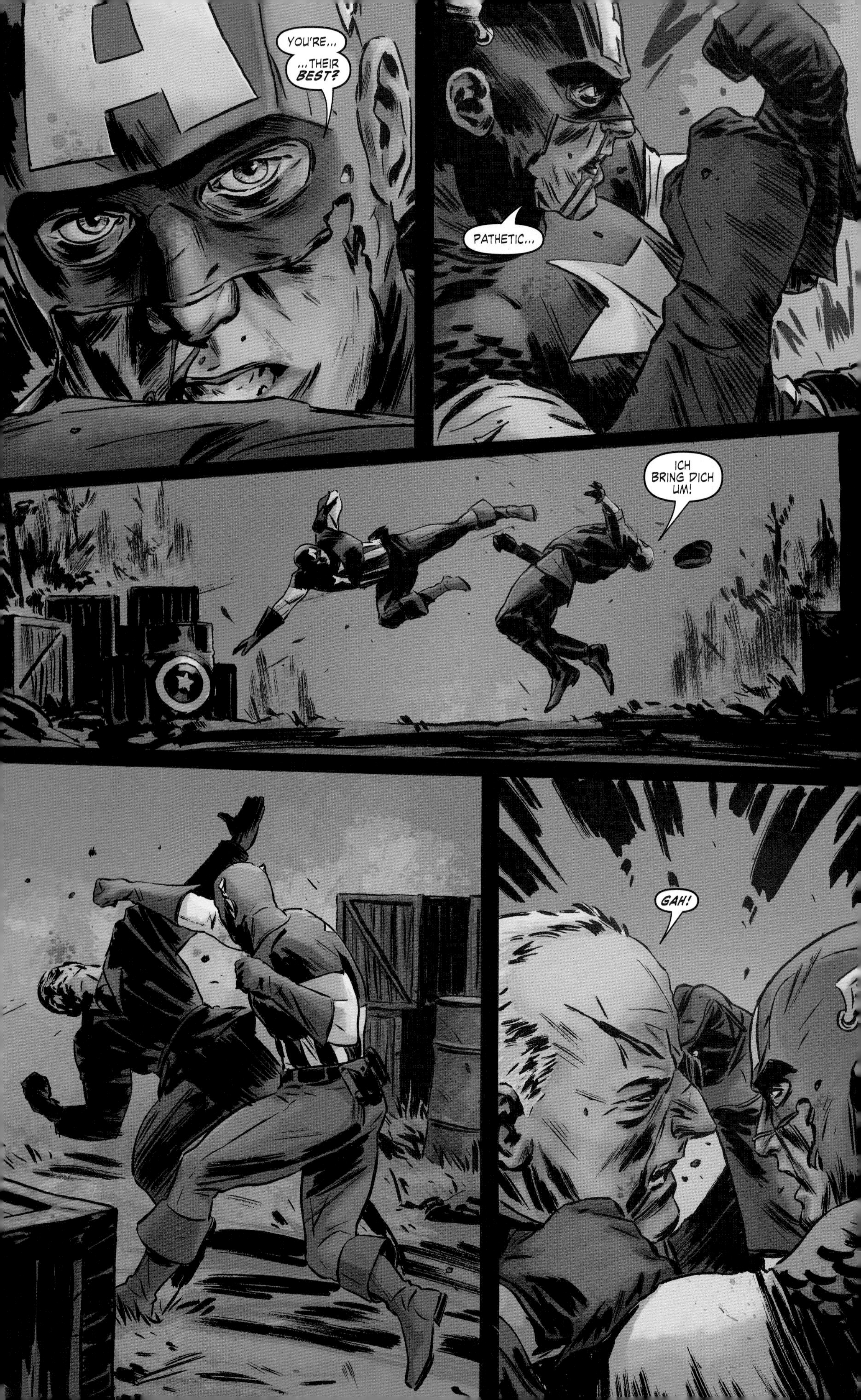
YOU'RE... ...THEIR BEST?
PATHETIC...
ICH BRING DICH UM!
GAH!

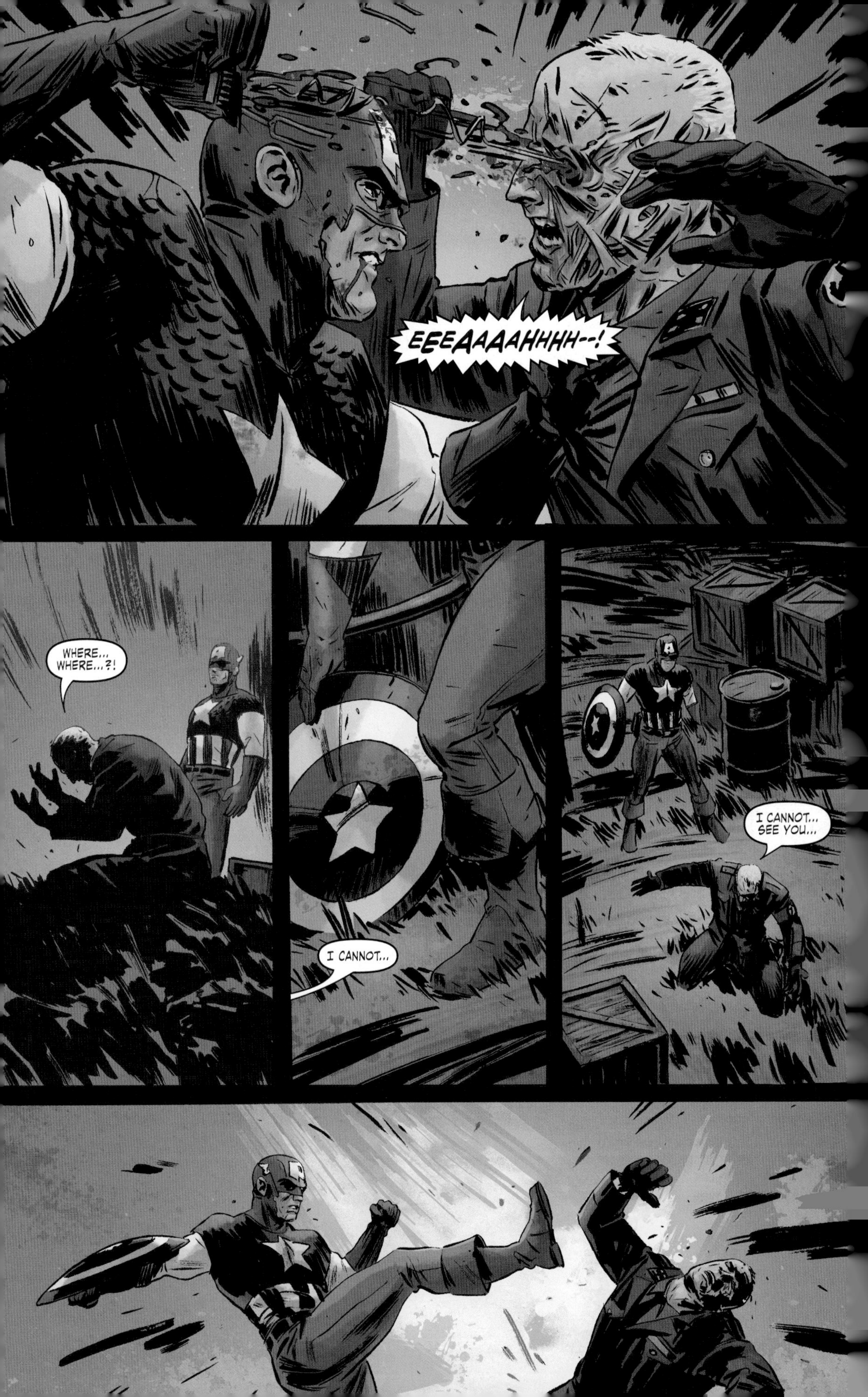
EEEAAAAHHHH--!
WHERE... WHERE...?!
I CANNOT...
I CANNOT... SEE YOU...

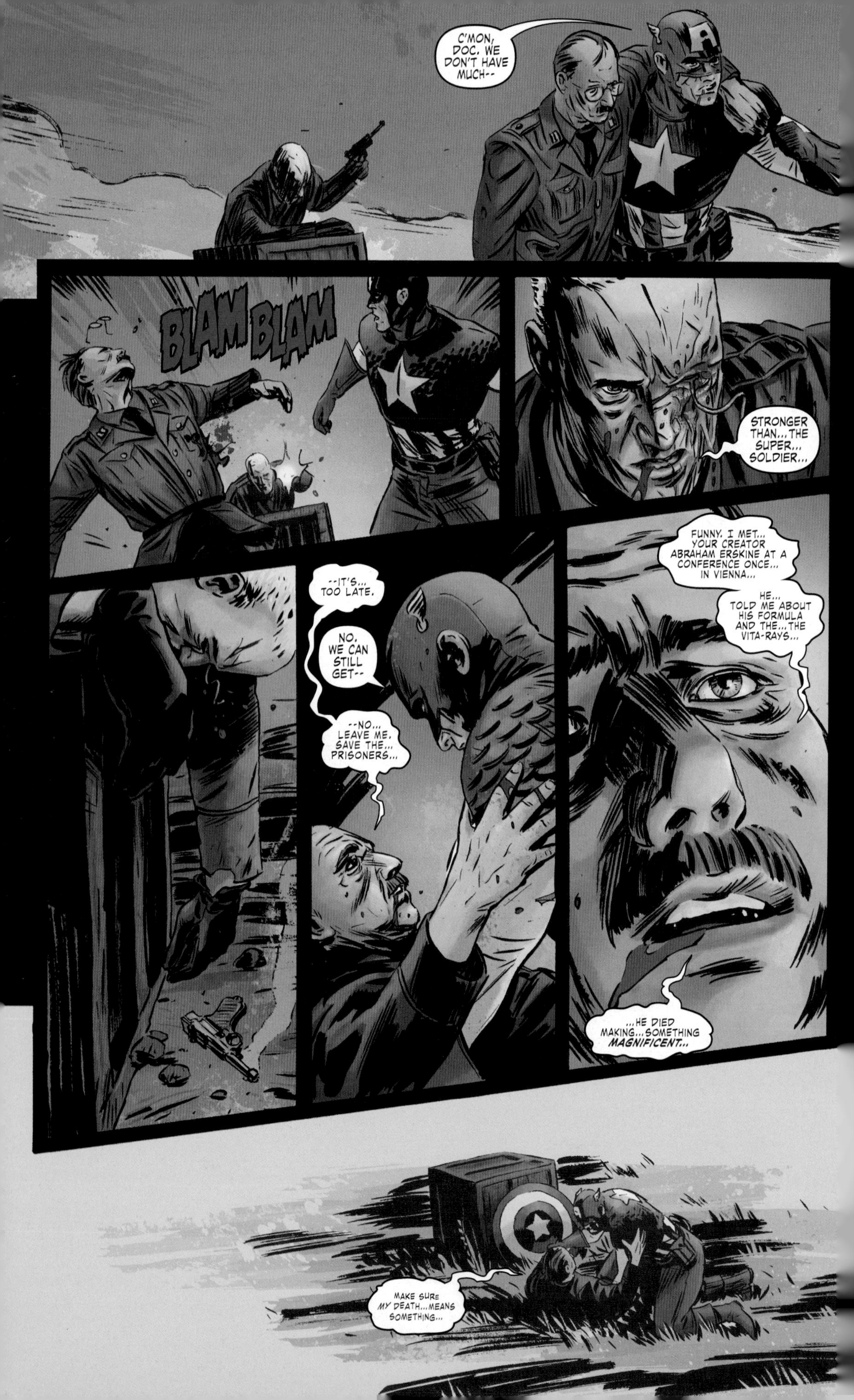
C'MON, DOC, WE DON'T HAVE MUCH--
BLAM BLAM
STRONGER THAN... THE SUPER... SOLDIER...
--IT'S... TOO LATE.
NO. WE CAN STILL GET--
--NO... LEAVE ME. SAVE THE... PRISONERS...
FUNNY. I MET... YOUR CREATOR ABRAHAM ERSKINE AT A CONFERENCE ONCE... IN VIENNA...
HE... TOLD ME ABOUT HIS FORMULA AND THE... THE VITA-RAYS...
...HE DIED MAKING... SOMETHING MAGNIFICENT...
MAKE SURE MY DEATH... MEANS SOMETHING...

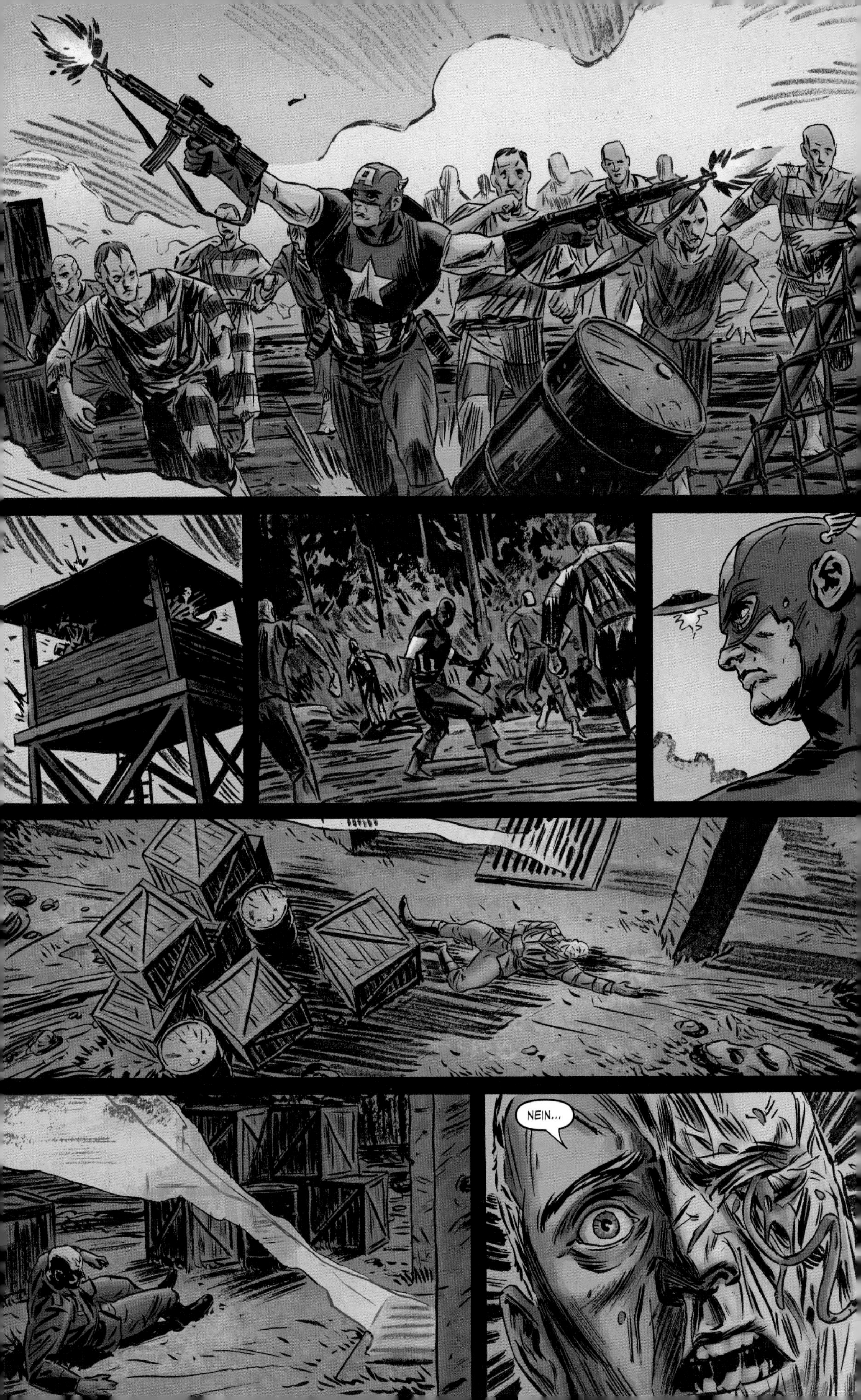
NEIN...

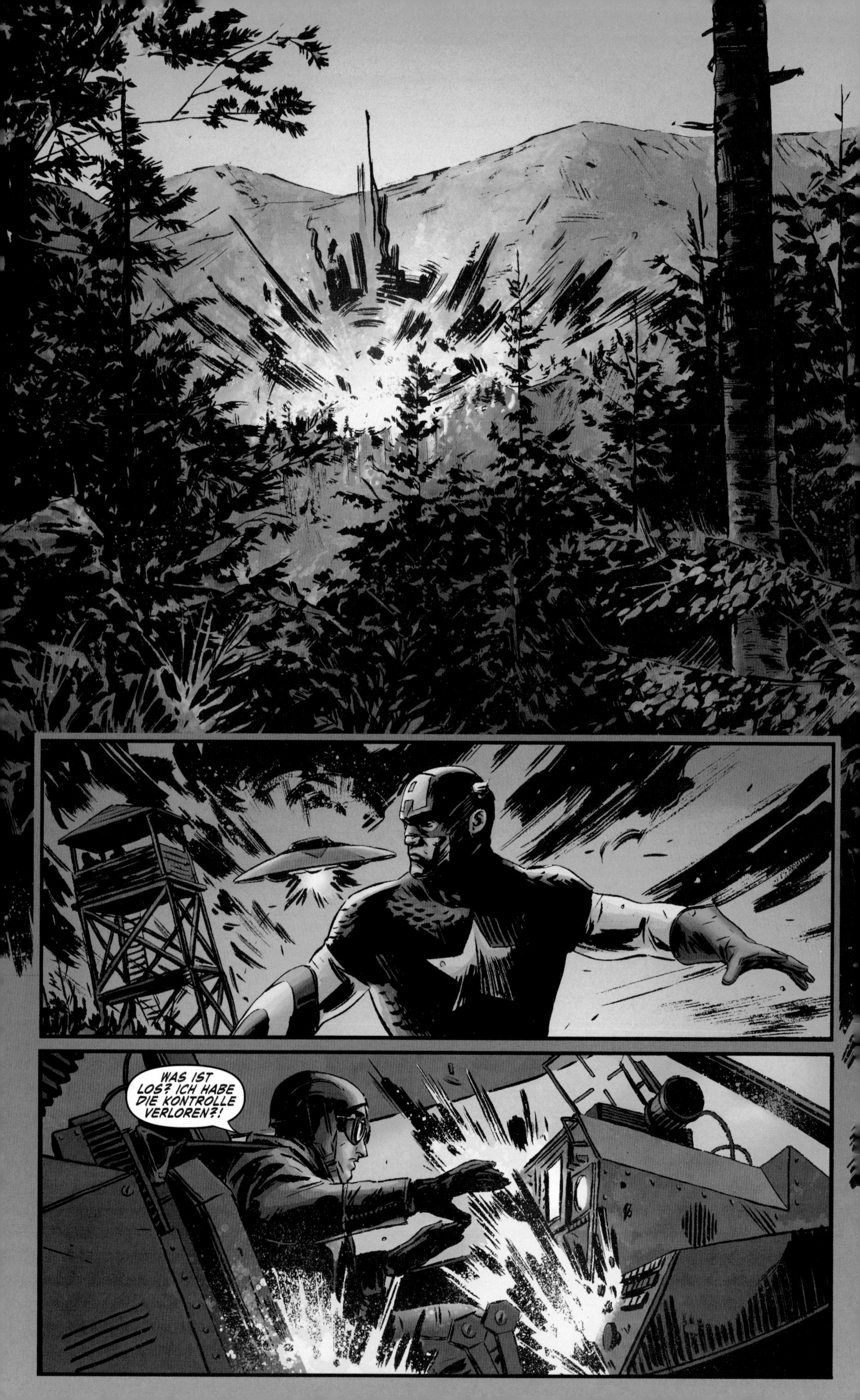
WAS IST LOS? ICH HABE DIE KONTROLLE VERLOREN?!

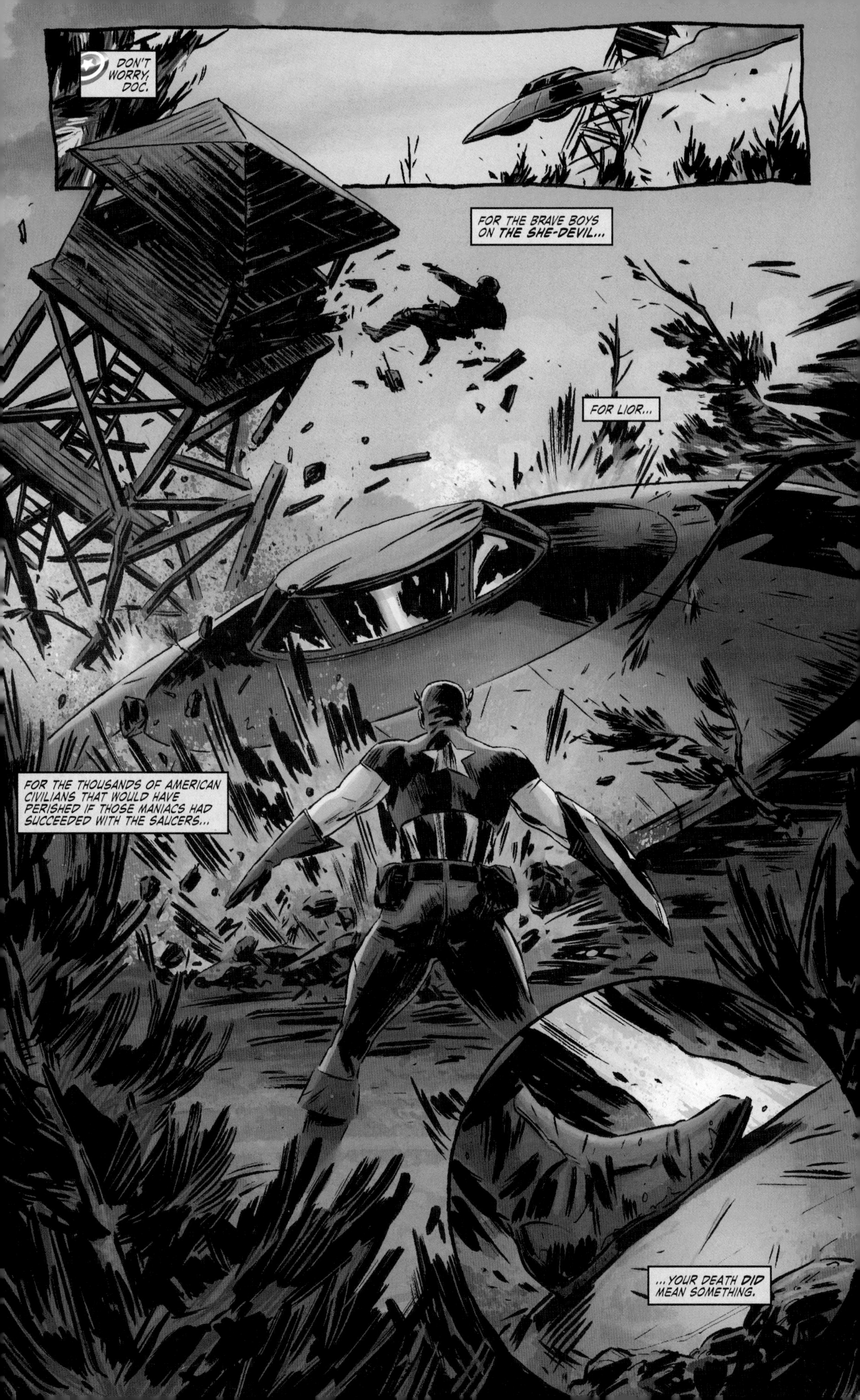
DON'T WORRY, DOC.
FOR THE BRAVE BOYS ON THE SHE-DEVIL...
FOR LIOR...
FOR THE THOUSANDS OF AMERICAN CIVILIANS THAT WOULD HAVE PERISHED IF THOSE MANIACS HAD SUCCEEDED WITH THE SAUCERS...
...YOUR DEATH DID MEAN SOMETHING.

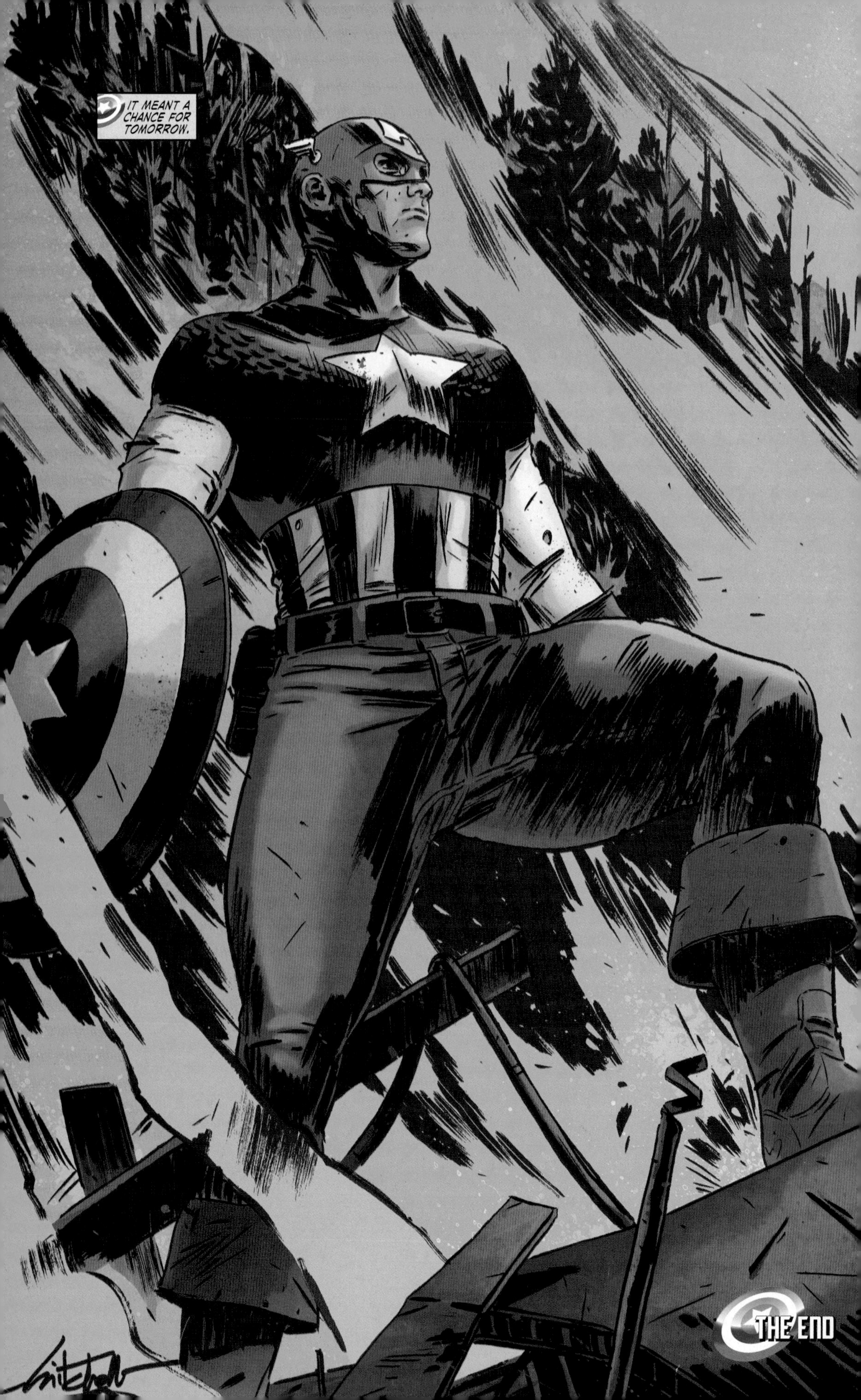
IT MEANT A CHANCE FOR TOMORROW.
THE END

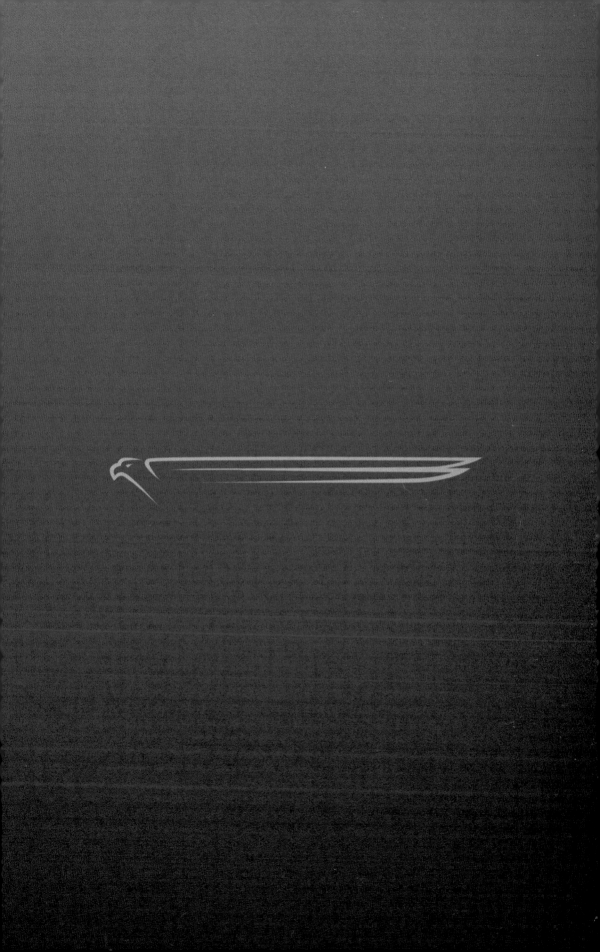

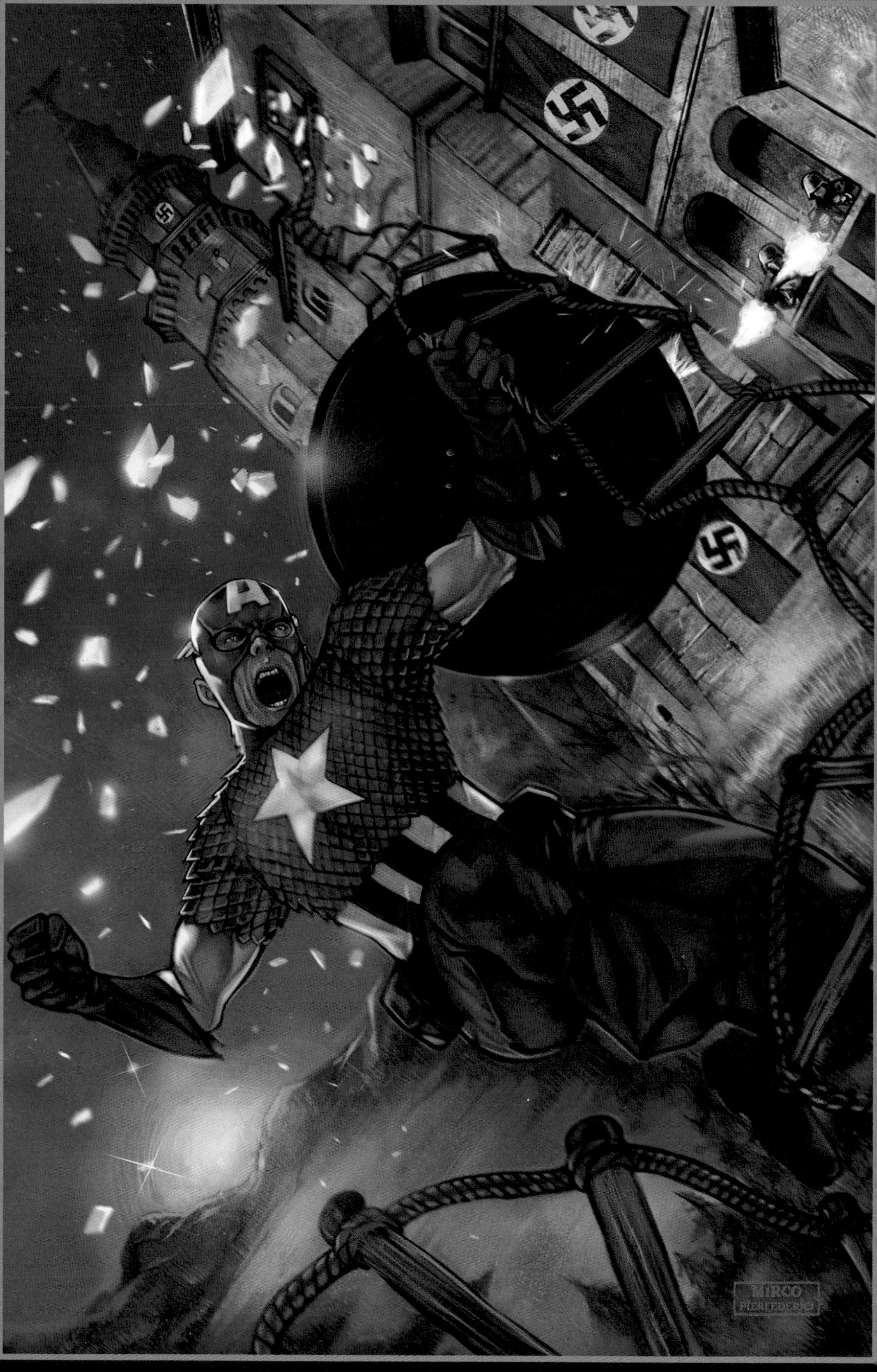
MIRCO PIERFEDERICI

PRISONERS OF DUTY

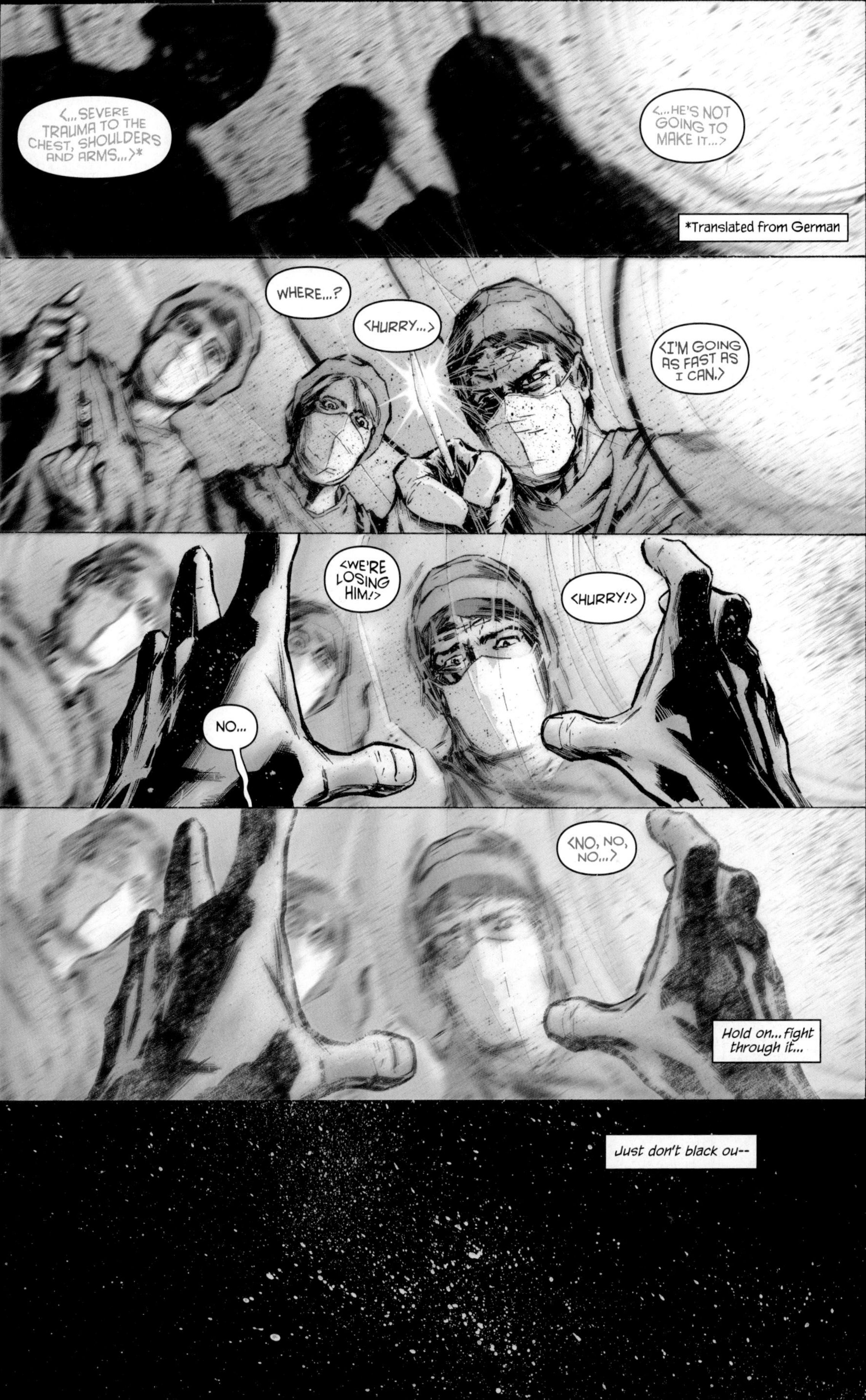
<... SEVERE TRAUMA TO THE CHEST, SHOULDERS AND ARMS...>*
<...HE'S NOT GOING TO MAKE IT...>
*Translated from German
WHERE...?
<HURRY...>
<I'M GOING AS FAST AS I CAN.>
<WE'RE LOSING HIM!>
<HURRY!>
NO...
<NO, NO, NO...>
Hold on... fight through it...
Just don't black ou--

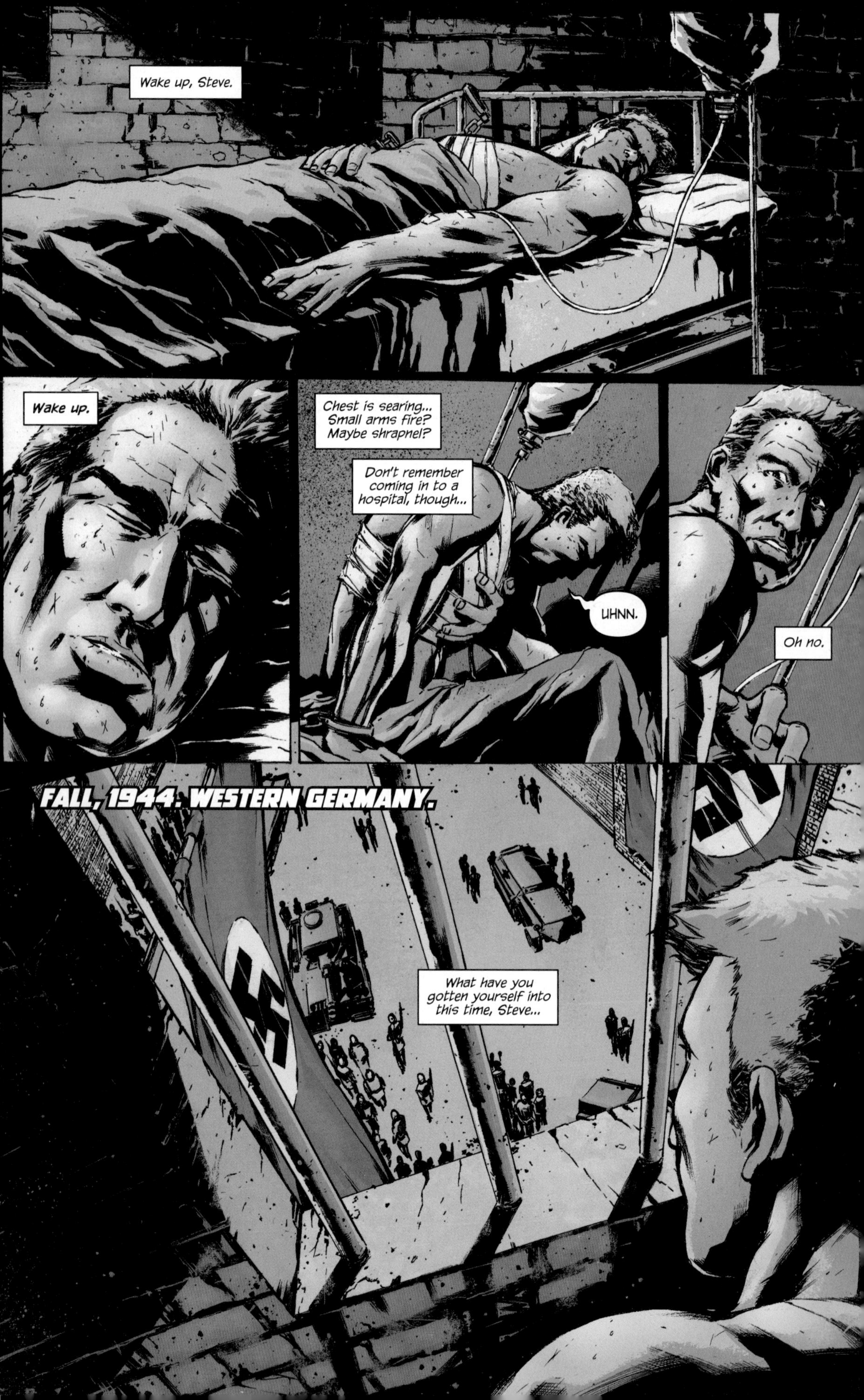
Wake up, Steve.
Wake up.
Chest is searing... Small arms fire? Maybe shrapnel?
Don't remember coming in to a hospital, though...
UHNN.
Oh no.
FALL, 1944. WESTERN GERMANY.
What have you gotten yourself into this time, Steve...

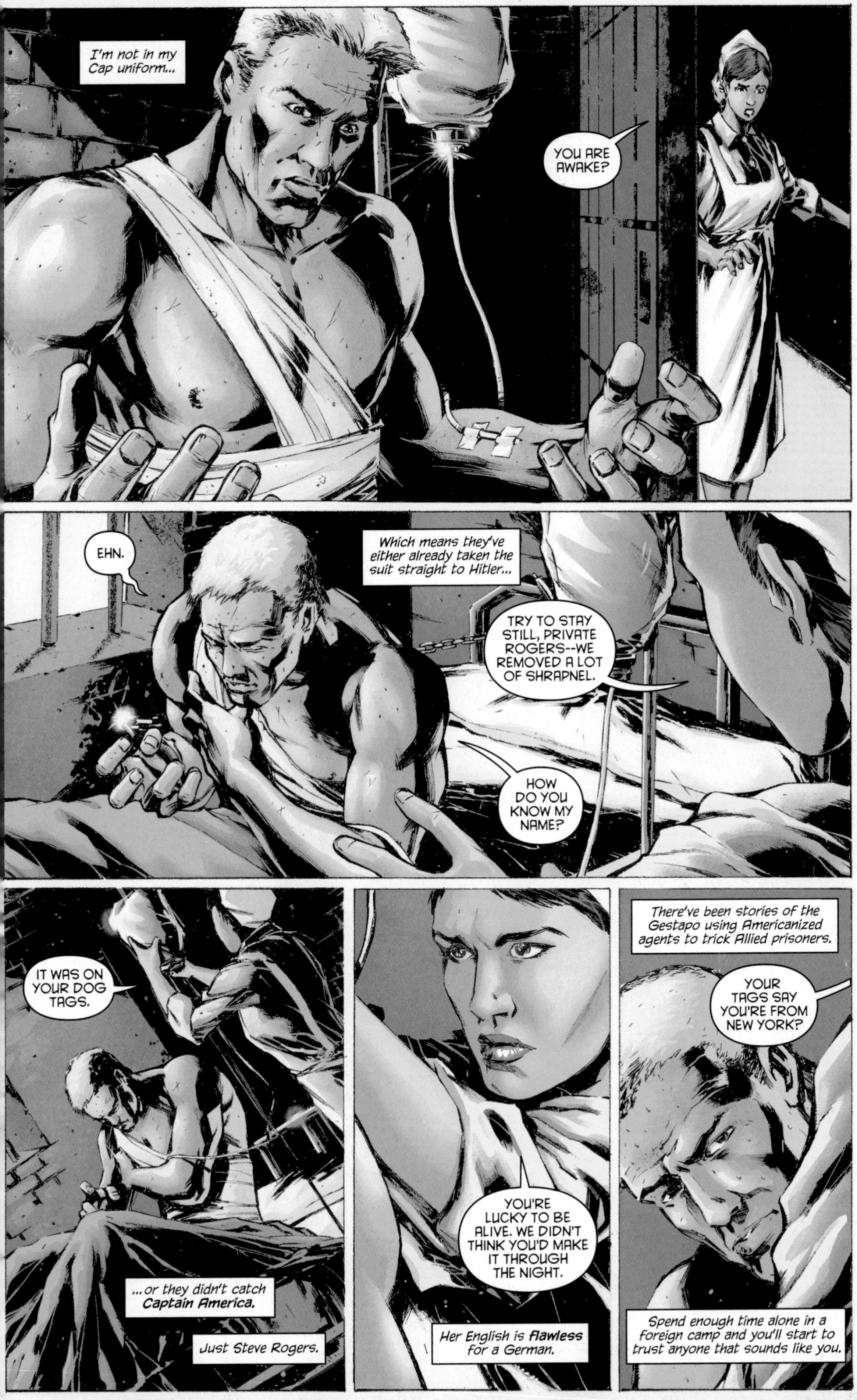
I'm not in my Cap uniform...
YOU ARE AWAKE?
EHN.
Which means they've either already taken the suit straight to Hitler...
TRY TO STAY STILL, PRIVATE ROGERS--WE REMOVED A LOT OF SHRAPNEL.
HOW DO YOU KNOW MY NAME?
IT WAS ON YOUR DOG TAGS.
...or they didn't catch Captain America.
Just Steve Rogers.
YOU'RE LUCKY TO BE ALIVE. WE DIDN'T THINK YOU'D MAKE IT THROUGH THE NIGHT.
Her English is flawless for a German.
There've been stories of the Gestapo using Americanized agents to trick Allied prisoners.
YOUR TAGS SAY YOU'RE FROM NEW YORK?
Spend enough time alone in a foreign camp and you'll start to trust anyone that sounds like you.

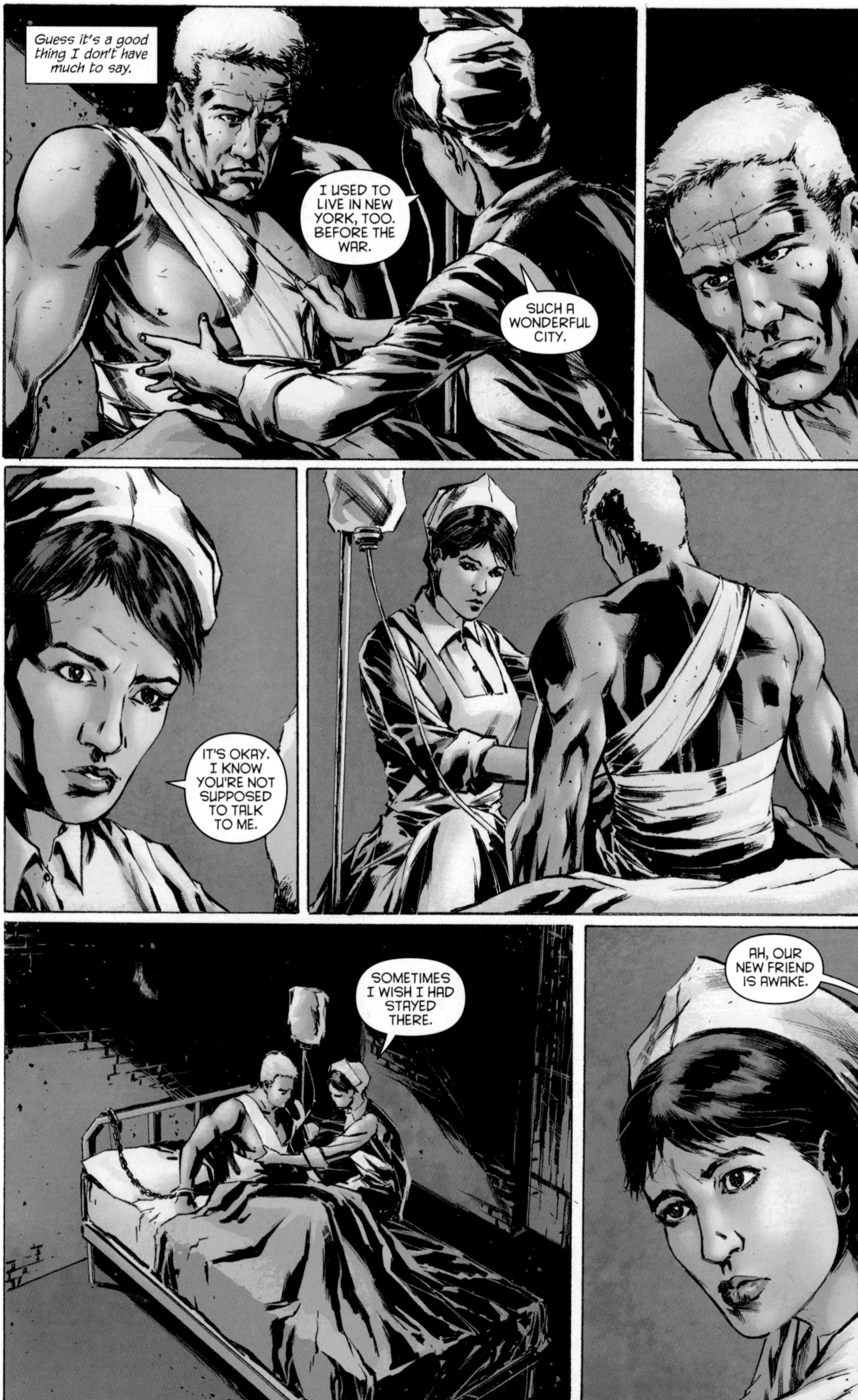
Guess it's a good thing I don't have much to say.
I USED TO LIVE IN NEW YORK, TOO. BEFORE THE WAR.
SUCH A WONDERFUL CITY.
IT'S OKAY. I KNOW YOU'RE NOT SUPPOSED TO TALK TO ME.
SOMETIMES I WISH I HAD STAYED THERE.
AH, OUR NEW FRIEND IS AWAKE.

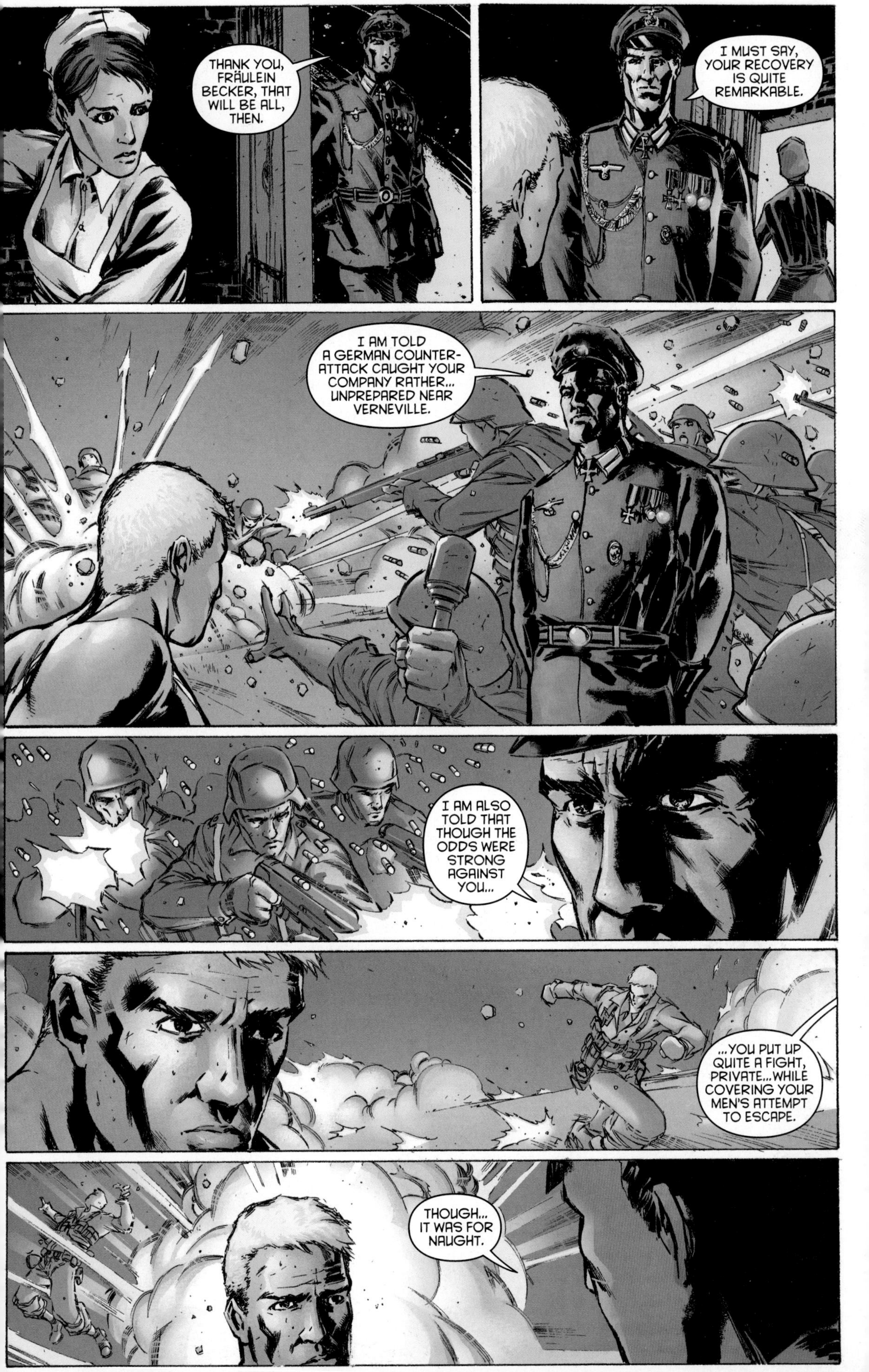
THANK YOU, FRÄULEIN BECKER, THAT WILL BE ALL, THEN.
I MUST SAY, YOUR RECOVERY IS QUITE REMARKABLE.
I AM TOLD A GERMAN COUNTER-ATTACK CAUGHT YOUR COMPANY RATHER... UNPREPARED NEAR VERNEVILLE.
I AM ALSO TOLD THAT THOUGH THE ODDS WERE STRONG AGAINST YOU...
...YOU PUT UP QUITE A FIGHT, PRIVATE...WHILE COVERING YOUR MEN'S ATTEMPT TO ESCAPE.
THOUGH... IT WAS FOR NAUGHT.

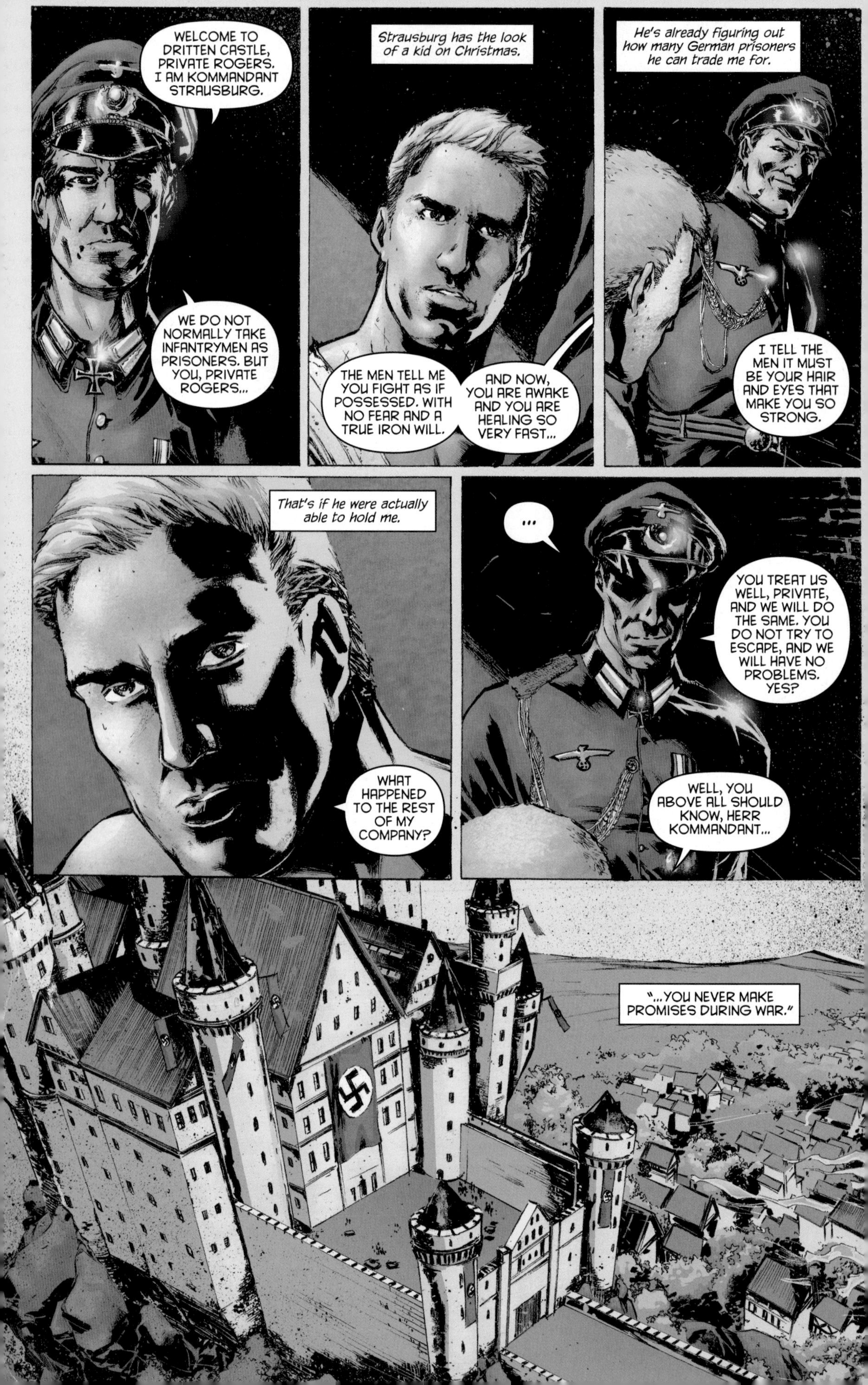
WELCOME TO DRITTEN CASTLE, PRIVATE ROGERS. I AM KOMMANDANT STRAUSBURG.
WE DO NOT NORMALLY TAKE INFANTRYMEN AS PRISONERS. BUT YOU, PRIVATE ROGERS...
Strausburg has the look of a kid on Christmas.
THE MEN TELL ME YOU FIGHT AS IF POSSESSED. WITH NO FEAR AND A TRUE IRON WILL.
AND NOW, YOU ARE AWAKE AND YOU ARE HEALING SO VERY FAST...
He's already figuring out how many German prisoners he can trade me for.
I TELL THE MEN IT MUST BE YOUR HAIR AND EYES THAT MAKE YOU SO STRONG.
That's if he were actually able to hold me.
WHAT HAPPENED TO THE REST OF MY COMPANY?
...
YOU TREAT US WELL, PRIVATE, AND WE WILL DO THE SAME. YOU DO NOT TRY TO ESCAPE, AND WE WILL HAVE NO PROBLEMS. YES?
WELL, YOU ABOVE ALL SHOULD KNOW, HERR KOMMANDANT...
"...YOU NEVER MAKE PROMISES DURING WAR."

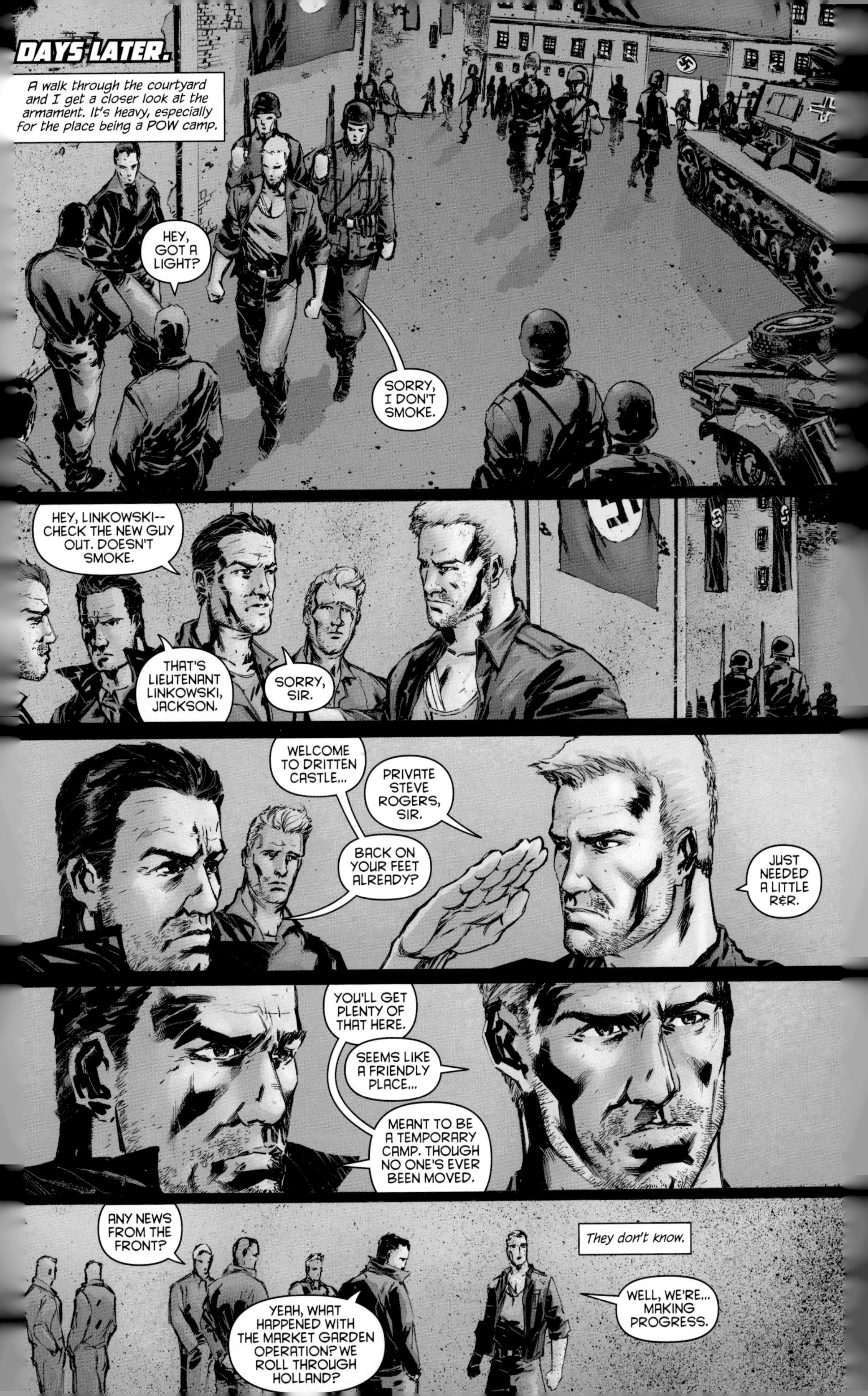
DAYS LATER.
A walk through the courtyard and I get a closer look at the armament. It's heavy, especially for the place being a POW camp.
HEY, GOT A LIGHT?
SORRY, I DON'T SMOKE.
HEY, LINKOWSKI-- CHECK THE NEW GUY OUT. DOESN'T SMOKE.
THAT'S LIEUTENANT LINKOWSKI, JACKSON.
SORRY, SIR.
WELCOME TO DRITTEN CASTLE...
PRIVATE STEVE ROGERS, SIR.
BACK ON YOUR FEET ALREADY?
JUST NEEDED A LITTLE R&R.
YOU'LL GET PLENTY OF THAT HERE.
SEEMS LIKE A FRIENDLY PLACE...
MEANT TO BE A TEMPORARY CAMP. THOUGH NO ONE'S EVER BEEN MOVED.
ANY NEWS FROM THE FRONT?
YEAH, WHAT HAPPENED WITH THE MARKET GARDEN OPERATION? WE ROLL THROUGH HOLLAND?
They don't know.
WELL, WE'RE... MAKING PROGRESS.

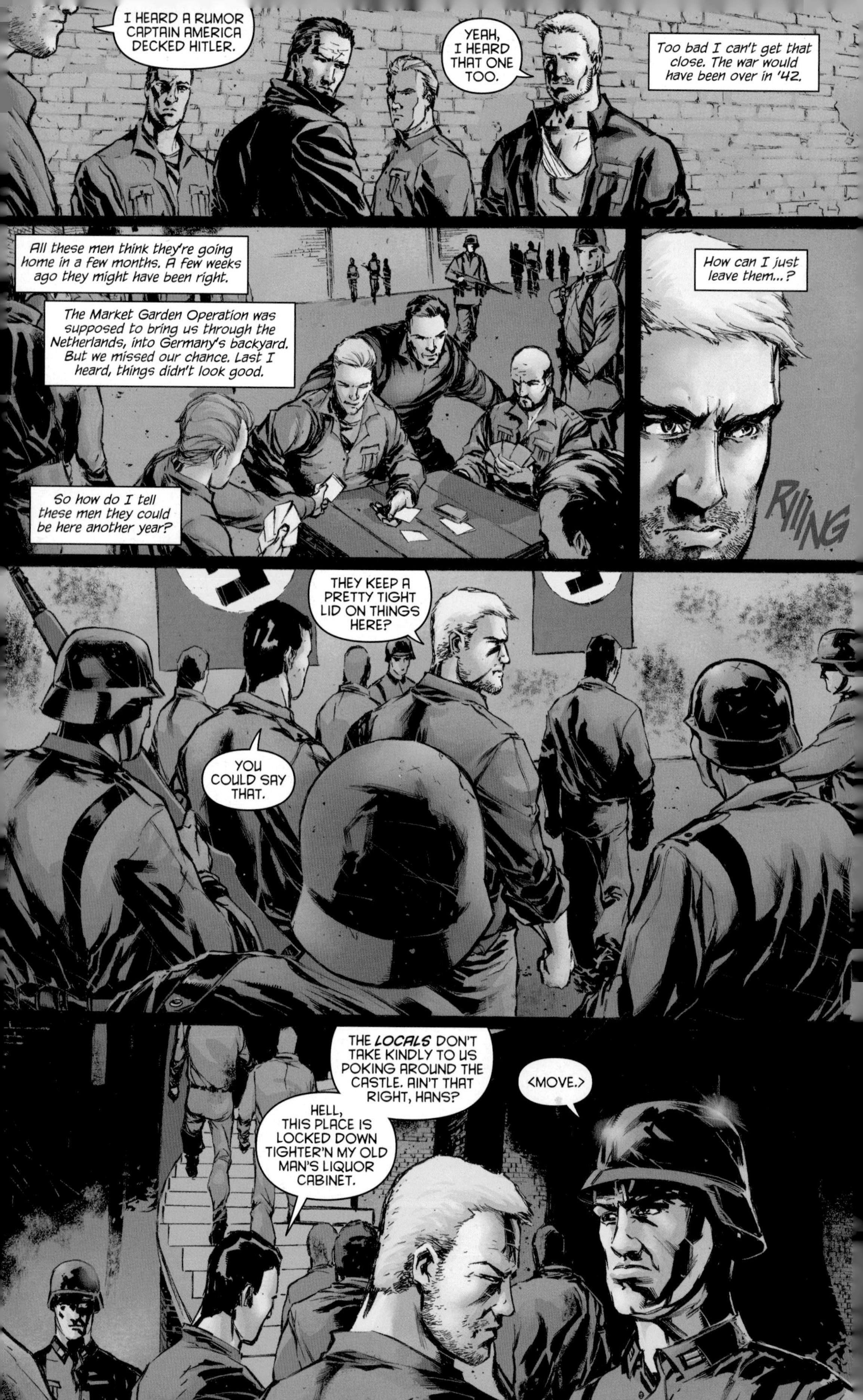
I HEARD A RUMOR CAPTAIN AMERICA DECKED HITLER.
YEAH, I HEARD THAT ONE TOO.
Too bad I can't get that close. The war would have been over in '42.
All these men think they're going home in a few months. A few weeks ago they might have been right.
The Market Garden Operation was supposed to bring us through the Netherlands, into Germany's backyard. But we missed our chance. Last I heard, things didn't look good.
So how do I tell these men they could be here another year?
How can I just leave them...?
RIIING
THEY KEEP A PRETTY TIGHT LID ON THINGS HERE?
YOU COULD SAY THAT.
THE LOCALS DON'T TAKE KINDLY TO US POKING AROUND THE CASTLE. AIN'T THAT RIGHT, HANS?
HELL, THIS PLACE IS LOCKED DOWN TIGHTER'N MY OLD MAN'S LIQUOR CABINET.
<MOVE.>

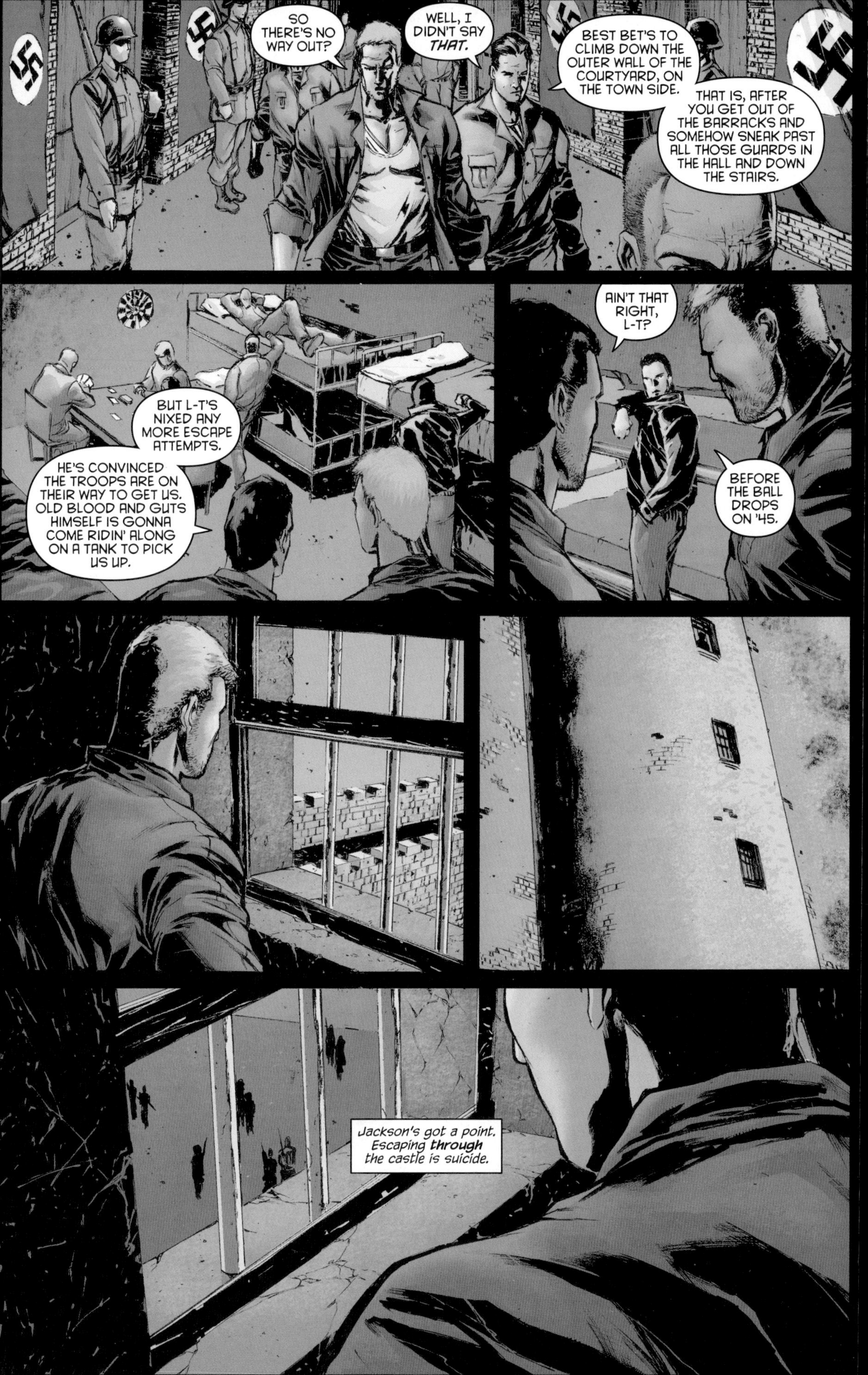
SO THERE'S NO WAY OUT?
WELL, I DIDN'T SAY *THAT.*
BEST BET'S TO CLIMB DOWN THE OUTER WALL OF THE COURTYARD, ON THE TOWN SIDE.
THAT IS, AFTER YOU GET OUT OF THE BARRACKS AND SOMEHOW SNEAK PAST ALL THOSE GUARDS IN THE HALL AND DOWN THE STAIRS.
BUT L-T'S NIXED ANY MORE ESCAPE ATTEMPTS.
HE'S CONVINCED THE TROOPS ARE ON THEIR WAY TO GET US. OLD BLOOD AND GUTS HIMSELF IS GONNA COME RIDIN' ALONG ON A TANK TO PICK US UP.
AIN'T THAT RIGHT, L-T?
BEFORE THE BALL DROPS ON '45.
Jackson's got a point. Escaping **through** the castle is suicide.

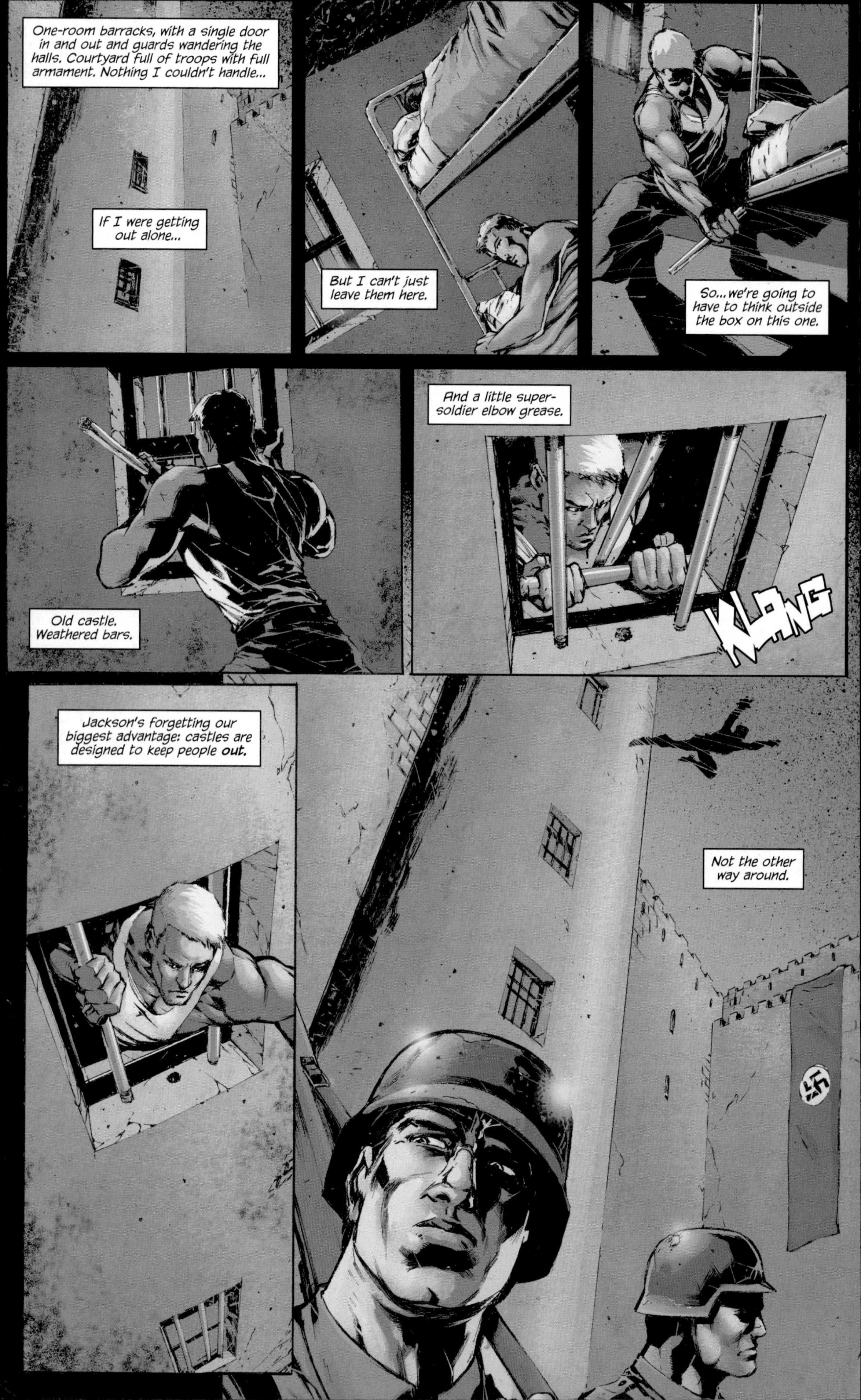
One-room barracks, with a single door in and out and guards wandering the halls. Courtyard full of troops with full armament. Nothing I couldn't handle...
If I were getting out alone...
But I can't just leave them here.
So...we're going to have to think outside the box on this one.
Old castle. Weathered bars.
And a little super-soldier elbow grease.
KLANG
Jackson's forgetting our biggest advantage: castles are designed to keep people **out.**
Not the other way around.

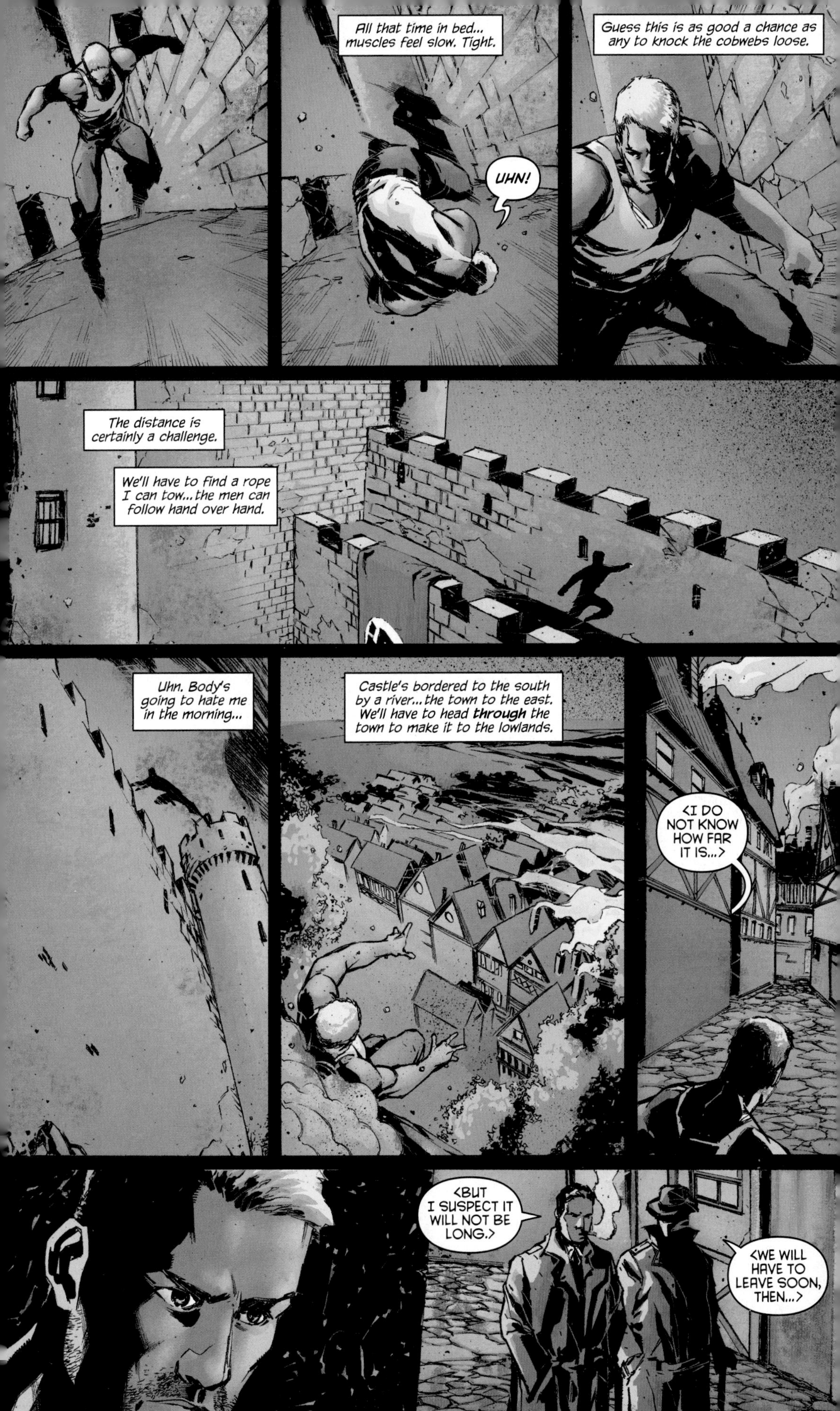
All that time in bed... muscles feel slow. Tight.
UHN!
Guess this is as good a chance as any to knock the cobwebs loose.
The distance is certainly a challenge.
We'll have to find a rope I can tow...the men can follow hand over hand.
Uhn. Body's going to hate me in the morning...
Castle's bordered to the south by a river...the town to the east. We'll have to head **through** the town to make it to the lowlands.
<I DO NOT KNOW HOW FAR IT IS...>
<BUT I SUSPECT IT WILL NOT BE LONG.>
<WE WILL HAVE TO LEAVE SOON, THEN...>

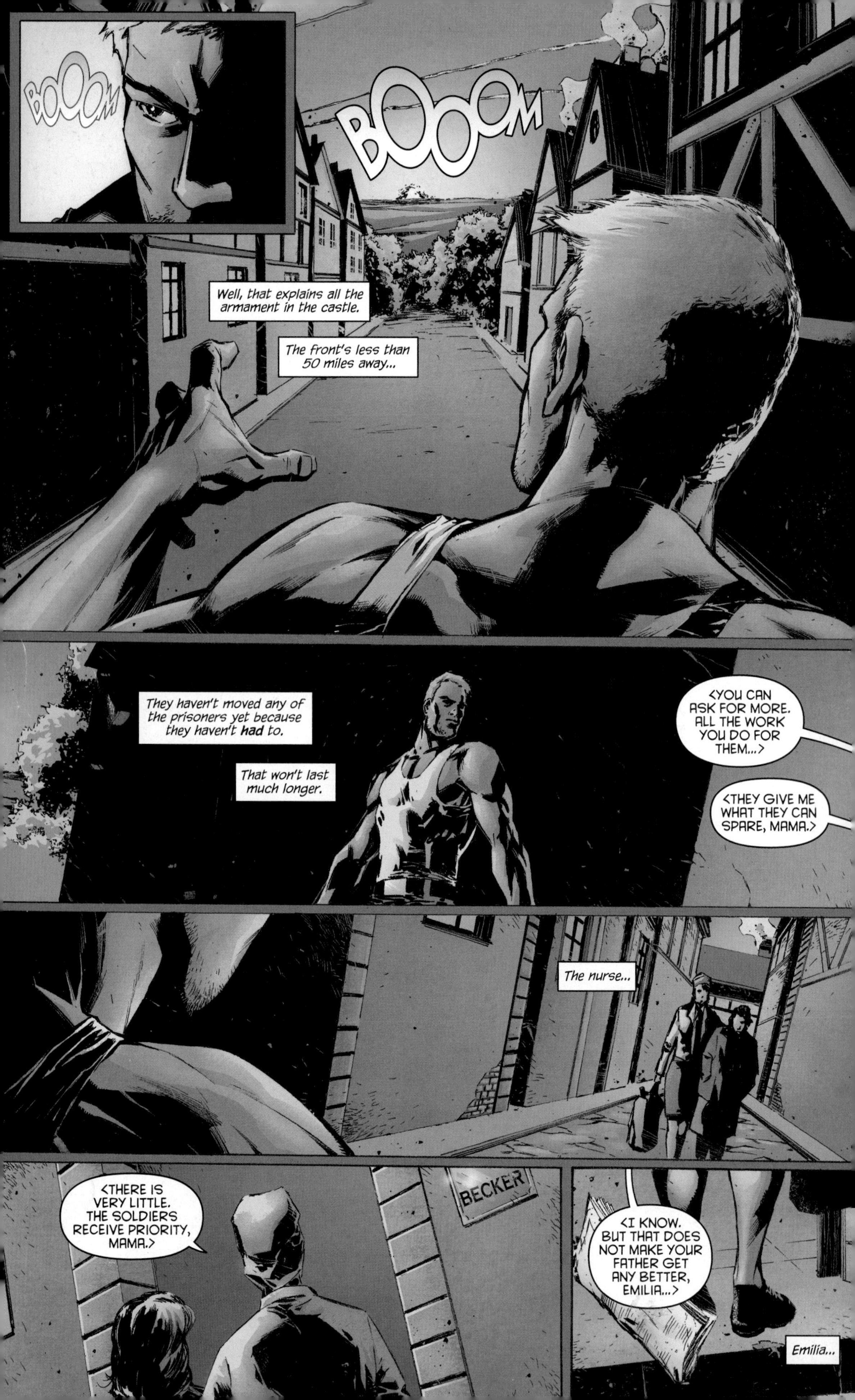
BOOOOM
BOOOOM
Well, that explains all the armament in the castle.
The front's less than 50 miles away...
They haven't moved any of the prisoners yet because they haven't **had** to.
That won't last much longer.
<YOU CAN ASK FOR MORE. ALL THE WORK YOU DO FOR THEM...>
<THEY GIVE ME WHAT THEY CAN SPARE, MAMA.>
The nurse...
<THERE IS VERY LITTLE. THE SOLDIERS RECEIVE PRIORITY, MAMA.>
BECKER
<I KNOW. BUT THAT DOES NOT MAKE YOUR FATHER GET ANY BETTER, EMILIA...>
Emilia...

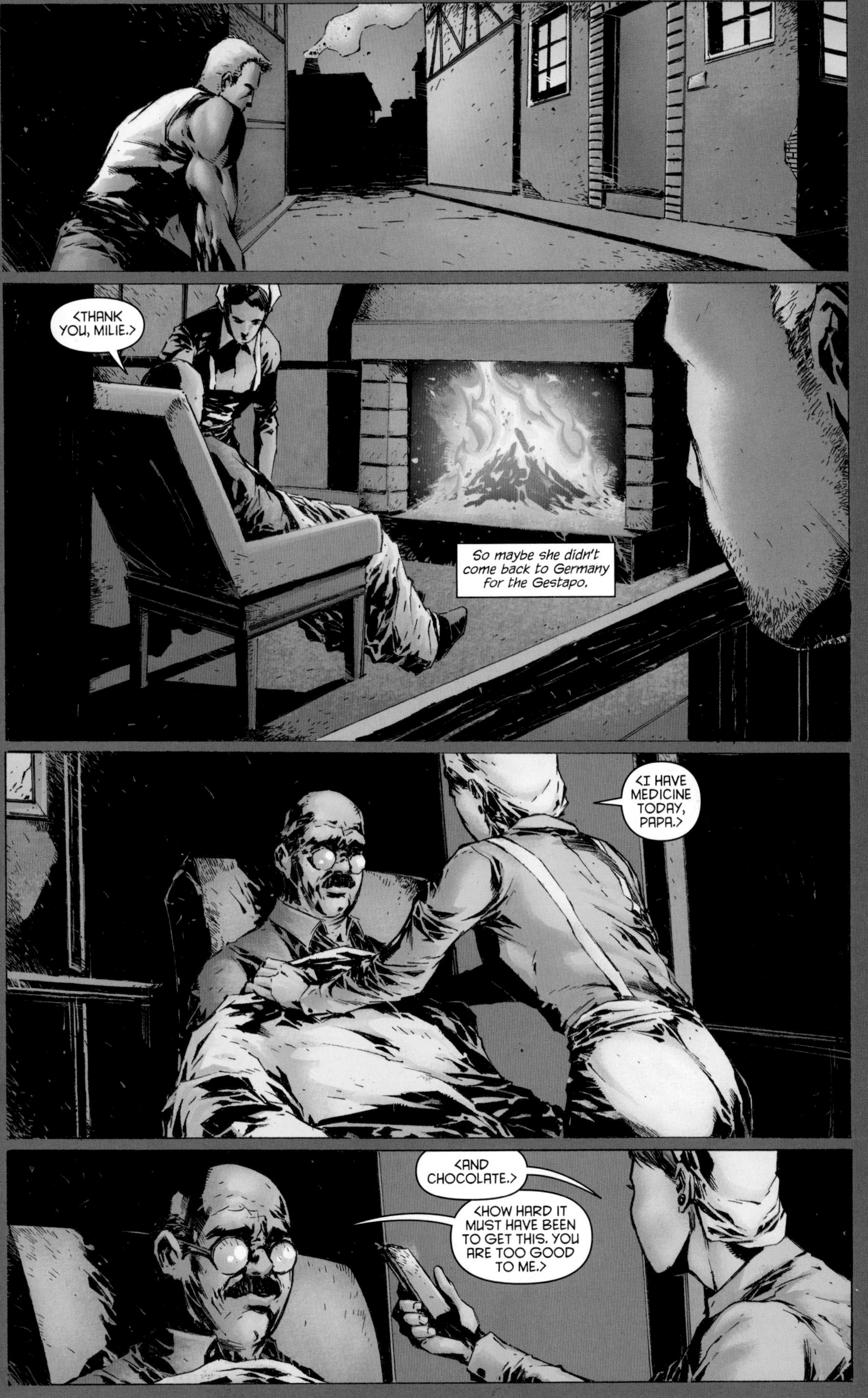

<THANK YOU, MILIE.>
So maybe she didn't come back to Germany for the Gestapo.
<I HAVE MEDICINE TODAY, PAPA.>
<AND CHOCOLATE.>
<HOW HARD IT MUST HAVE BEEN TO GET THIS. YOU ARE TOO GOOD TO ME.>

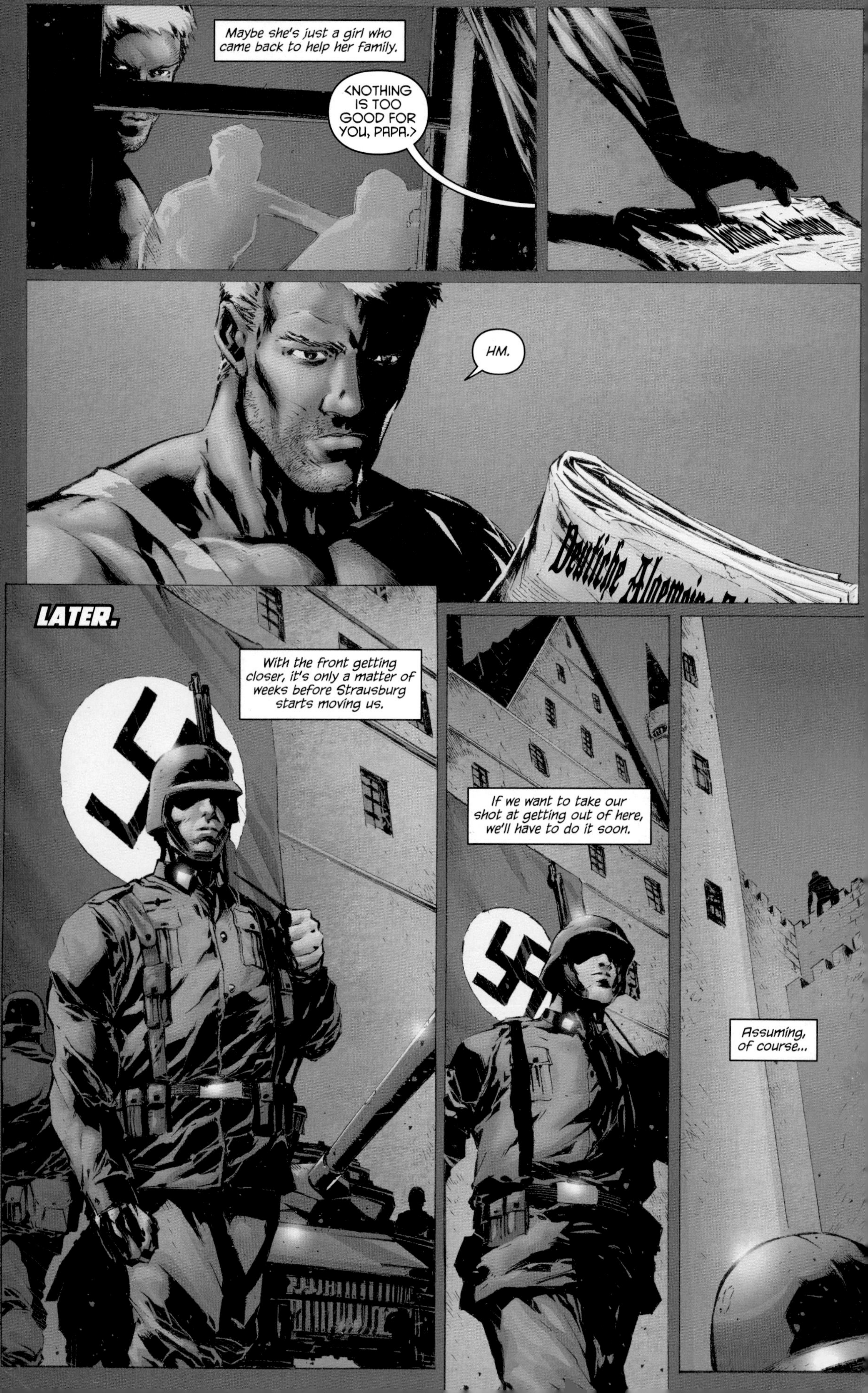
Maybe she's just a girl who came back to help her family.
<NOTHING IS TOO GOOD FOR YOU, PAPA.>
HM.
LATER.
With the front getting closer, it's only a matter of weeks before Strausburg starts moving us.
If we want to take our shot at getting out of here, we'll have to do it soon.
Assuming, of course...

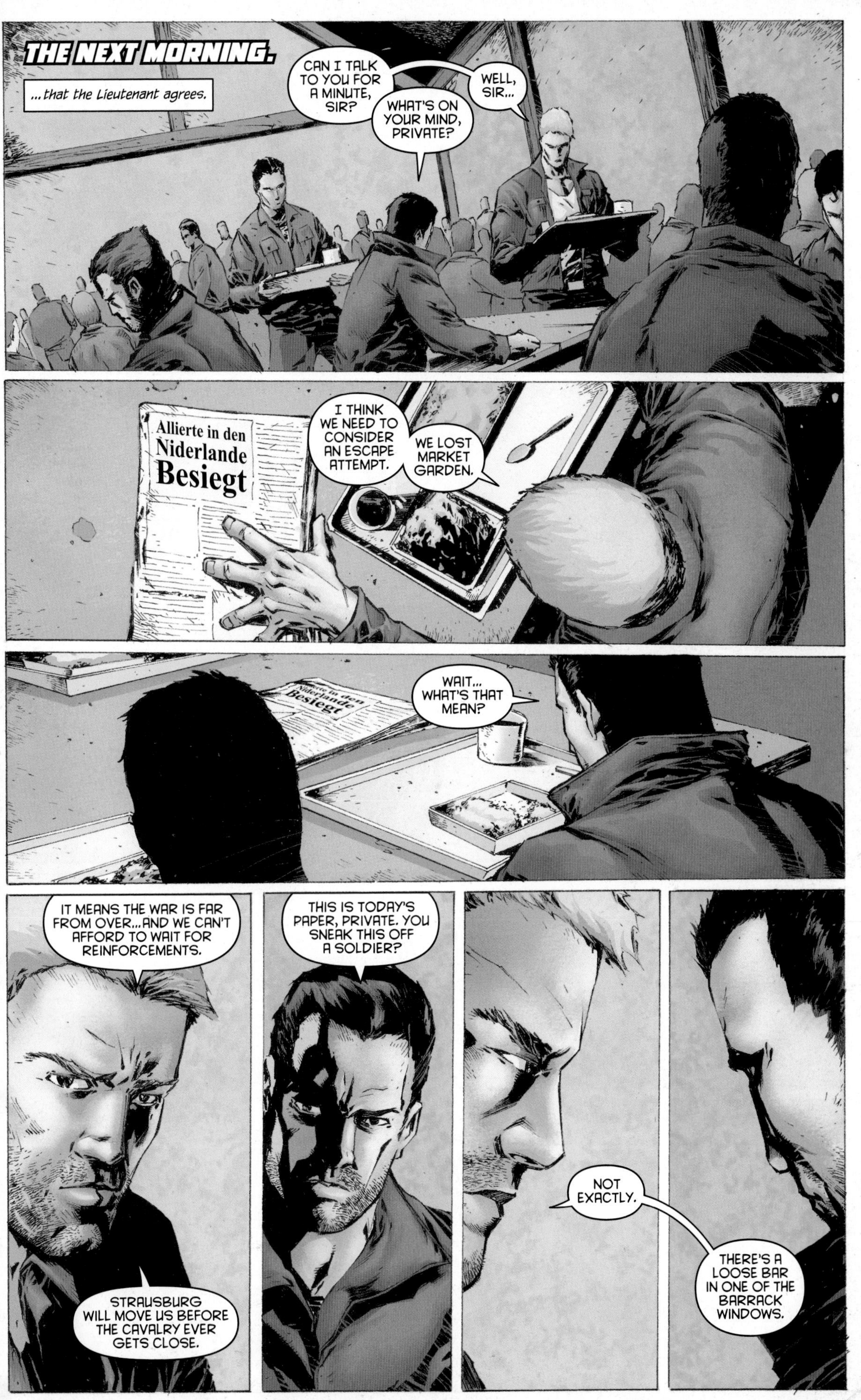
THE NEXT MORNING.
...that the Lieutenant agrees.
CAN I TALK TO YOU FOR A MINUTE, SIR?
WHAT'S ON YOUR MIND, PRIVATE?
WELL, SIR...
Allierte in den Niderlande Besiegt
I THINK WE NEED TO CONSIDER AN ESCAPE ATTEMPT.
WE LOST MARKET GARDEN.
Allierte in den Niderlande Besiegt
WAIT... WHAT'S THAT MEAN?
IT MEANS THE WAR IS FAR FROM OVER...AND WE CAN'T AFFORD TO WAIT FOR REINFORCEMENTS.
STRAUSBURG WILL MOVE US BEFORE THE CAVALRY EVER GETS CLOSE.
THIS IS TODAY'S PAPER, PRIVATE. YOU SNEAK THIS OFF A SOLDIER?
NOT EXACTLY.
THERE'S A LOOSE BAR IN ONE OF THE BARRACK WINDOWS.

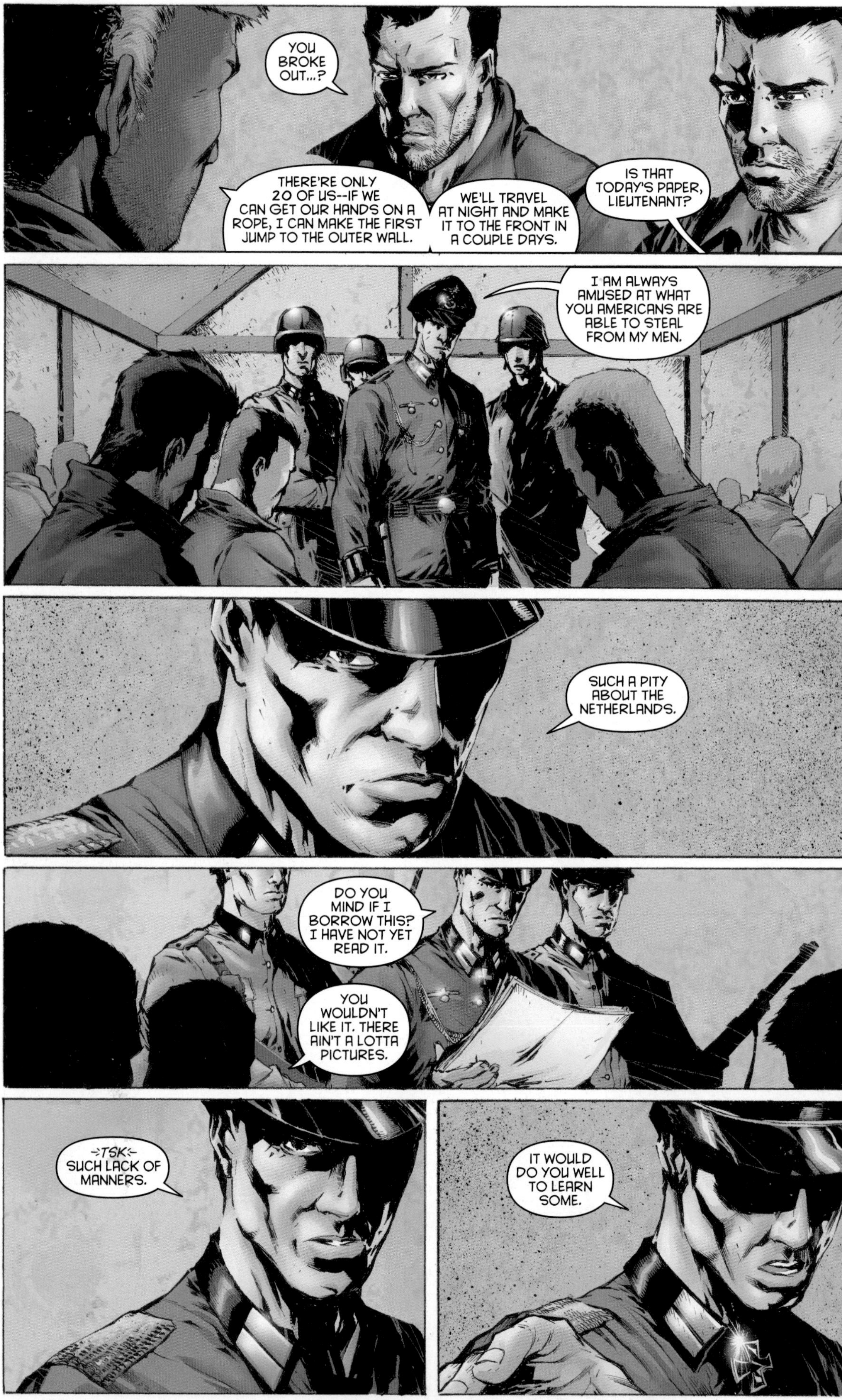
YOU BROKE OUT...?
THERE'RE ONLY 20 OF US--IF WE CAN GET OUR HANDS ON A ROPE, I CAN MAKE THE FIRST JUMP TO THE OUTER WALL.
WE'LL TRAVEL AT NIGHT AND MAKE IT TO THE FRONT IN A COUPLE DAYS.
IS THAT TODAY'S PAPER, LIEUTENANT?
I AM ALWAYS AMUSED AT WHAT YOU AMERICANS ARE ABLE TO STEAL FROM MY MEN.
SUCH A PITY ABOUT THE NETHERLANDS.
DO YOU MIND IF I BORROW THIS? I HAVE NOT YET READ IT.
YOU WOULDN'T LIKE IT. THERE AIN'T A LOTTA PICTURES.
-TSK- SUCH LACK OF MANNERS.
IT WOULD DO YOU WELL TO LEARN SOME.

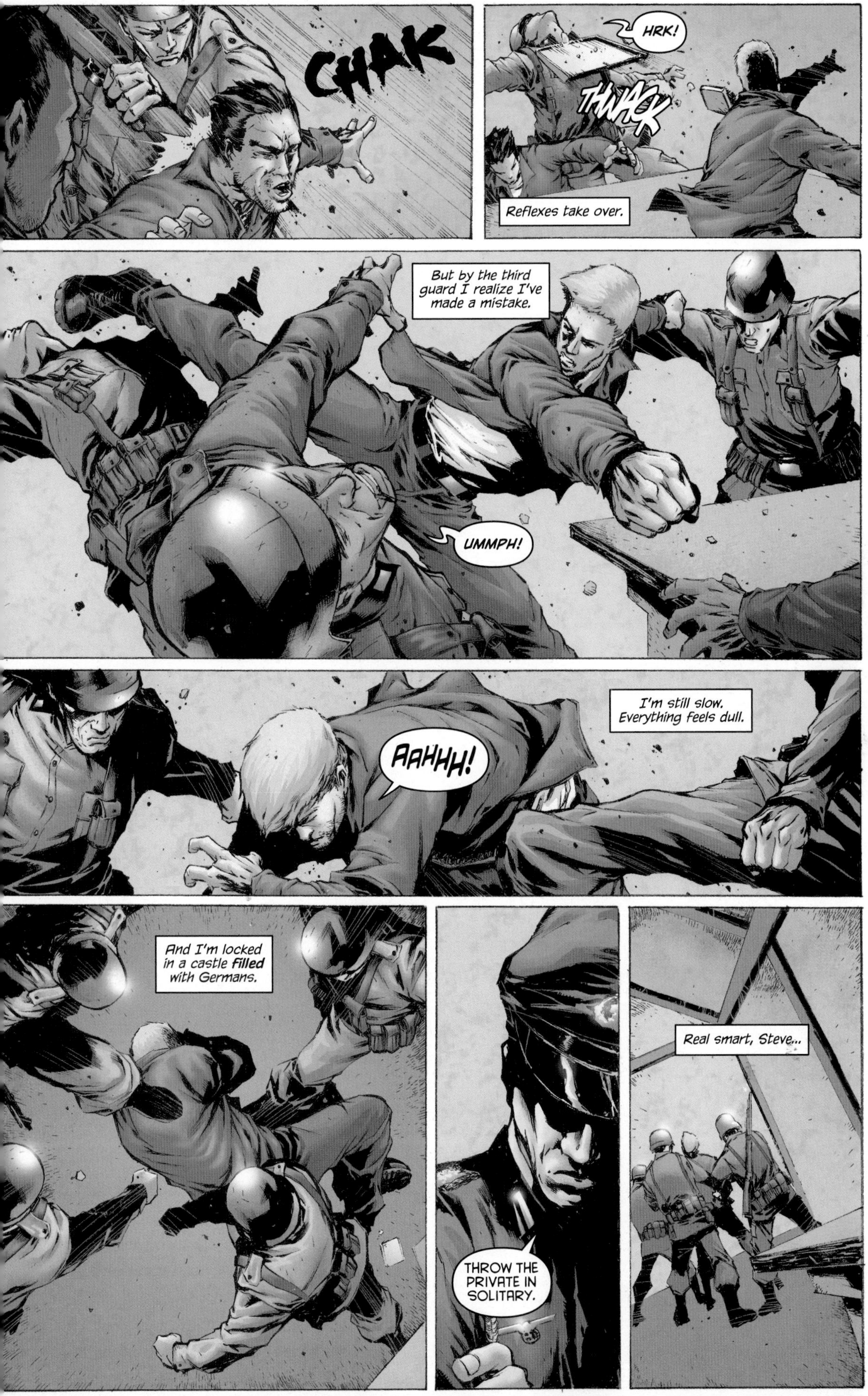
CHAK
HRK!
THWACK
Reflexes take over.
But by the third guard I realize I've made a mistake.
UMMPH!
I'm still slow. Everything feels dull.
AAHHH!
And I'm locked in a castle **filled** with Germans.
THROW THE PRIVATE IN SOLITARY.
Real smart, Steve...

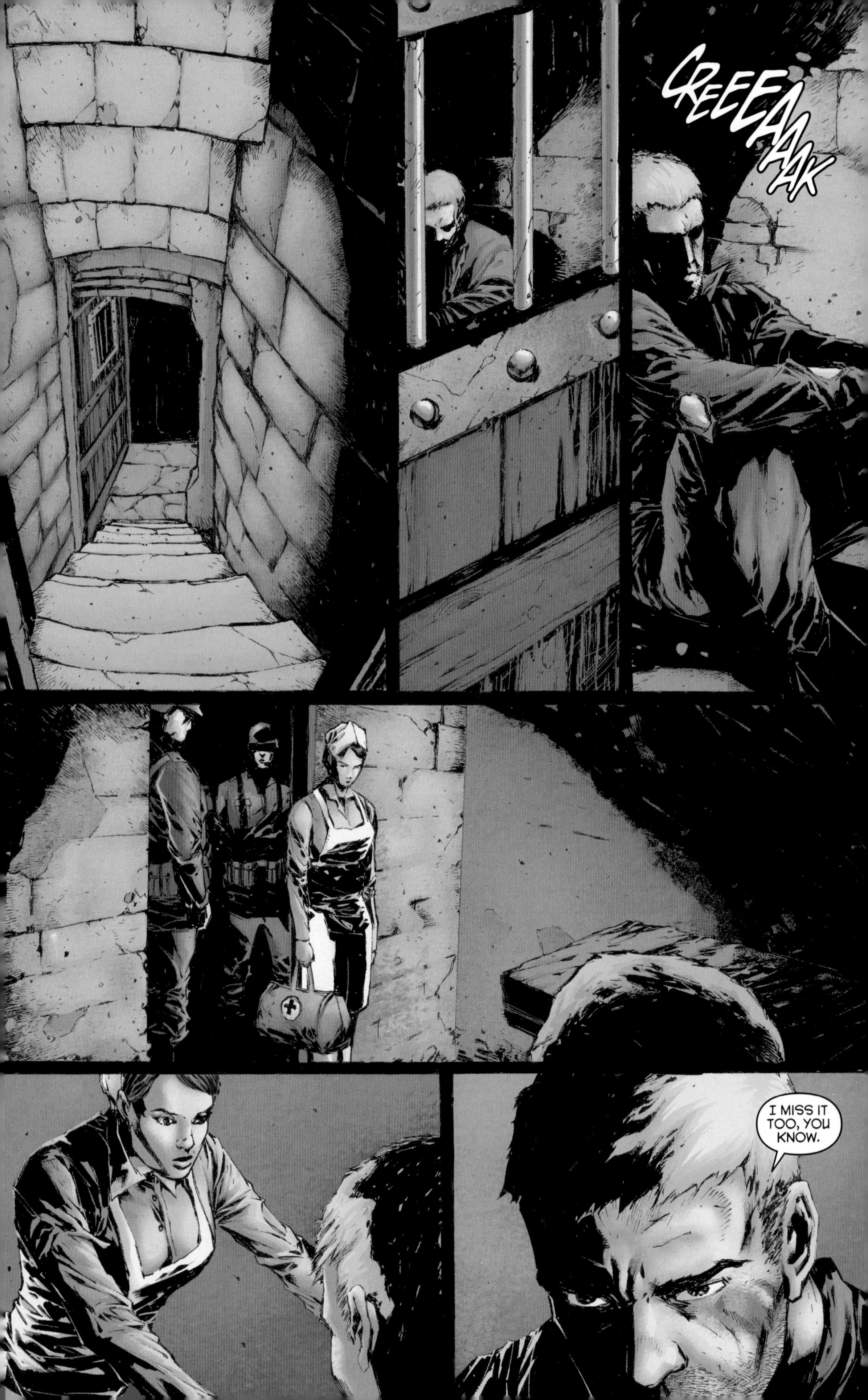
CREEEAAAAK
I MISS IT TOO, YOU KNOW.

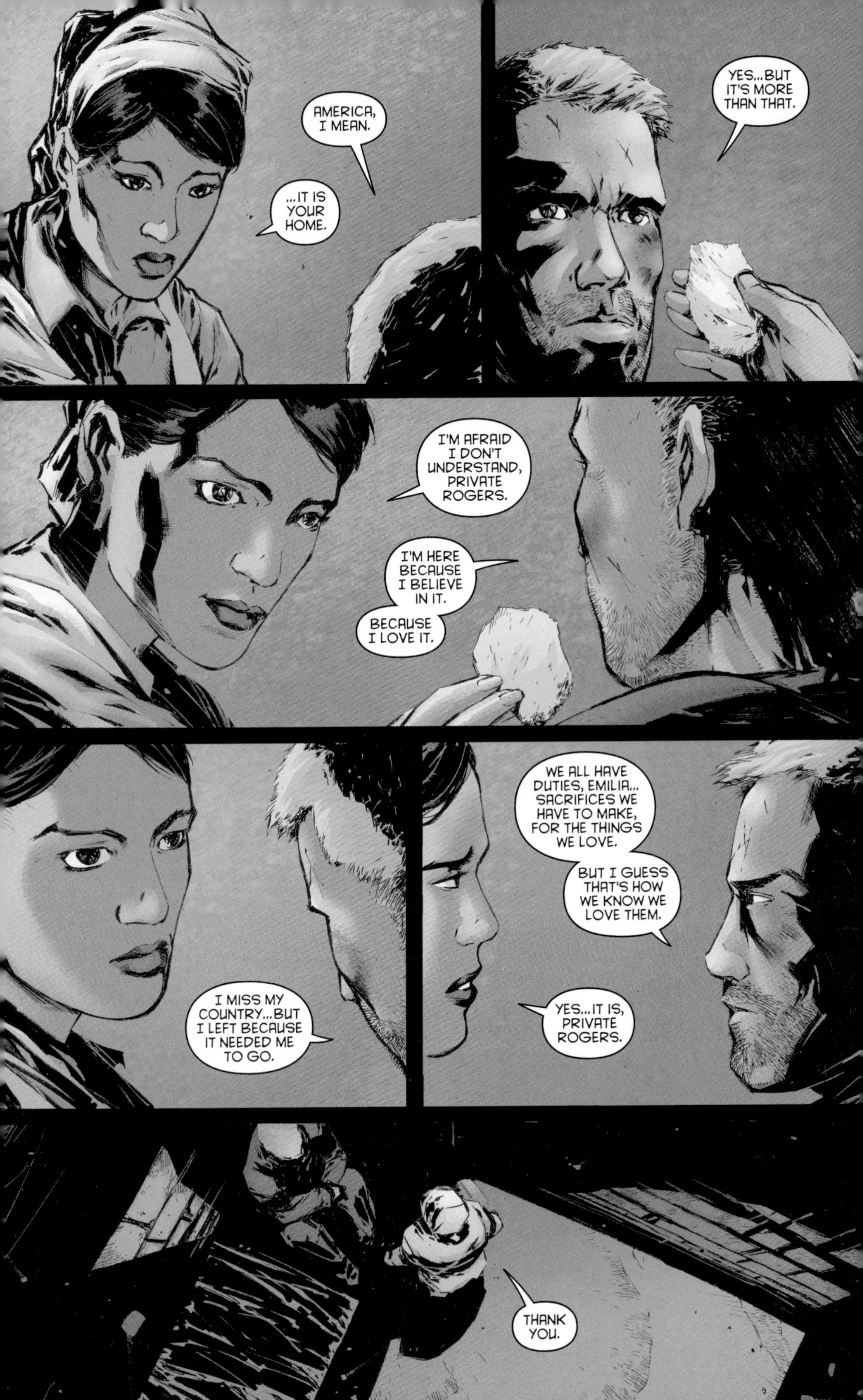
AMERICA, I MEAN.
...IT IS YOUR HOME.
YES...BUT IT'S MORE THAN THAT.
I'M AFRAID I DON'T UNDERSTAND, PRIVATE ROGERS.
I'M HERE BECAUSE I BELIEVE IN IT.
BECAUSE I LOVE IT.
I MISS MY COUNTRY...BUT I LEFT BECAUSE IT NEEDED ME TO GO.
WE ALL HAVE DUTIES, EMILIA... SACRIFICES WE HAVE TO MAKE, FOR THE THINGS WE LOVE.
BUT I GUESS THAT'S HOW WE KNOW WE LOVE THEM.
YES...IT IS, PRIVATE ROGERS.
THANK YOU.

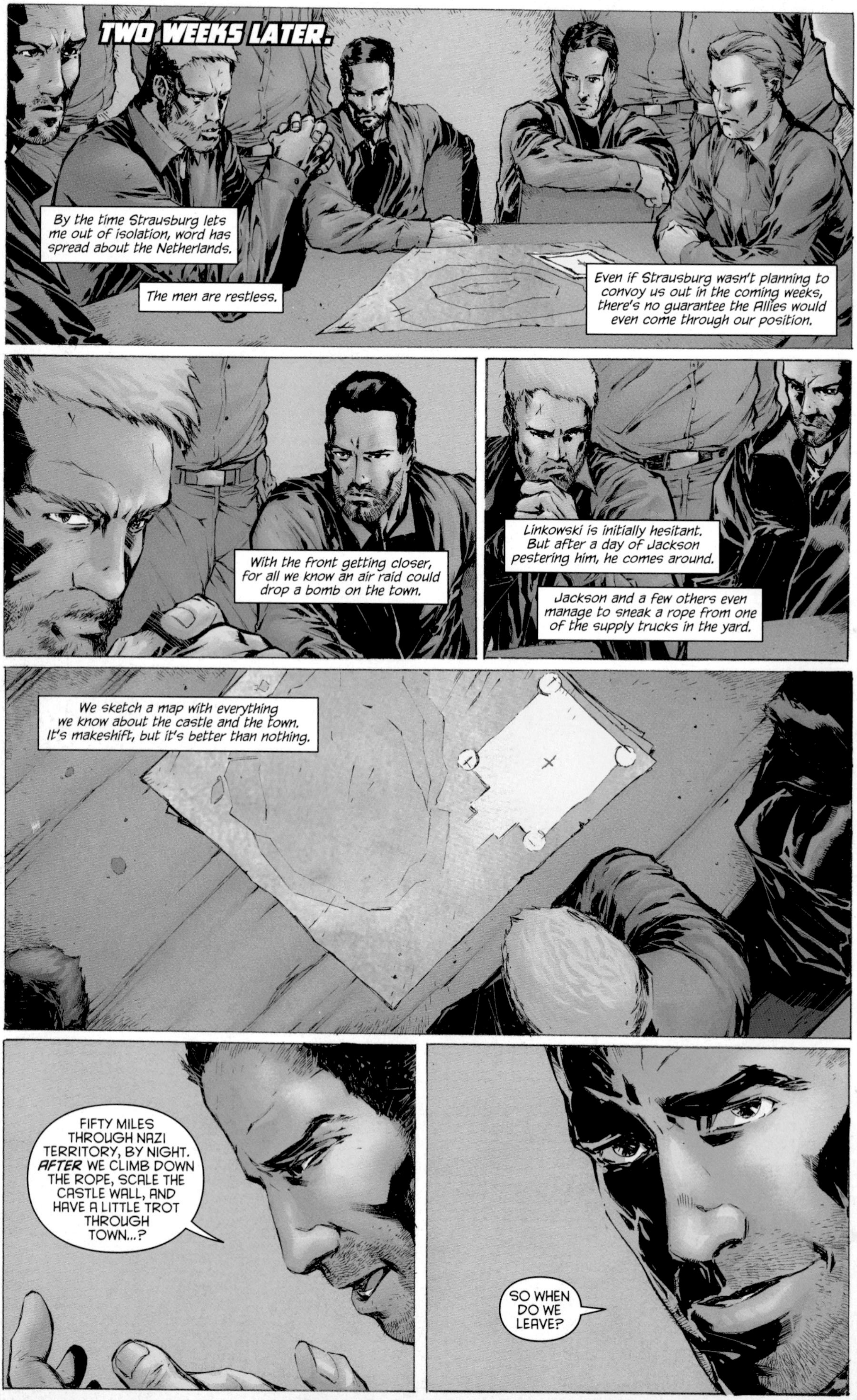
TWO WEEKS LATER.
By the time Strausburg lets me out of isolation, word has spread about the Netherlands.
The men are restless.
Even if Strausburg wasn't planning to convoy us out in the coming weeks, there's no guarantee the Allies would even come through our position.
With the front getting closer, for all we know an air raid could drop a bomb on the town.
Linkowski is initially hesitant. But after a day of Jackson pestering him, he comes around.
Jackson and a few others even manage to sneak a rope from one of the supply trucks in the yard.
We sketch a map with everything we know about the castle and the town. It's makeshift, but it's better than nothing.
FIFTY MILES THROUGH NAZI TERRITORY, BY NIGHT. AFTER WE CLIMB DOWN THE ROPE, SCALE THE CASTLE WALL, AND HAVE A LITTLE TROT THROUGH TOWN...?
SO WHEN DO WE LEAVE?

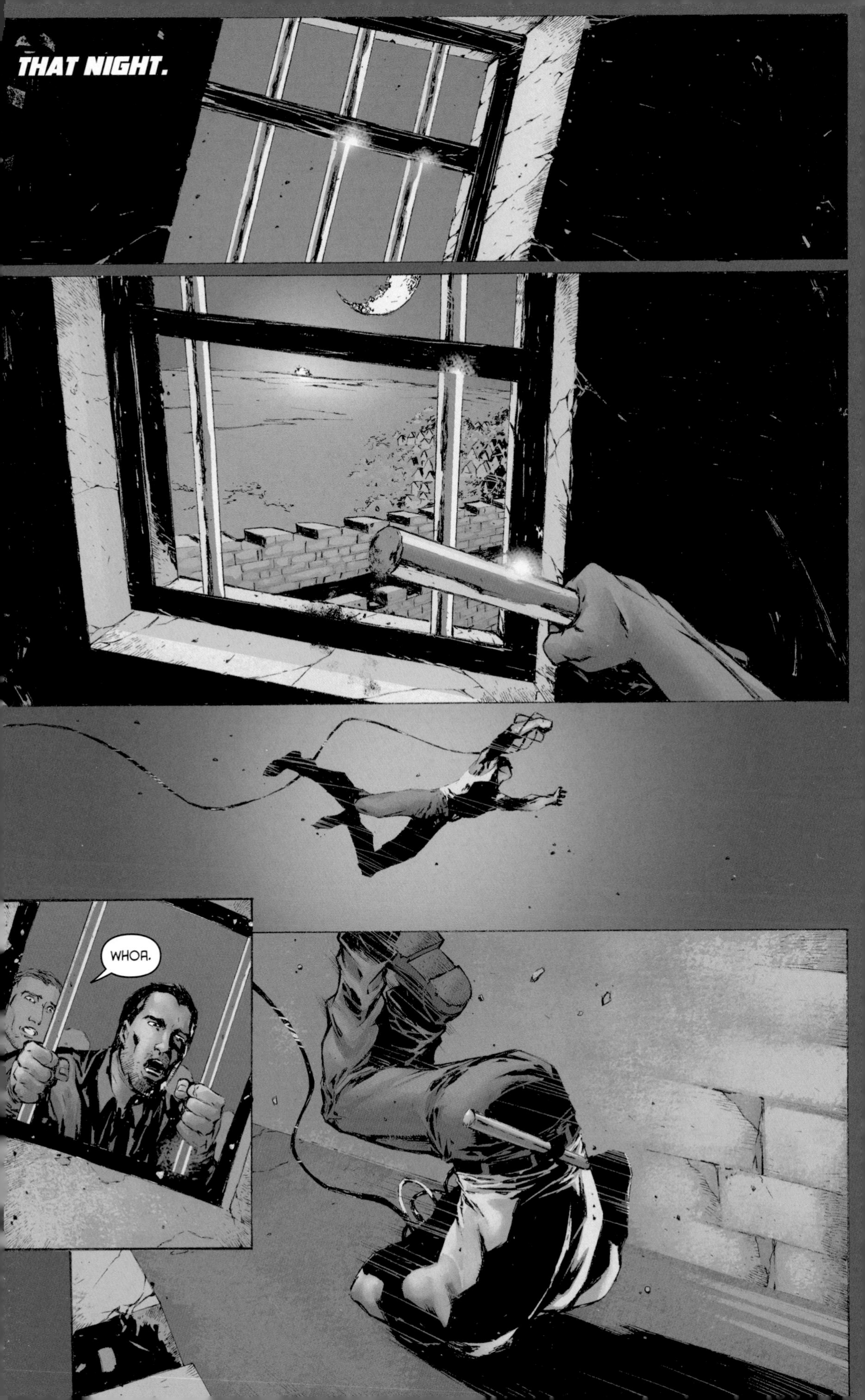
THAT NIGHT.
WHOA.

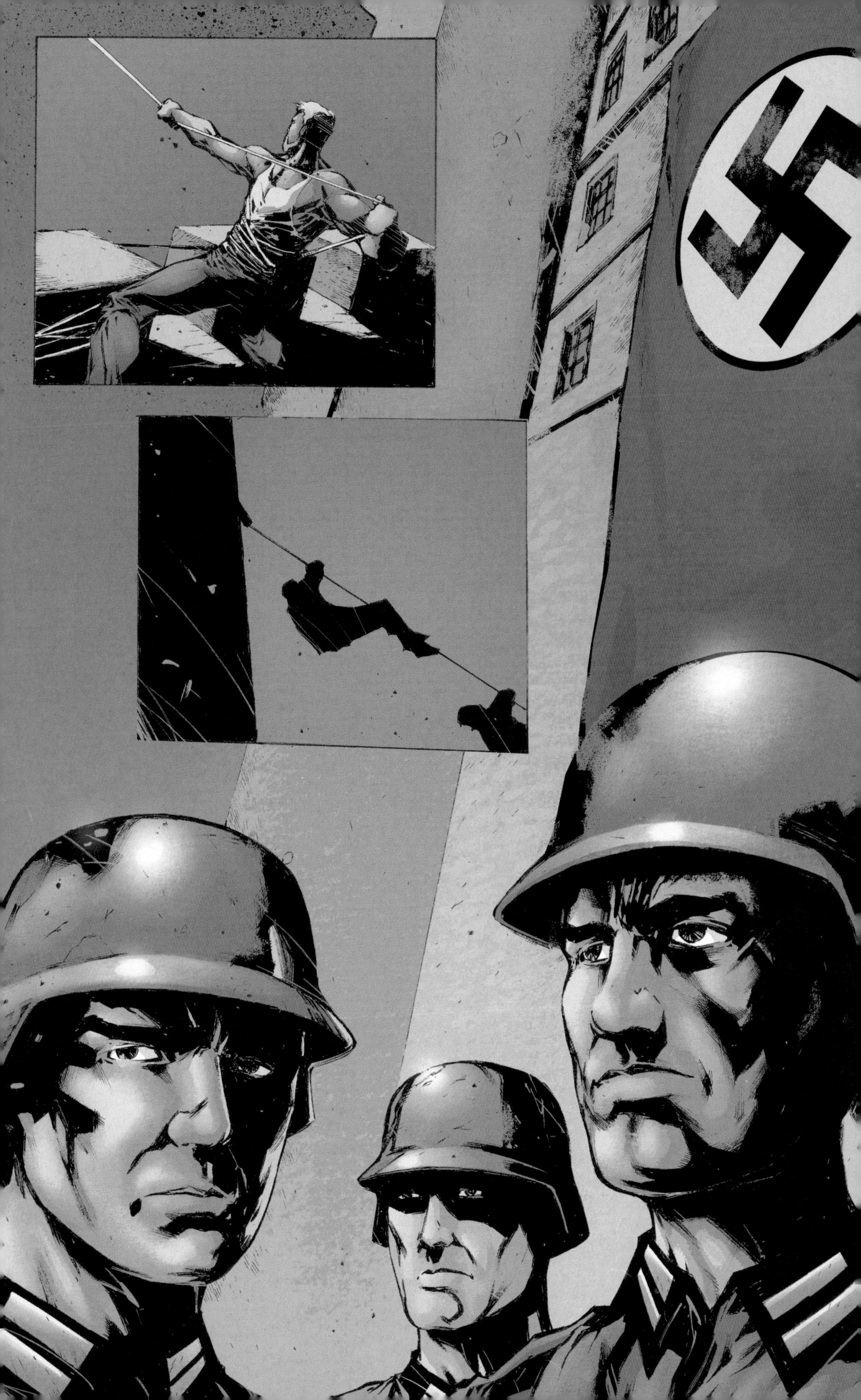

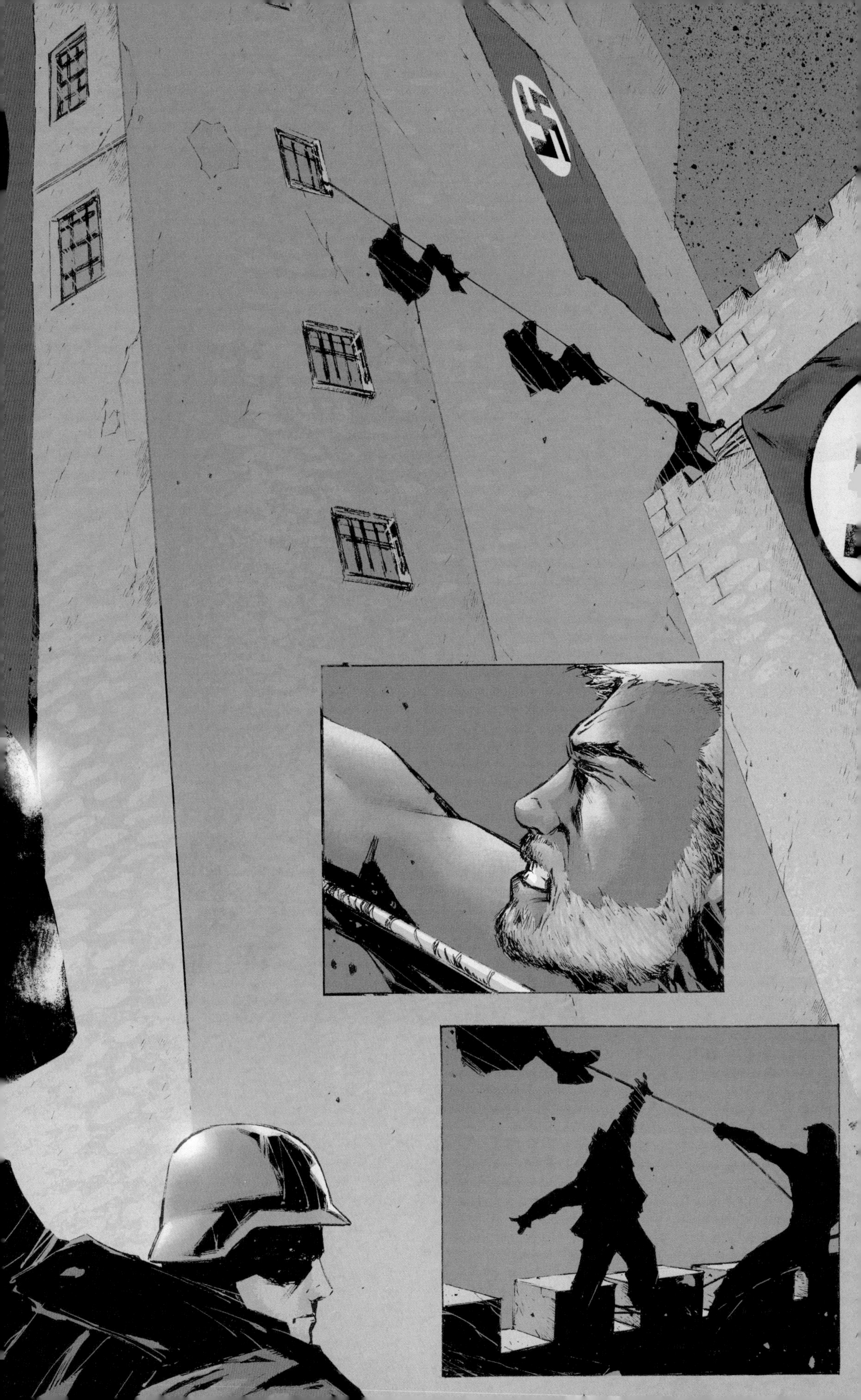

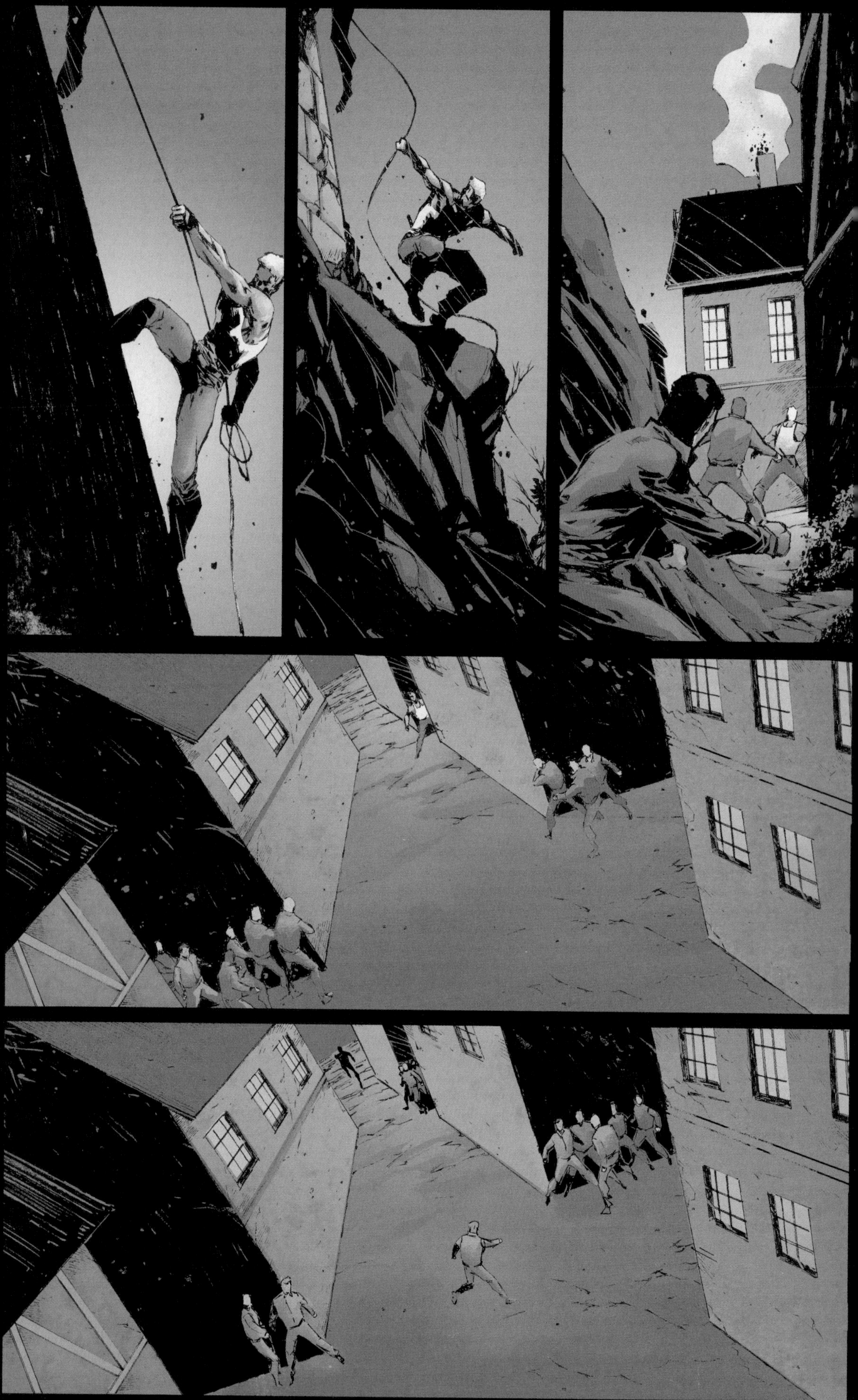

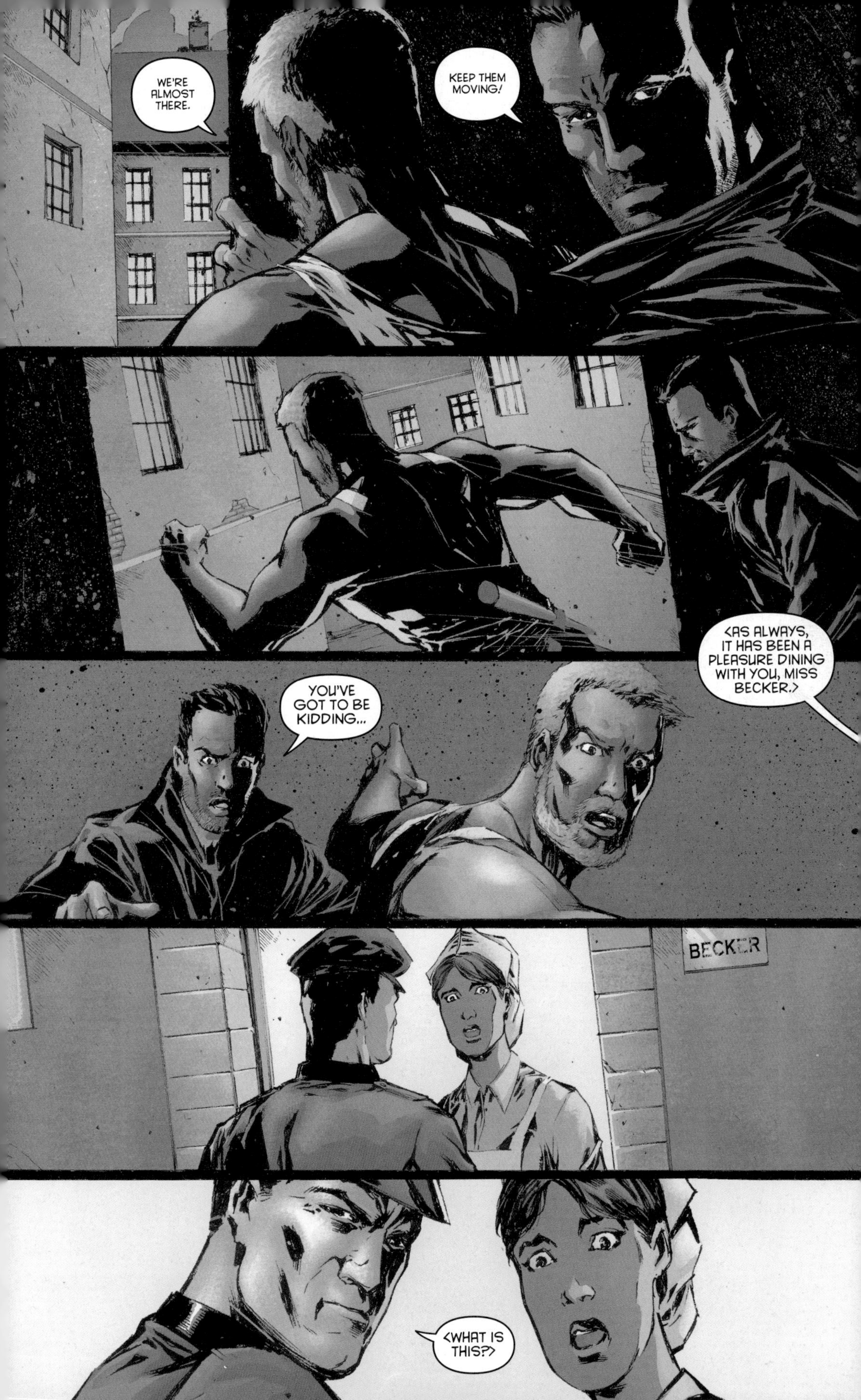
WE'RE ALMOST THERE.
KEEP THEM MOVING!
YOU'VE GOT TO BE KIDDING...
<AS ALWAYS, IT HAS BEEN A PLEASURE DINING WITH YOU, MISS BECKER.>
BECKER
<WHAT IS THIS?>

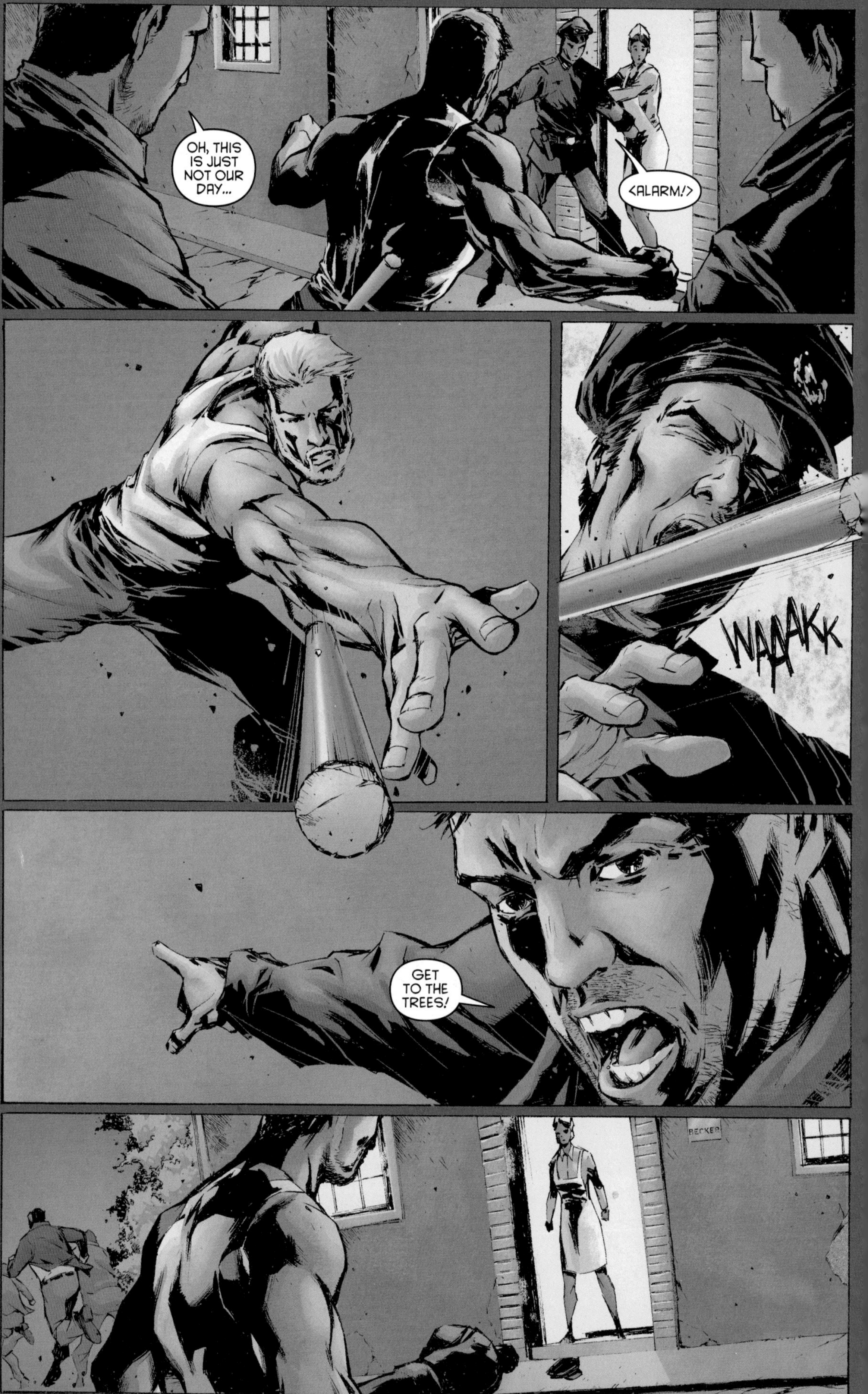
OH, THIS IS JUST NOT OUR DAY...
<ALARM!>
WAAAKK
GET TO THE TREES!

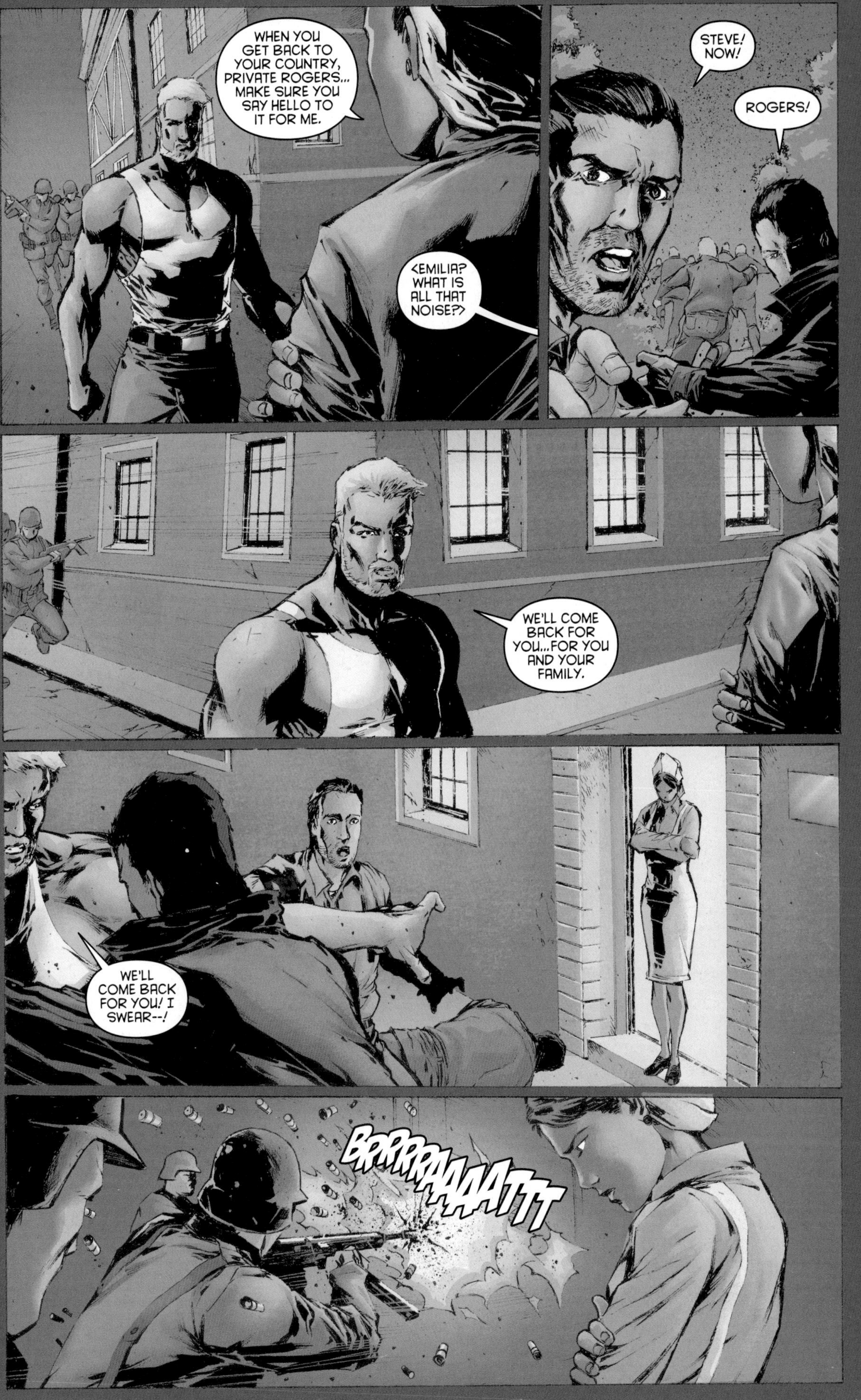

WHEN YOU GET BACK TO YOUR COUNTRY, PRIVATE ROGERS... MAKE SURE YOU SAY HELLO TO IT FOR ME.
<EMILIA? WHAT IS ALL THAT NOISE?>
STEVE! NOW!
ROGERS!
WE'LL COME BACK FOR YOU...FOR YOU AND YOUR FAMILY.
WE'LL COME BACK FOR YOU! I SWEAR--!
BRRRRAAAAATTT

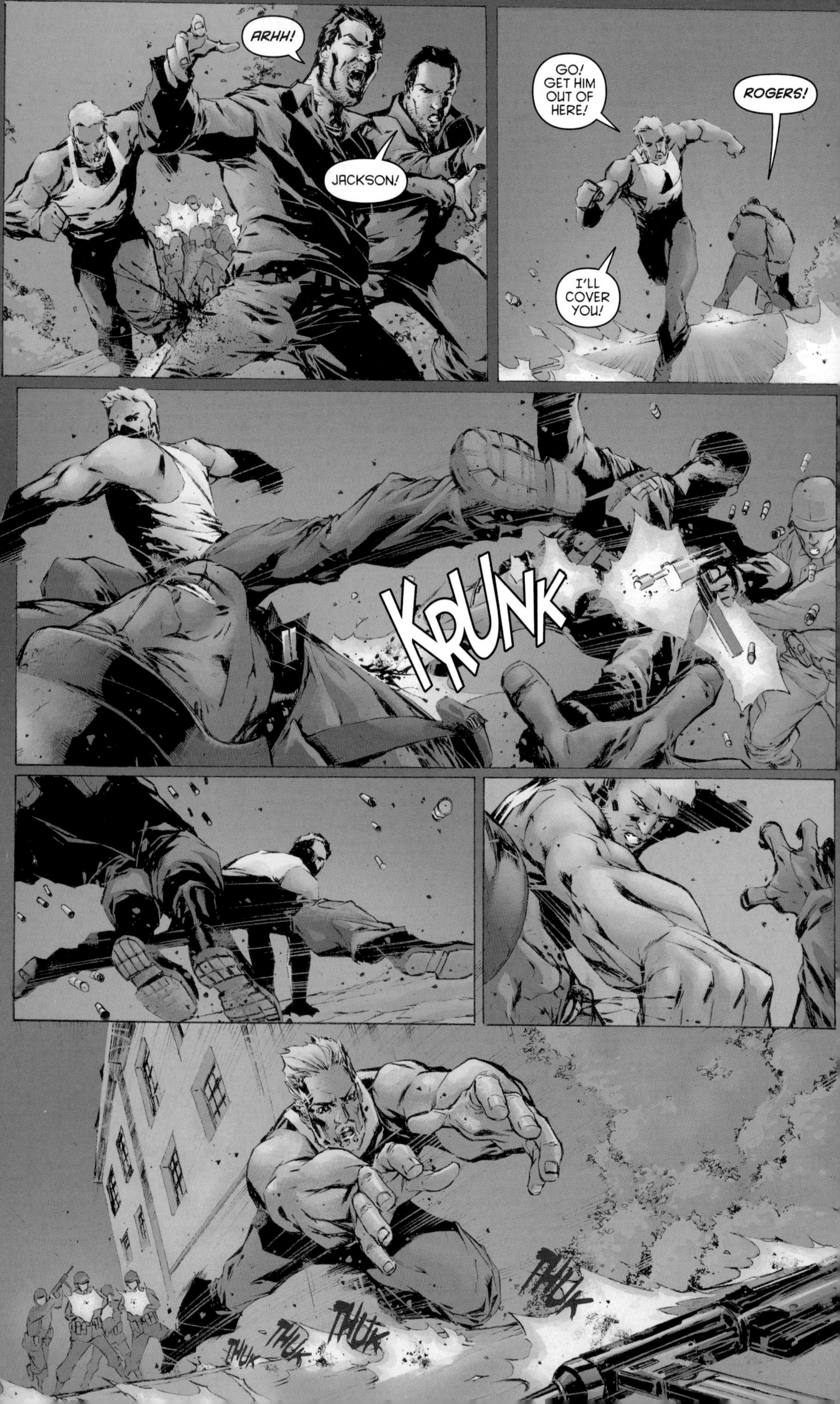
ARHH!
JACKSON!
GO! GET HIM OUT OF HERE!
ROGERS!
I'LL COVER YOU!
KRUNK
THUK
THUK
THUK
THUK

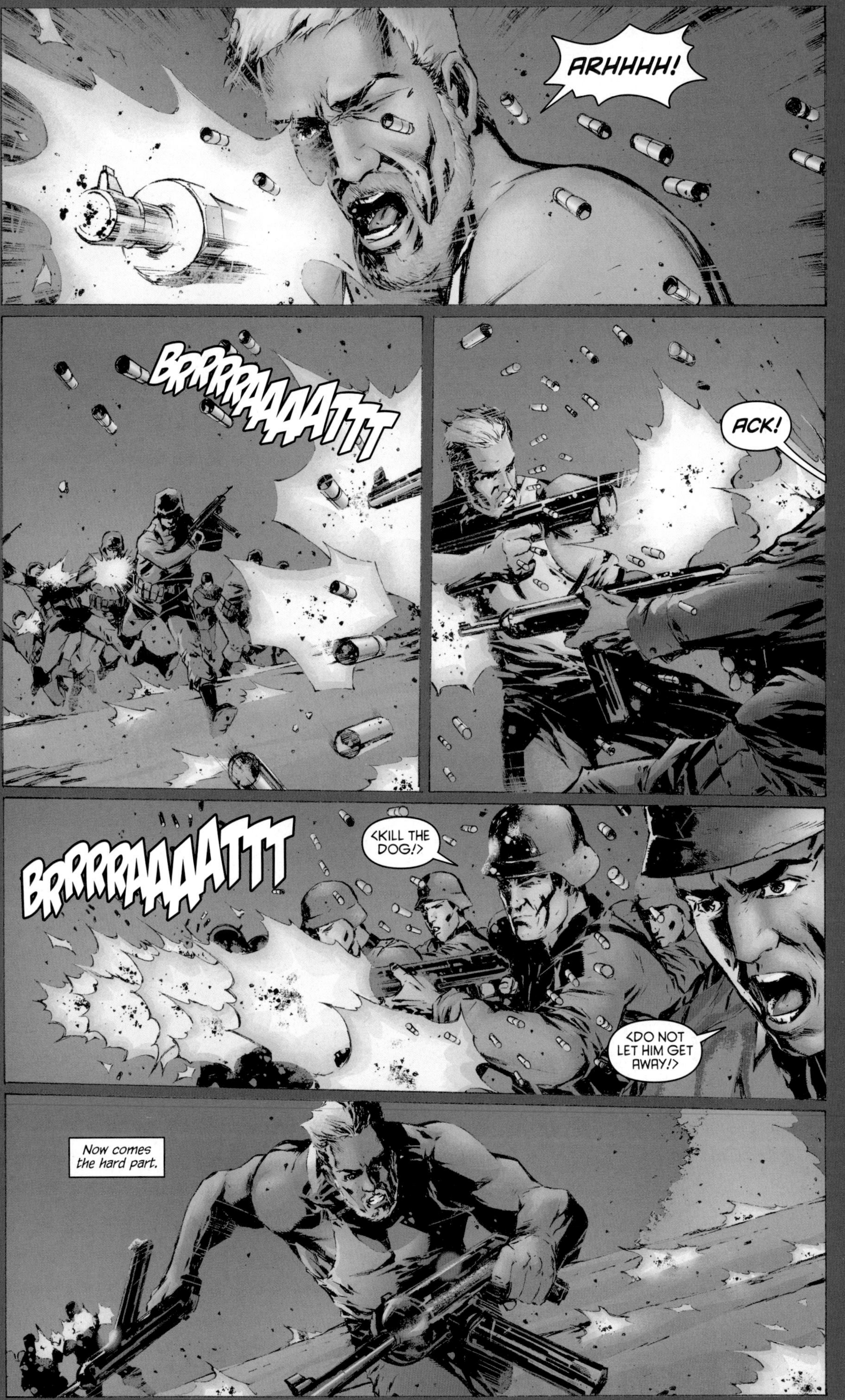
ARHHHH!
BRRRRAAAATTT
ACK!
BRRRRAAAATTT
<KILL THE DOG!>
<DO NOT LET HIM GET AWAY!>
Now comes the hard part.

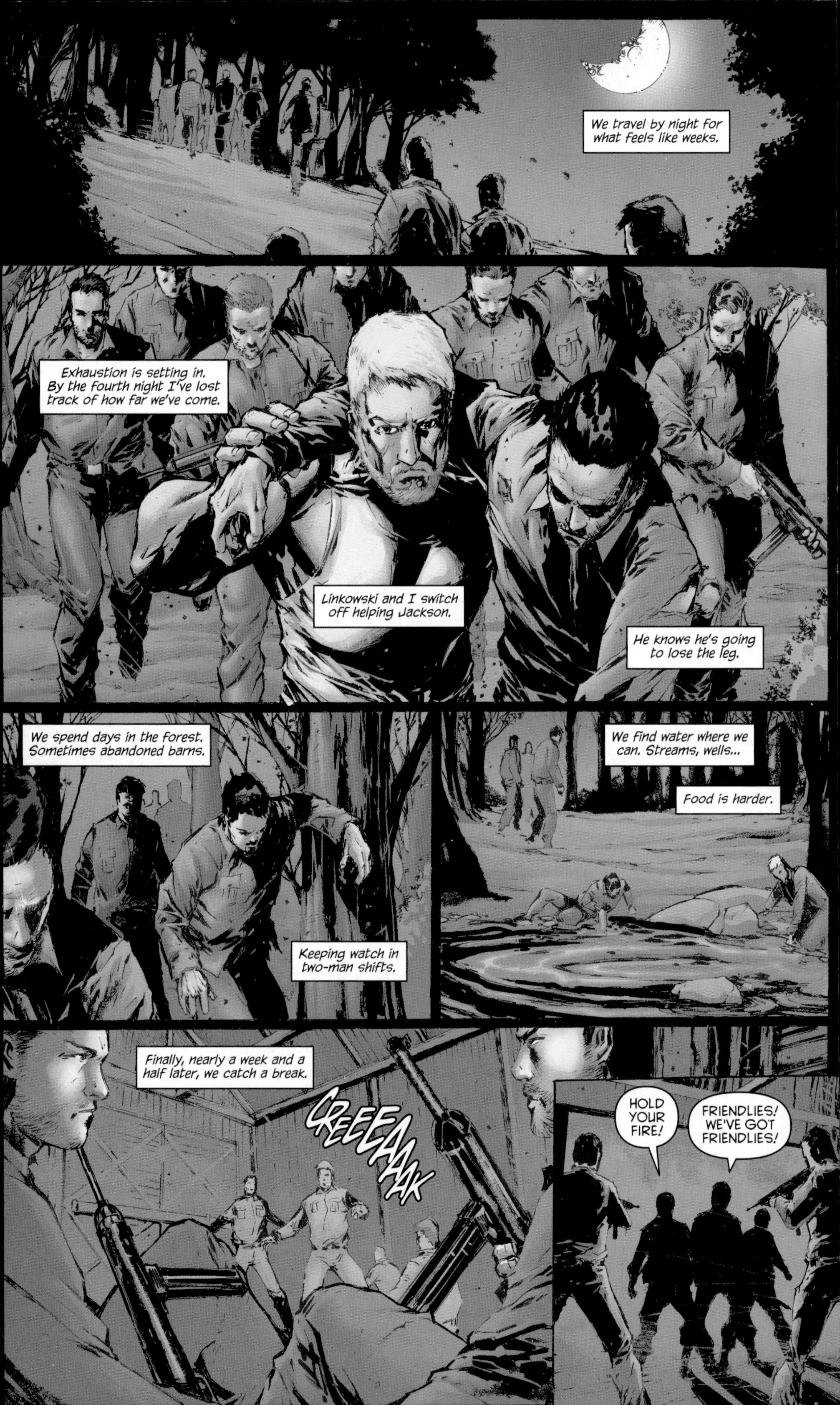

We travel by night for what feels like weeks.
Exhaustion is setting in. By the fourth night I've lost track of how far we've come.
Linkowski and I switch off helping Jackson.
He knows he's going to lose the leg.
We spend days in the forest. Sometimes abandoned barns.
Keeping watch in two-man shifts.
We find water where we can. Streams, wells...
Food is harder.
Finally, nearly a week and a half later, we catch a break.
CREEEAAAK
HOLD YOUR FIRE!
FRIENDLIES! WE'VE GOT FRIENDLIES!

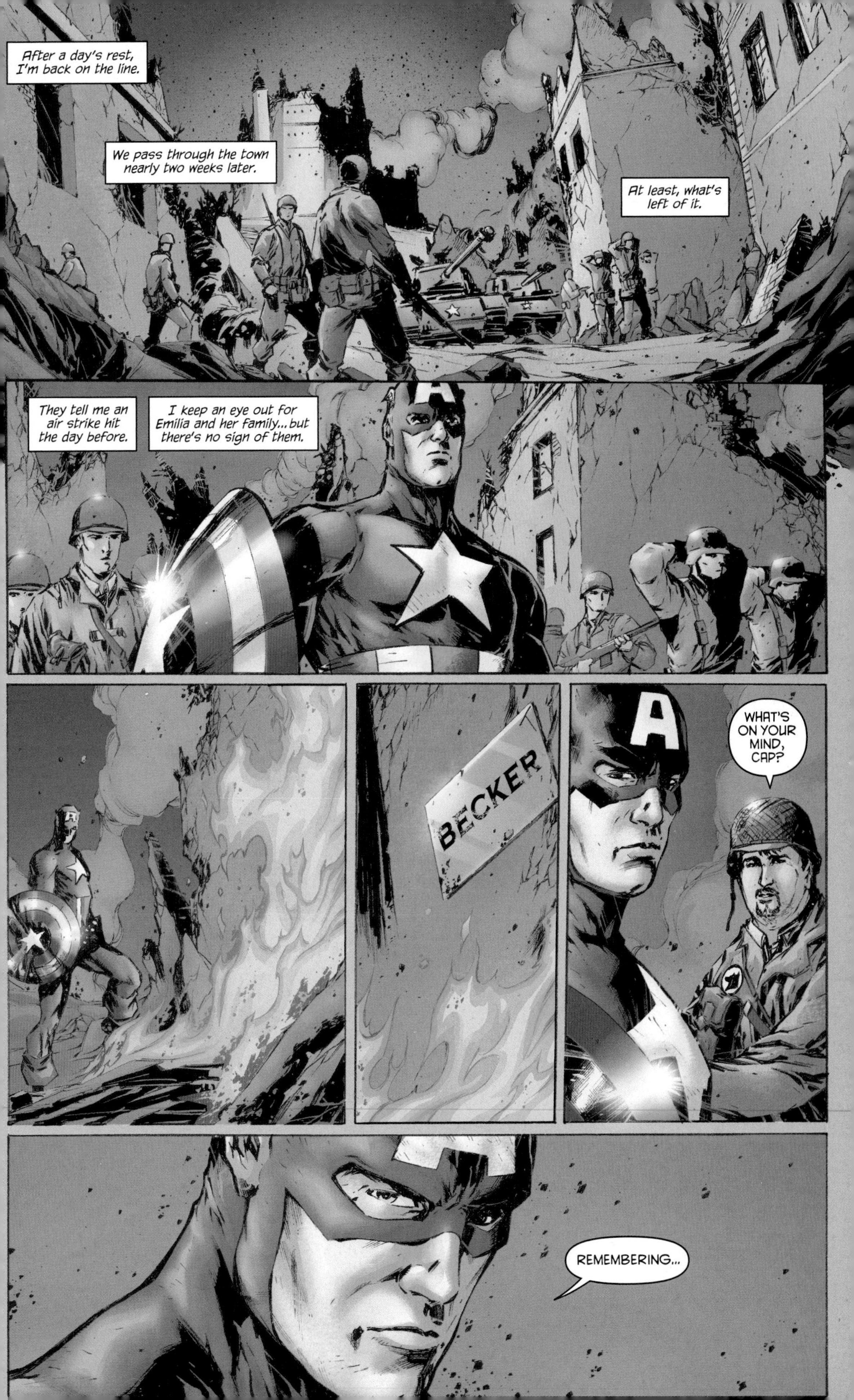
After a day's rest, I'm back on the line.
We pass through the town nearly two weeks later.
At least, what's left of it.
They tell me an air strike hit the day before.
I keep an eye out for Emilia and her family... but there's no sign of them.
BECKER
WHAT'S ON YOUR MIND, CAP?
REMEMBERING...

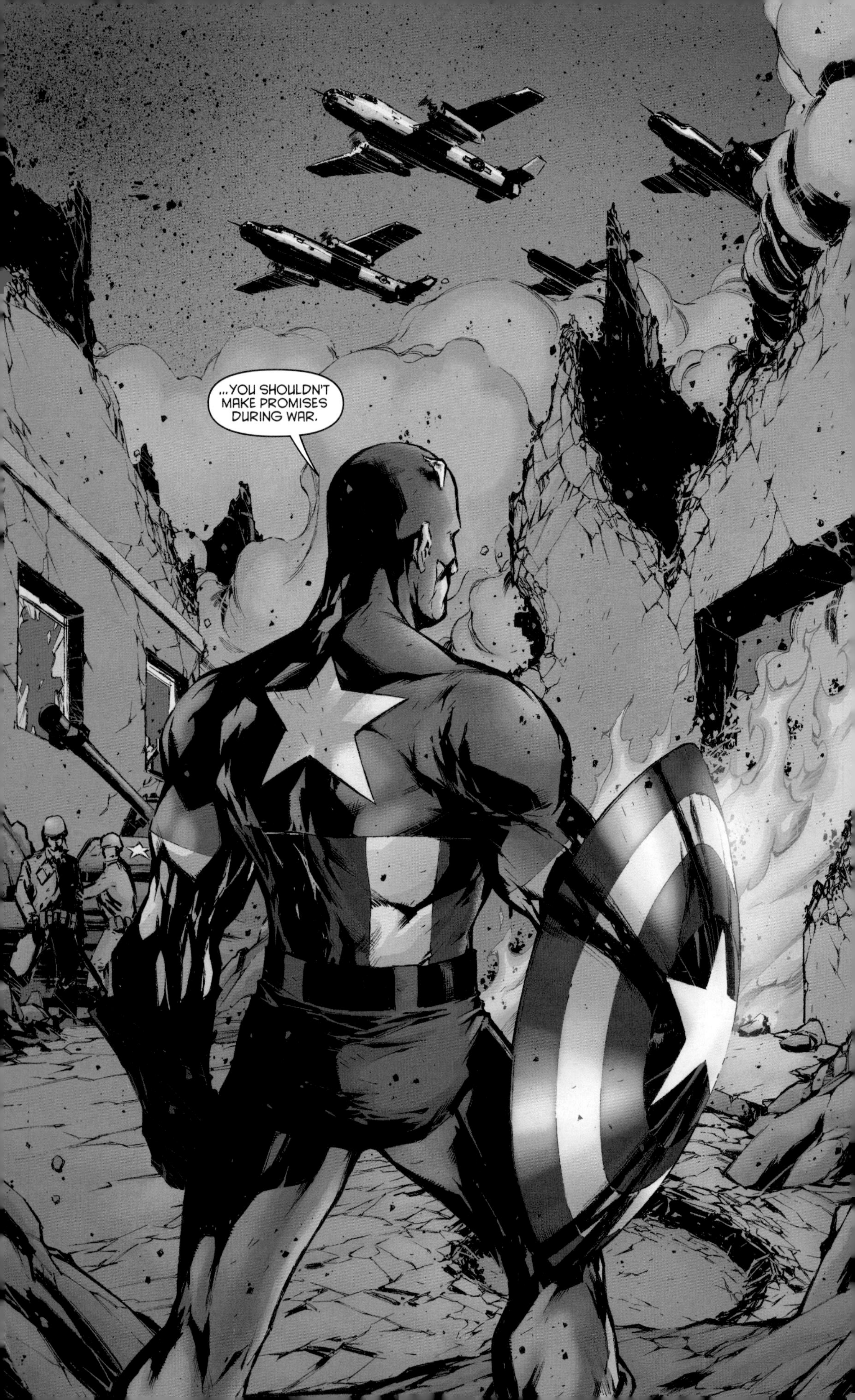
...YOU SHOULDN'T MAKE PROMISES DURING WAR.

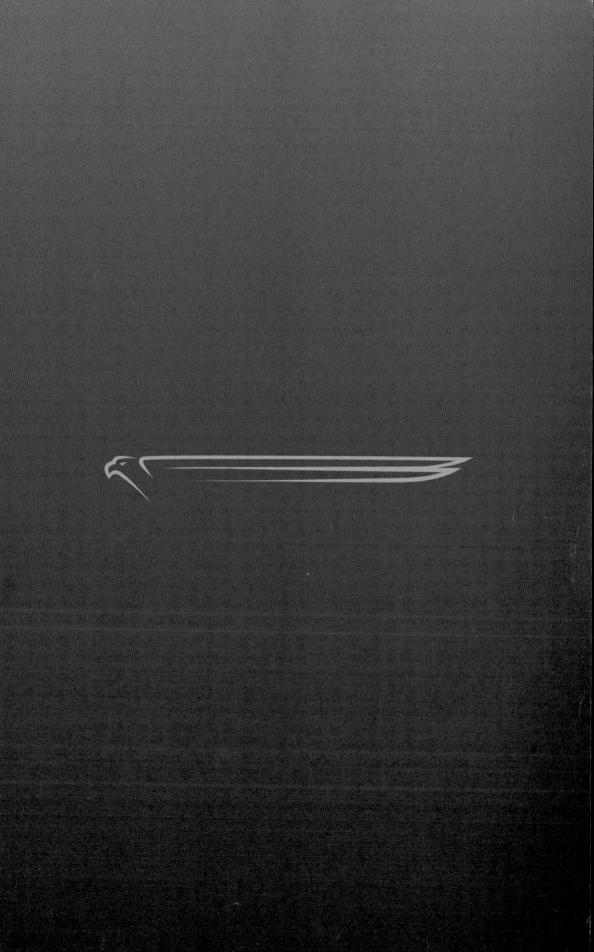

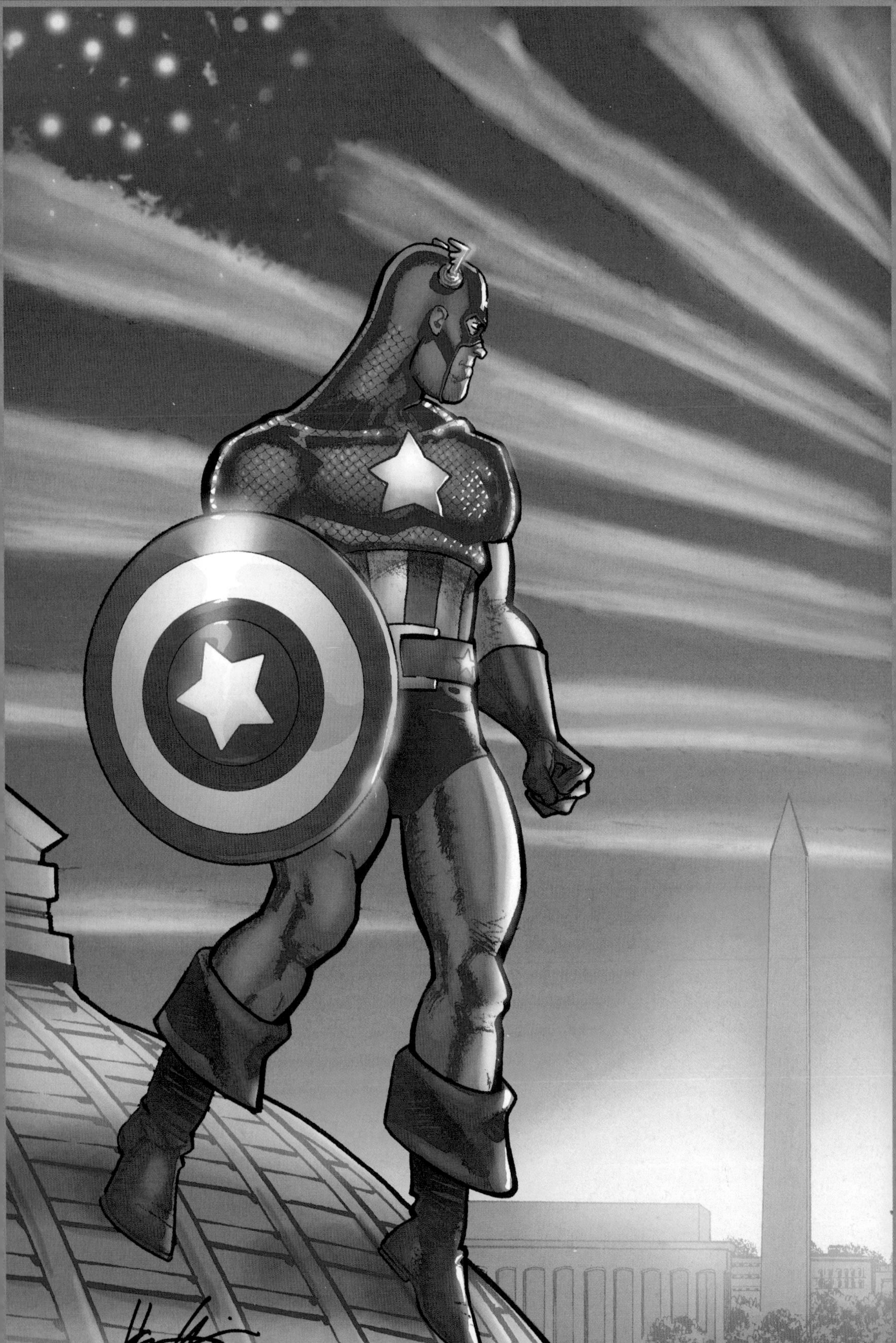
delgado

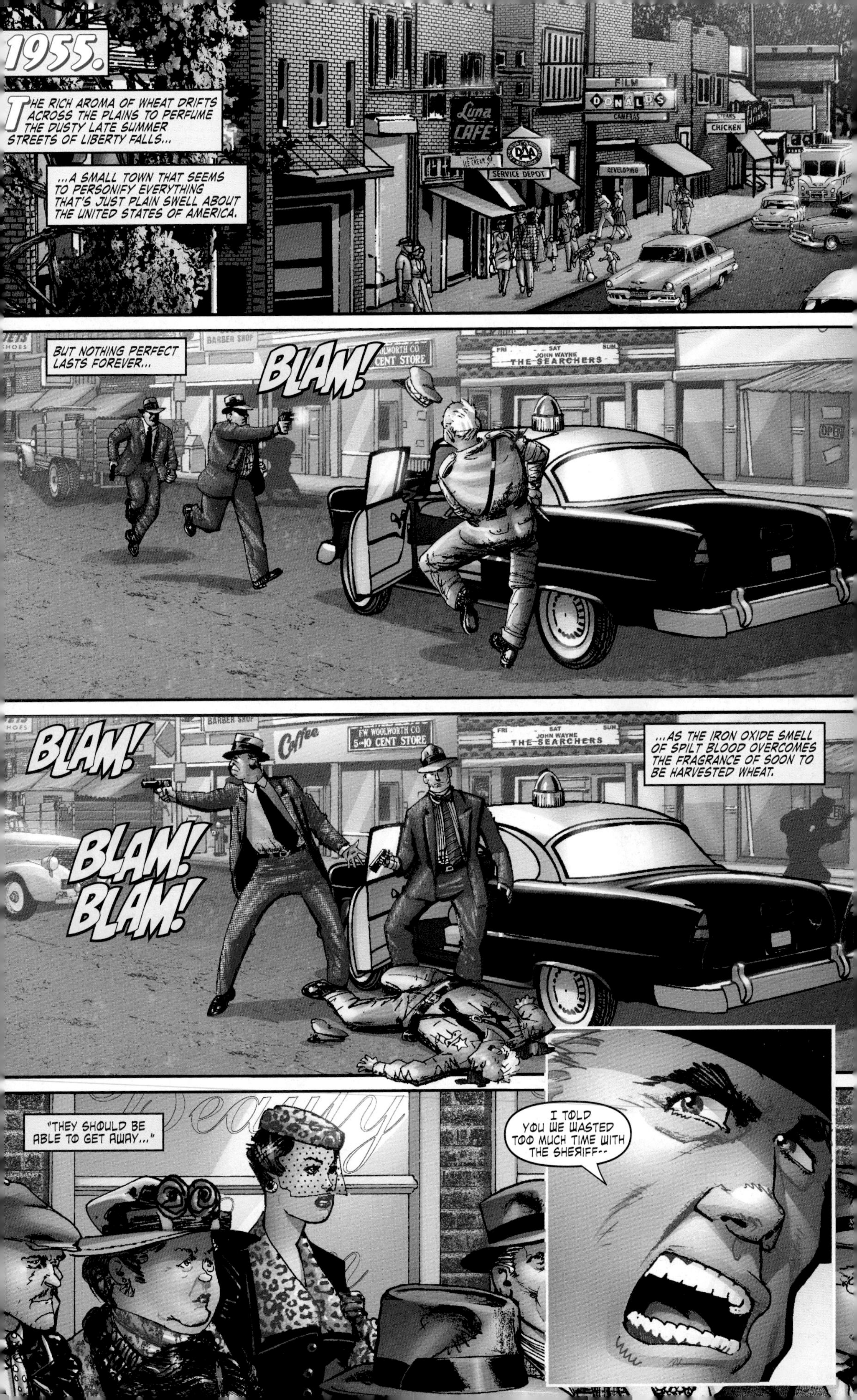
1955.
THE RICH AROMA OF WHEAT DRIFTS ACROSS THE PLAINS TO PERFUME THE DUSTY LATE SUMMER STREETS OF LIBERTY FALLS...
...A SMALL TOWN THAT SEEMS TO PERSONIFY EVERYTHING THAT'S JUST PLAIN SWELL ABOUT THE UNITED STATES OF AMERICA.
BUT NOTHING PERFECT LASTS FOREVER...
BLAM!
BLAM!
BLAM!
BLAM!
...AS THE IRON OXIDE SMELL OF SPILT BLOOD OVERCOMES THE FRAGRANCE OF SOON TO BE HARVESTED WHEAT.
"THEY SHOULD BE ABLE TO GET AWAY..."
I TOLD YOU WE WASTED TOO MUCH TIME WITH THE SHERIFF--

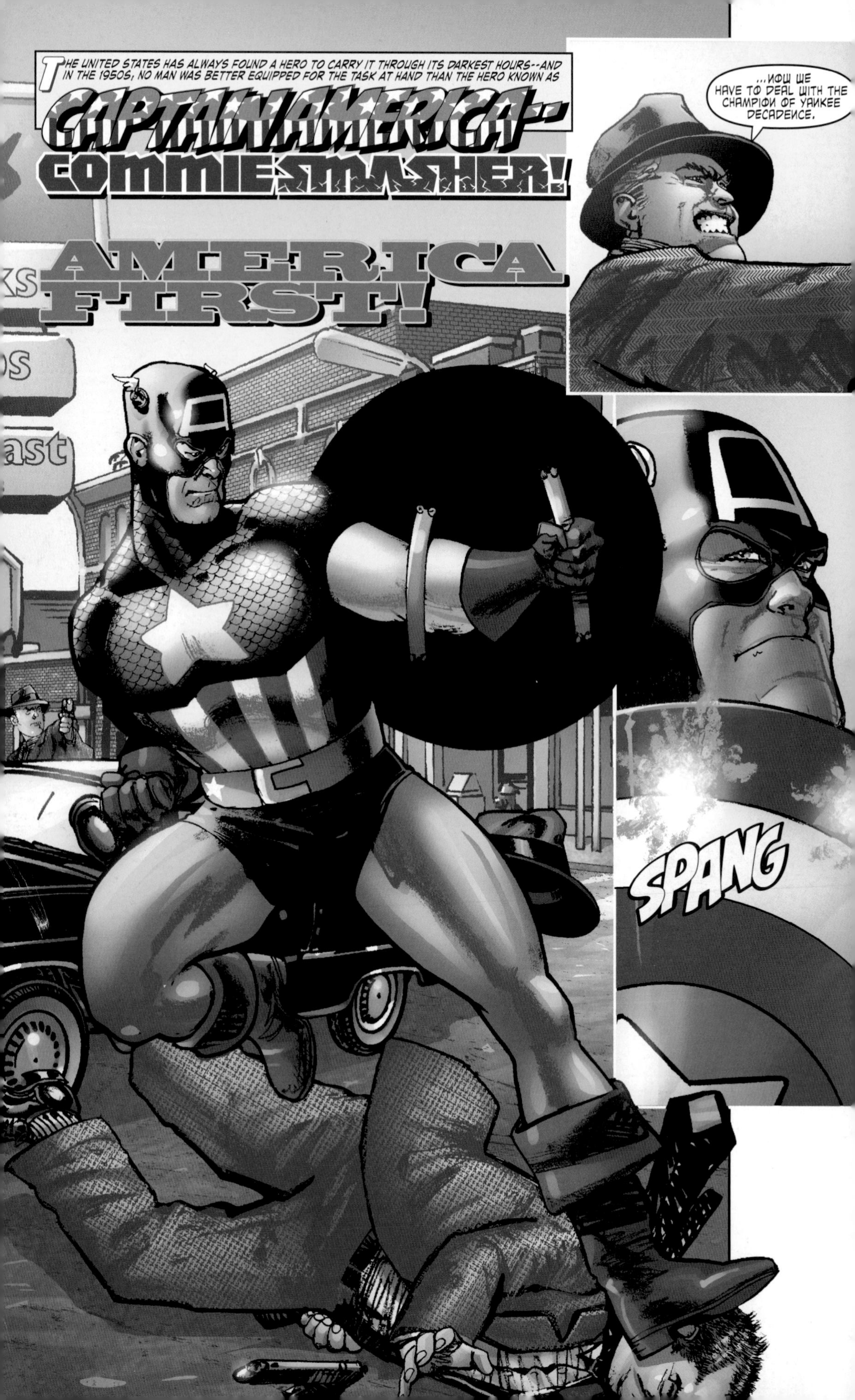
THE UNITED STATES HAS ALWAYS FOUND A HERO TO CARRY IT THROUGH ITS DARKEST HOURS--AND IN THE 1950S, NO MAN WAS BETTER EQUIPPED FOR THE TASK AT HAND THAN THE HERO KNOWN AS
CAPTAIN AMERICA--
COMMIE SMASHER!
AMERICA FIRST!
...NOW WE HAVE TO DEAL WITH THE CHAMPION OF YANKEE DECADENCE.
SPANG

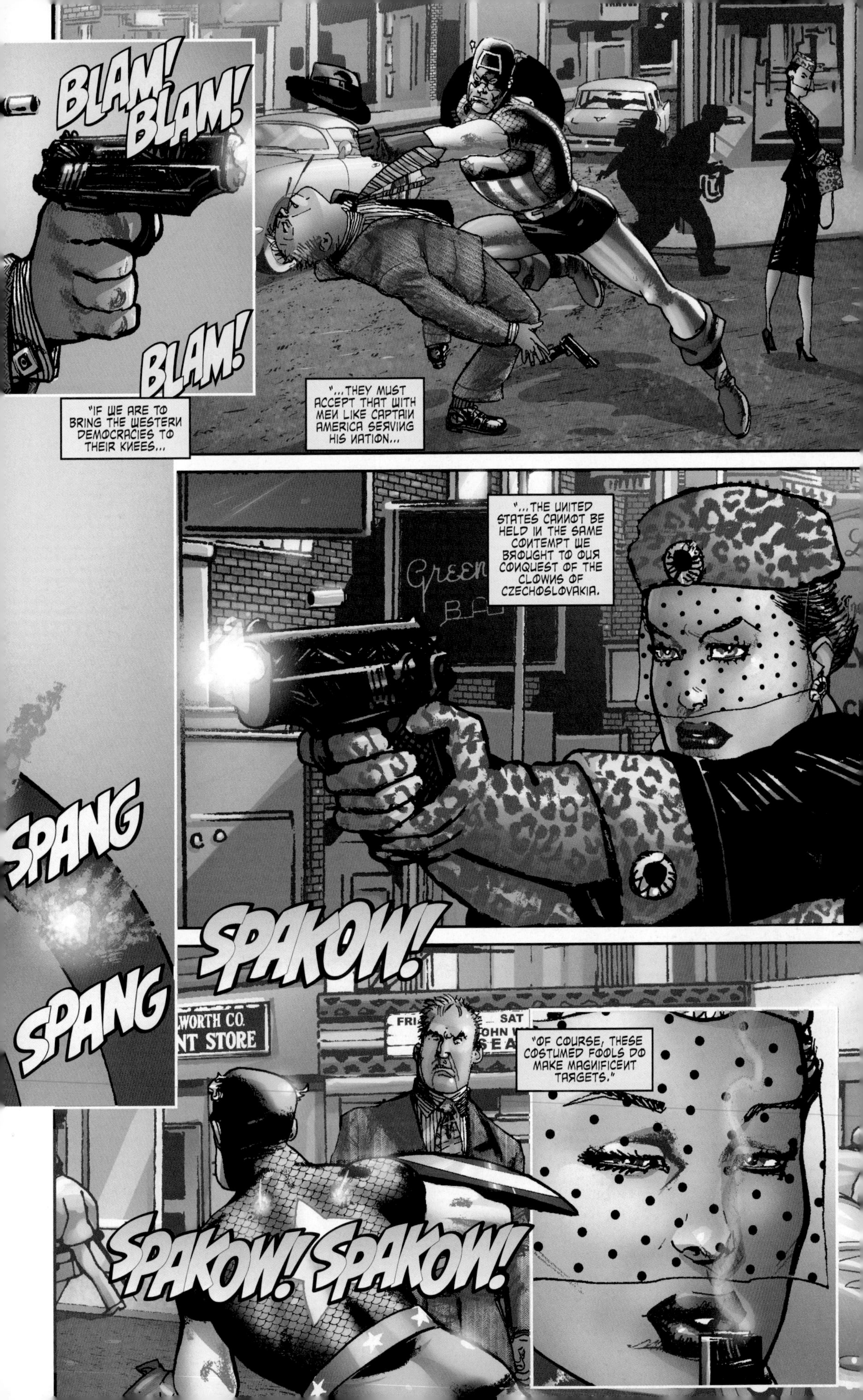
BLAM! BLAM!
BLAM!
"IF WE ARE TO BRING THE WESTERN DEMOCRACIES TO THEIR KNEES...
"...THEY MUST ACCEPT THAT WITH MEN LIKE CAPTAIN AMERICA SERVING HIS NATION...
"...THE UNITED STATES CANNOT BE HELD IN THE SAME CONTEMPT WE BROUGHT TO OUR CONQUEST OF THE CLOWNS OF CZECHOSLOVAKIA.
Green
SPANG
SPAKOW!
SPANG
WORTH CO.
NT STORE
FRI
SAT
"OF COURSE, THESE COSTUMED FOOLS DO MAKE MAGNIFICENT TARGETS."
SPAKOW! SPAKOW!

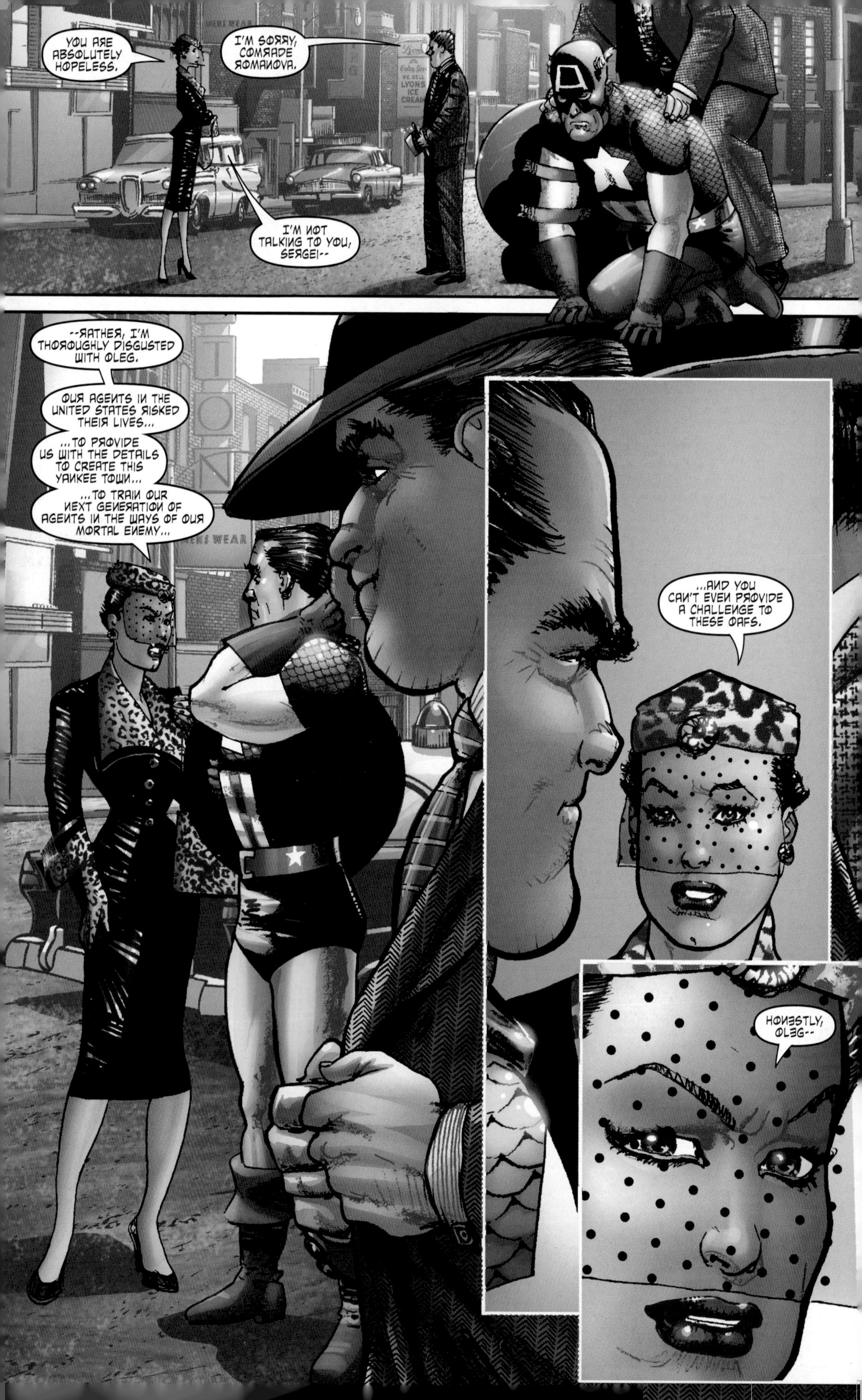
YOU ARE ABSOLUTELY HOPELESS.
I'M SORRY, COMRADE ROMANOVA.
I'M NOT TALKING TO YOU, SERGEI--
--RATHER, I'M THOROUGHLY DISGUSTED WITH OLEG.
OUR AGENTS IN THE UNITED STATES RISKED THEIR LIVES...
...TO PROVIDE US WITH THE DETAILS TO CREATE THIS YANKEE TOWN...
...TO TRAIN OUR NEXT GENERATION OF AGENTS IN THE WAYS OF OUR MORTAL ENEMY...
...AND YOU CAN'T EVEN PROVIDE A CHALLENGE TO THESE OAFS.
HONESTLY, OLEG--

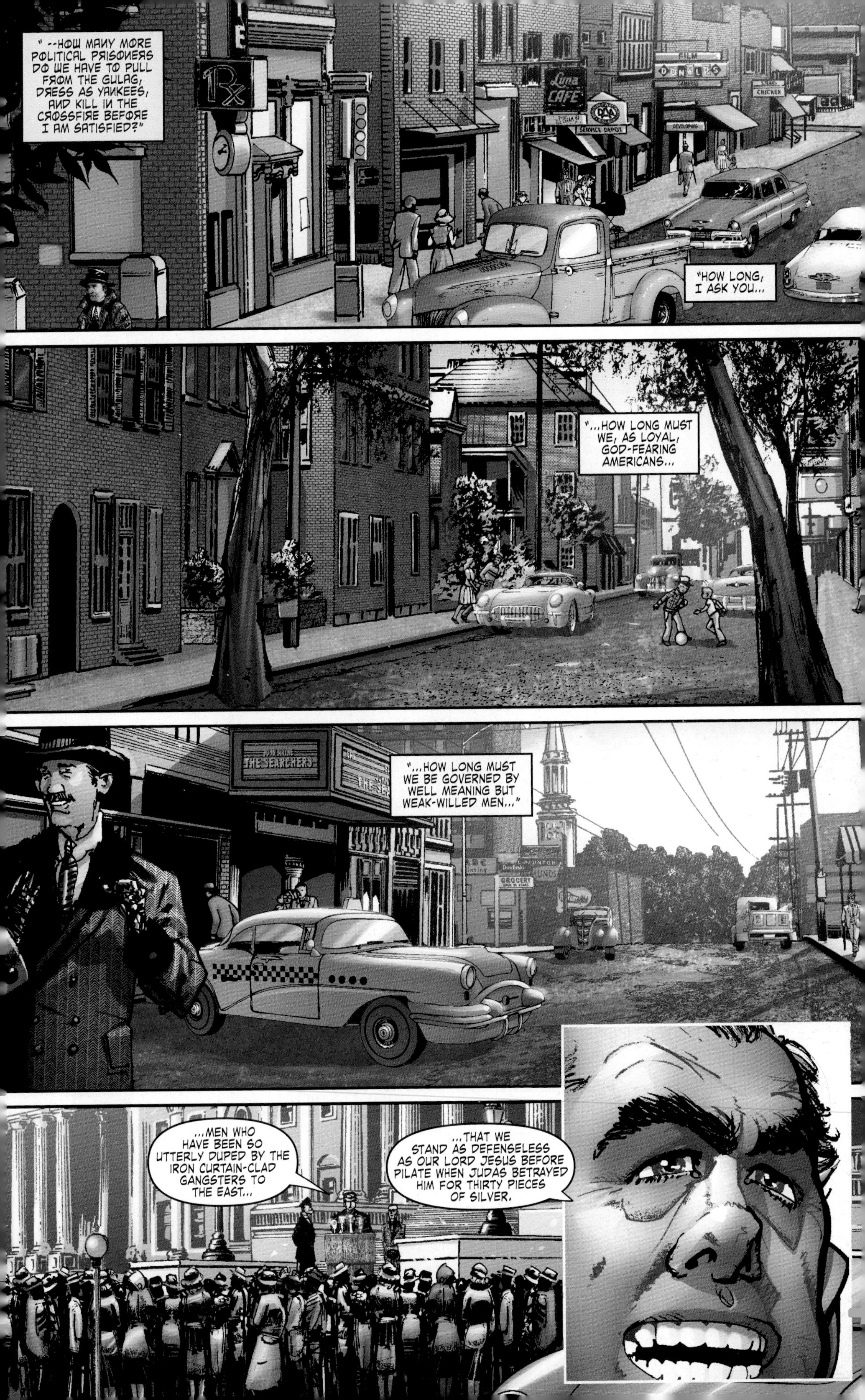
" --HOW MANY MORE POLITICAL PRISONERS DO WE HAVE TO PULL FROM THE GULAG, DRESS AS YANKEES, AND KILL IN THE CROSSFIRE BEFORE I AM SATISFIED?"
CAFE
SERVICE DEPOT
DEVELOPING
CHICKEN
"HOW LONG, I ASK YOU...
"...HOW LONG MUST WE, AS LOYAL, GOD-FEARING AMERICANS...
THE SEARCHERS
GROCERY
"...HOW LONG MUST WE BE GOVERNED BY WELL MEANING BUT WEAK-WILLED MEN..."
...MEN WHO HAVE BEEN SO UTTERLY DUPED BY THE IRON CURTAIN-CLAD GANGSTERS TO THE EAST...
...THAT WE STAND AS DEFENSELESS AS OUR LORD JESUS BEFORE PILATE WHEN JUDAS BETRAYED HIM FOR THIRTY PIECES OF SILVER.

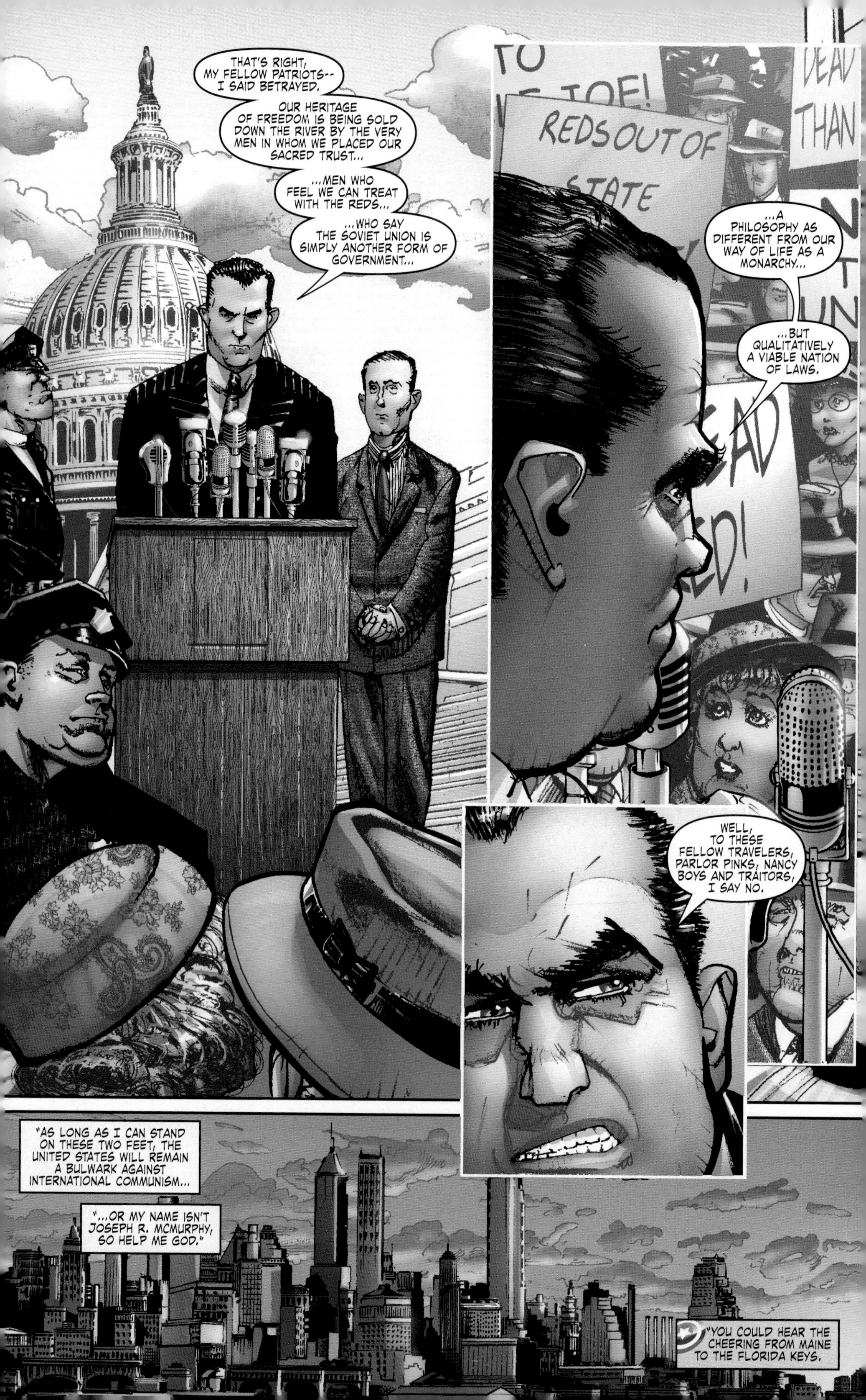
THAT'S RIGHT, MY FELLOW PATRIOTS-- I SAID BETRAYED.
OUR HERITAGE OF FREEDOM IS BEING SOLD DOWN THE RIVER BY THE VERY MEN IN WHOM WE PLACED OUR SACRED TRUST...
...MEN WHO FEEL WE CAN TREAT WITH THE REDS...
...WHO SAY THE SOVIET UNION IS SIMPLY ANOTHER FORM OF GOVERNMENT...
REDS OUT OF STATE
...A PHILOSOPHY AS DIFFERENT FROM OUR WAY OF LIFE AS A MONARCHY...
...BUT QUALITATIVELY A VIABLE NATION OF LAWS.
WELL, TO THESE FELLOW TRAVELERS, PARLOR PINKS, NANCY BOYS AND TRAITORS, I SAY NO.
"AS LONG AS I CAN STAND ON THESE TWO FEET, THE UNITED STATES WILL REMAIN A BULWARK AGAINST INTERNATIONAL COMMUNISM...
"...OR MY NAME ISN'T JOSEPH R. MCMURPHY, SO HELP ME GOD."
"YOU COULD HEAR THE CHEERING FROM MAINE TO THE FLORIDA KEYS.

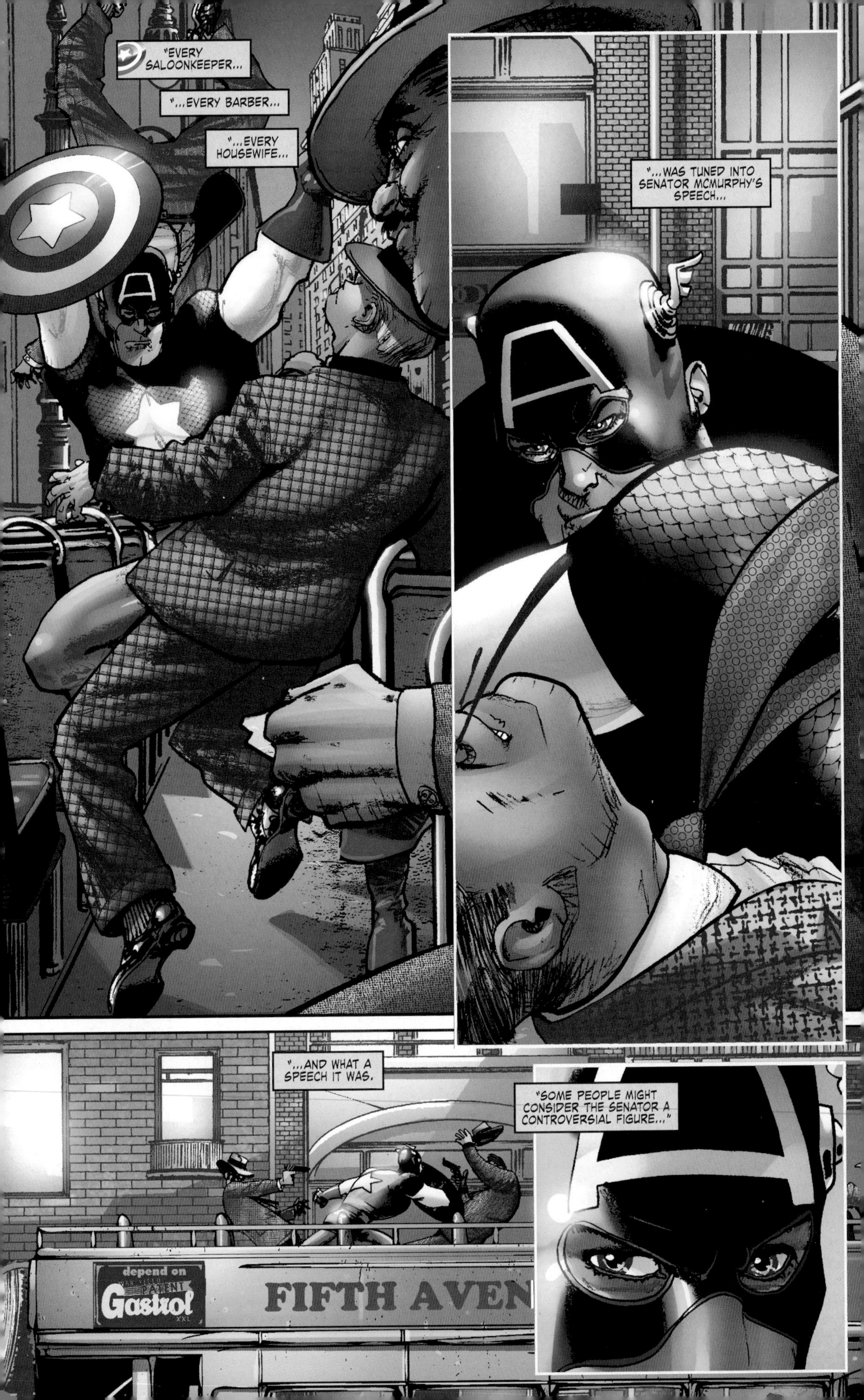
"EVERY SALOONKEEPER...
"...EVERY BARBER...
"...EVERY HOUSEWIFE...
"...WAS TUNED INTO SENATOR MCMURPHY'S SPEECH...
"...AND WHAT A SPEECH IT WAS.
depend on
PATENT
Gastrol
FIFTH AVEN
"SOME PEOPLE MIGHT CONSIDER THE SENATOR A CONTROVERSIAL FIGURE..."

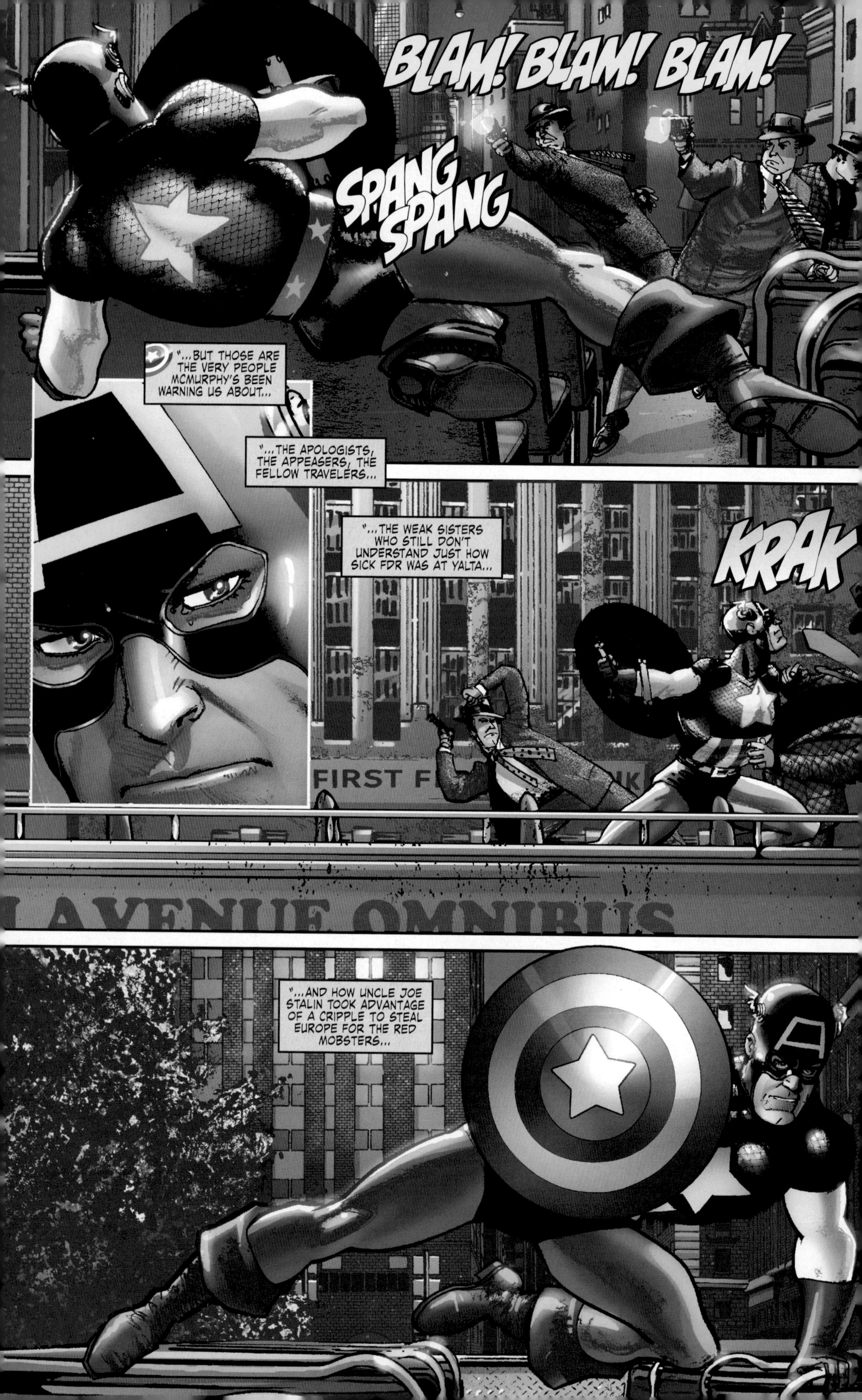
BLAM! BLAM! BLAM!
SPANG SPANG
"...BUT THOSE ARE THE VERY PEOPLE MCMURPHY'S BEEN WARNING US ABOUT...
"...THE APOLOGISTS, THE APPEASERS, THE FELLOW TRAVELERS...
"...THE WEAK SISTERS WHO STILL DON'T UNDERSTAND JUST HOW SICK FDR WAS AT YALTA...
KRAK
FIRST F
AVENUE OMNIBUS
"...AND HOW UNCLE JOE STALIN TOOK ADVANTAGE OF A CRIPPLE TO STEAL EUROPE FOR THE RED MOBSTERS...

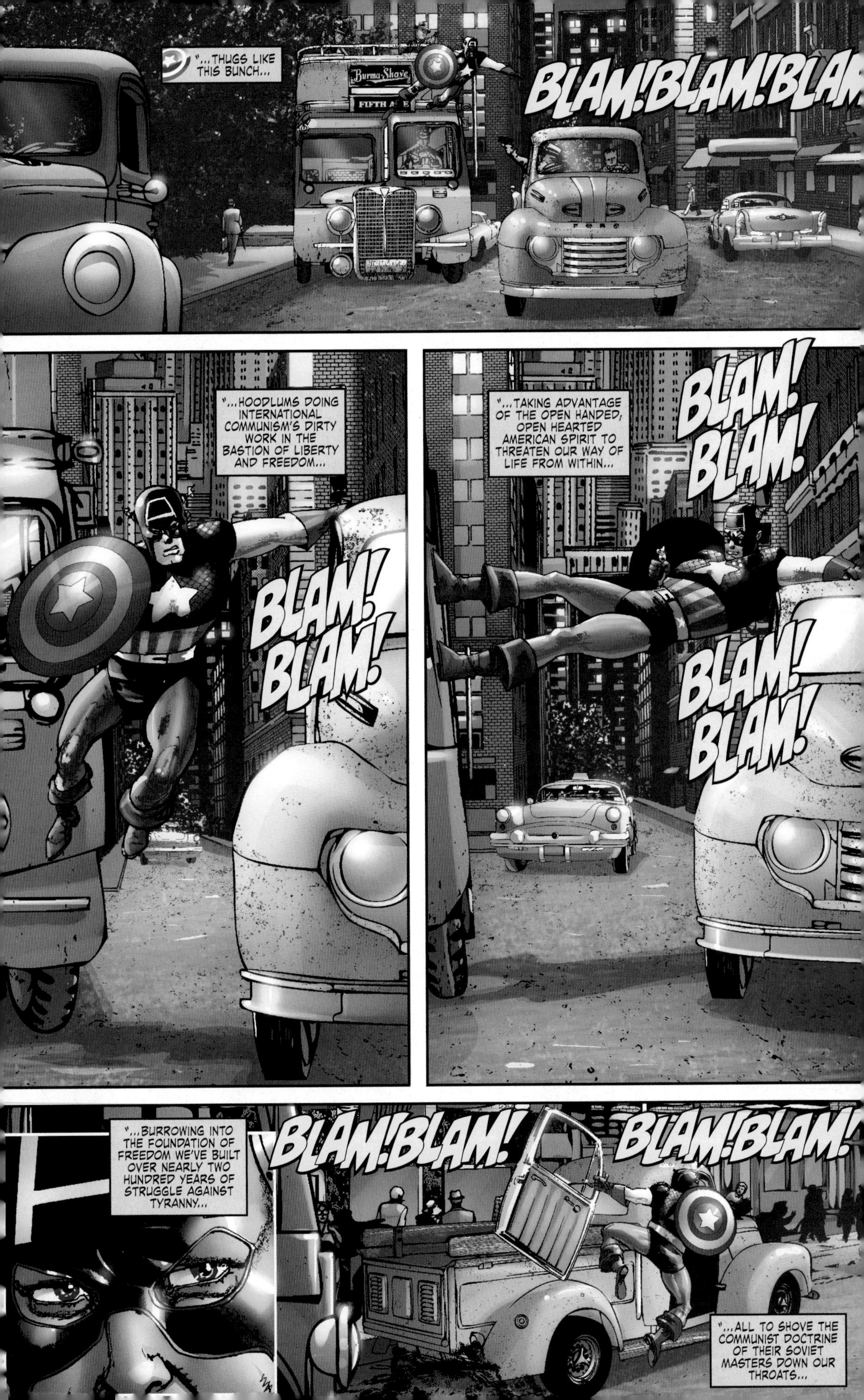
"...THUGS LIKE THIS BUNCH...
Burma-Shave
FIFTH AVE
BLAM! BLAM! BLAM
"...HOODLUMS DOING INTERNATIONAL COMMUNISM'S DIRTY WORK IN THE BASTION OF LIBERTY AND FREEDOM...
BLAM! BLAM!
"...TAKING ADVANTAGE OF THE OPEN HANDED, OPEN HEARTED AMERICAN SPIRIT TO THREATEN OUR WAY OF LIFE FROM WITHIN...
BLAM! BLAM!
BLAM! BLAM!
"...BURROWING INTO THE FOUNDATION OF FREEDOM WE'VE BUILT OVER NEARLY TWO HUNDRED YEARS OF STRUGGLE AGAINST TYRANNY...
BLAM! BLAM!
BLAM! BLAM!
"...ALL TO SHOVE THE COMMUNIST DOCTRINE OF THEIR SOVIET MASTERS DOWN OUR THROATS...

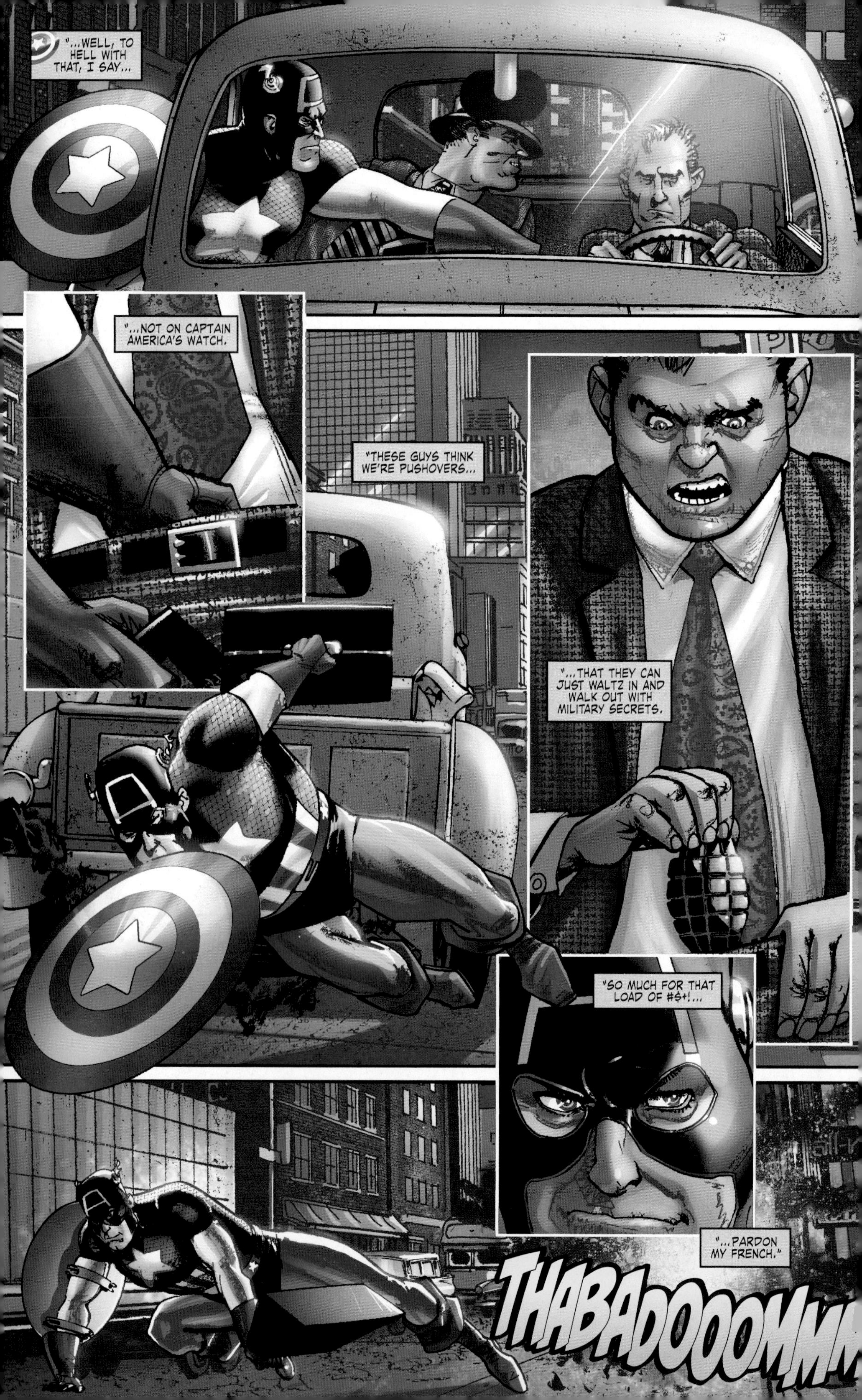
"...WELL, TO HELL WITH THAT, I SAY...
"...NOT ON CAPTAIN AMERICA'S WATCH.
"THESE GUYS THINK WE'RE PUSHOVERS...
"...THAT THEY CAN JUST WALTZ IN AND WALK OUT WITH MILITARY SECRETS.
"SO MUCH FOR THAT LOAD OF #$+!...
"...PARDON MY FRENCH."
THABADOOOMMM

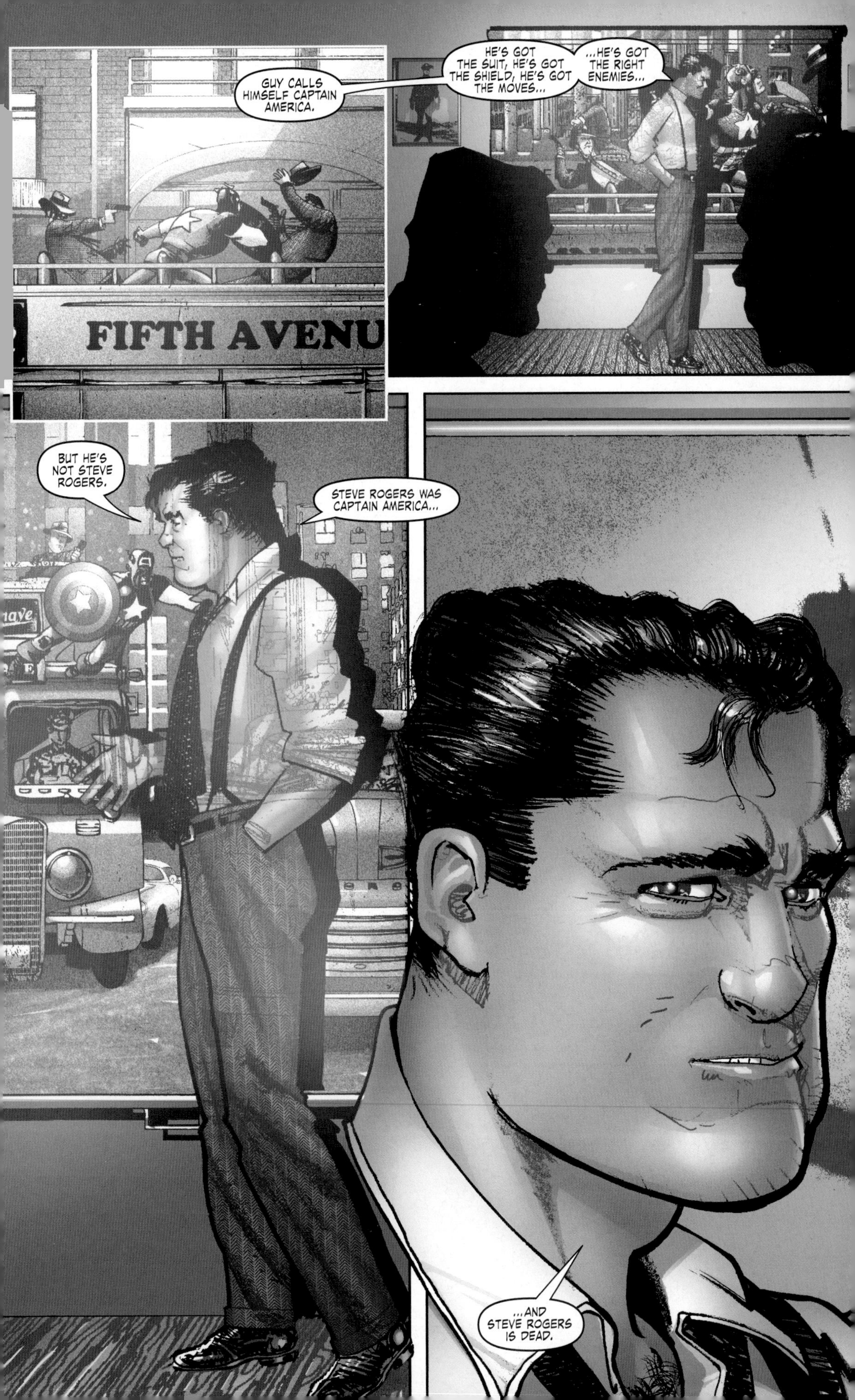
GUY CALLS HIMSELF CAPTAIN AMERICA.
HE'S GOT THE SUIT, HE'S GOT THE SHIELD, HE'S GOT THE MOVES...
...HE'S GOT THE RIGHT ENEMIES...
FIFTH AVENU
BUT HE'S NOT STEVE ROGERS.
STEVE ROGERS WAS CAPTAIN AMERICA...
...AND STEVE ROGERS IS DEAD.

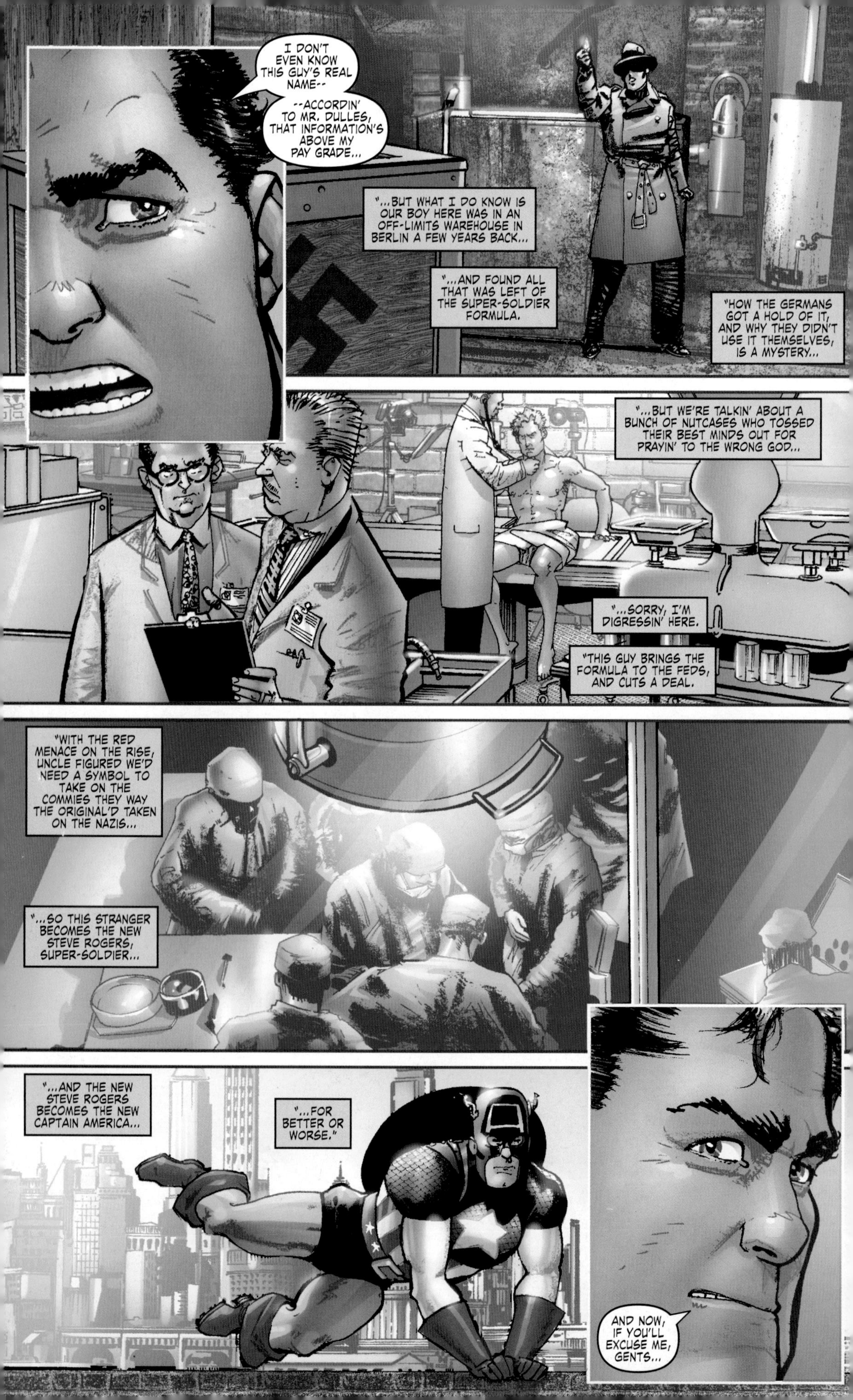
I DON'T EVEN KNOW THIS GUY'S REAL NAME--
--ACCORDIN' TO MR. DULLES, THAT INFORMATION'S ABOVE MY PAY GRADE...
"...BUT WHAT I DO KNOW IS OUR BOY HERE WAS IN AN OFF-LIMITS WAREHOUSE IN BERLIN A FEW YEARS BACK...
"...AND FOUND ALL THAT WAS LEFT OF THE SUPER-SOLDIER FORMULA.
"HOW THE GERMANS GOT A HOLD OF IT, AND WHY THEY DIDN'T USE IT THEMSELVES, IS A MYSTERY...
"...BUT WE'RE TALKIN' ABOUT A BUNCH OF NUTCASES WHO TOSSED THEIR BEST MINDS OUT FOR PRAYIN' TO THE WRONG GOD...
"...SORRY, I'M DIGRESSIN' HERE.
"THIS GUY BRINGS THE FORMULA TO THE FEDS, AND CUTS A DEAL.
"WITH THE RED MENACE ON THE RISE, UNCLE FIGURED WE'D NEED A SYMBOL TO TAKE ON THE COMMIES THEY WAY THE ORIGINAL'D TAKEN ON THE NAZIS...
"...SO THIS STRANGER BECOMES THE NEW STEVE ROGERS, SUPER-SOLDIER...
"...AND THE NEW STEVE ROGERS BECOMES THE NEW CAPTAIN AMERICA...
"...FOR BETTER OR WORSE."
AND NOW, IF YOU'LL EXCUSE ME, GENTS...

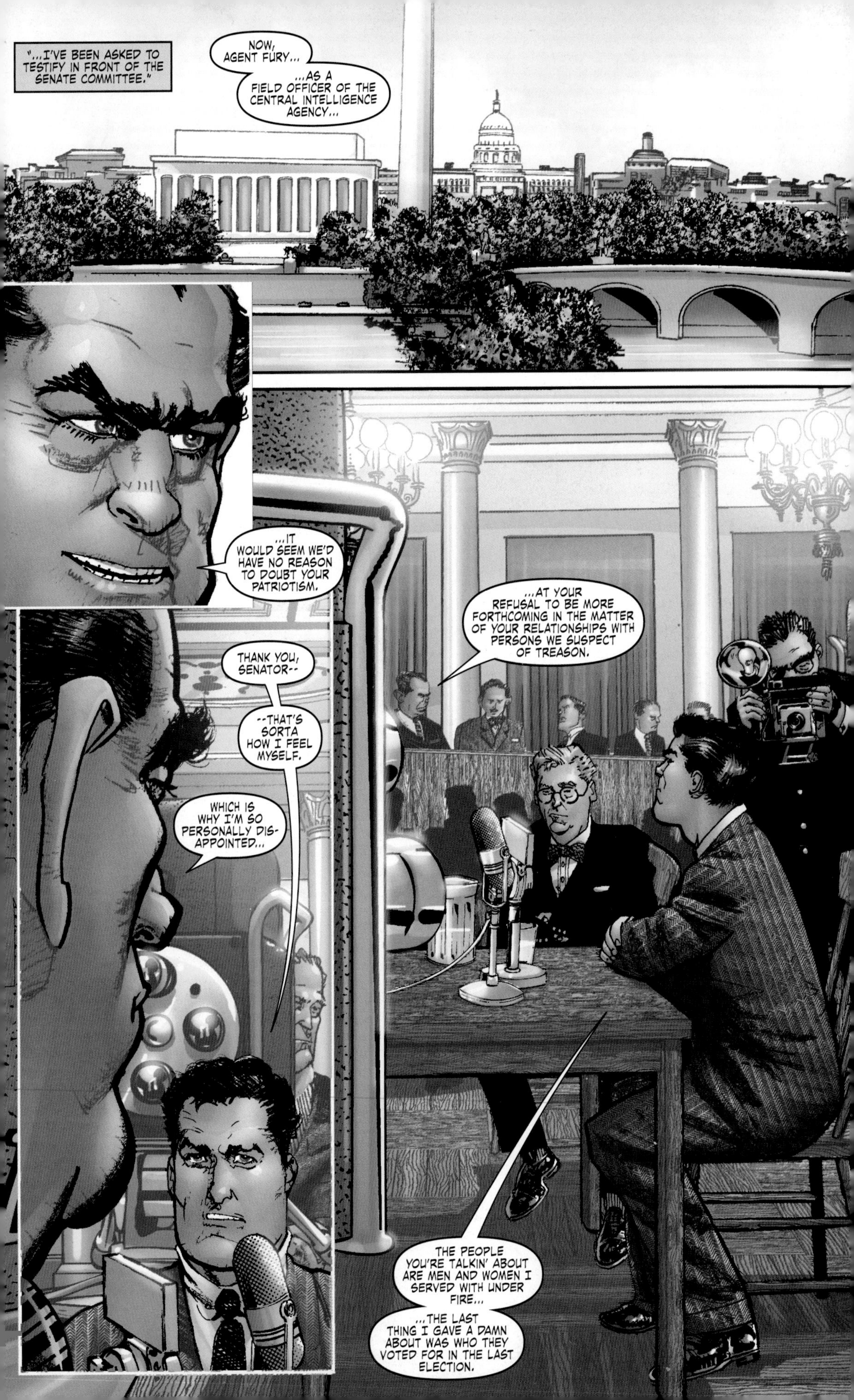
"...I'VE BEEN ASKED TO TESTIFY IN FRONT OF THE SENATE COMMITTEE."
NOW, AGENT FURY...
...AS A FIELD OFFICER OF THE CENTRAL INTELLIGENCE AGENCY...
...IT WOULD SEEM WE'D HAVE NO REASON TO DOUBT YOUR PATRIOTISM.
THANK YOU, SENATOR--
--THAT'S SORTA HOW I FEEL MYSELF.
WHICH IS WHY I'M SO PERSONALLY DIS-APPOINTED...
...AT YOUR REFUSAL TO BE MORE FORTHCOMING IN THE MATTER OF YOUR RELATIONSHIPS WITH PERSONS WE SUSPECT OF TREASON.
THE PEOPLE YOU'RE TALKIN' ABOUT ARE MEN AND WOMEN I SERVED WITH UNDER FIRE...
...THE LAST THING I GAVE A DAMN ABOUT WAS WHO THEY VOTED FOR IN THE LAST ELECTION.

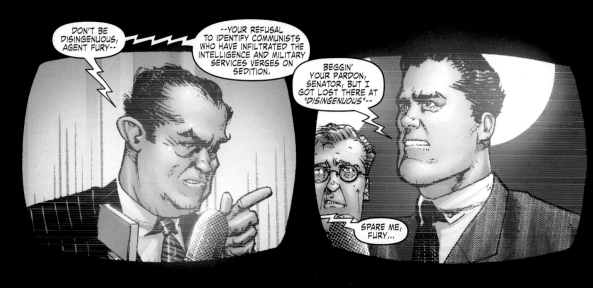

DON'T BE DISINGENUOUS, AGENT FURY--

--YOUR REFUSAL TO IDENTIFY COMMUNISTS WHO HAVE INFILTRATED THE INTELLIGENCE AND MILITARY SERVICES VERGES ON SEDITION.

BEGGIN' YOUR PARDON, SENATOR, BUT I GOT LOST THERE AT "DISINGENUOUS"--

SPARE ME, FURY...

...THAT "DESE DEMS AND DOSE" ACT MAY WORK ON SOME LITTLE OLD LADY FROM DUBUQUE, BUT I'VE BEEN AROUND THE BLOCK A FEW TIMES, PAL.

I GOT NO DOUBT IN MY MIND ABOUT THAT, SENATOR MCMURPHY...

...BUT I'M BETTIN' THAT BLOCK DON'T INCLUDE OMAHA BEACH, THE HURTGEN FOREST OR THE ARDENNES...

THIS IS IRRELEVANT--

I DON'T KNOW ABOUT THAT.

IT SEEMS TO ME WHILE YOU WERE SITTING ON YOUR FAT KEISTER OVER HERE--

BAM! BAM!

POINT OF ORDER!

--THE GUYS YOU'RE SMEARIN' WERE DYIN' OVER THERE TO GIVE YOU THE RIGHT TO SAY WHAT YOU PLEASE--

I WARN YOU, FURY--

--YOU'RE IN CONTEMPT...

BAM! BAM!

...AND THEIR COMBAT DUTY GIVES THEM THE RIGHT TO VOTE HOWEVER THEY PLEASE, TOO.

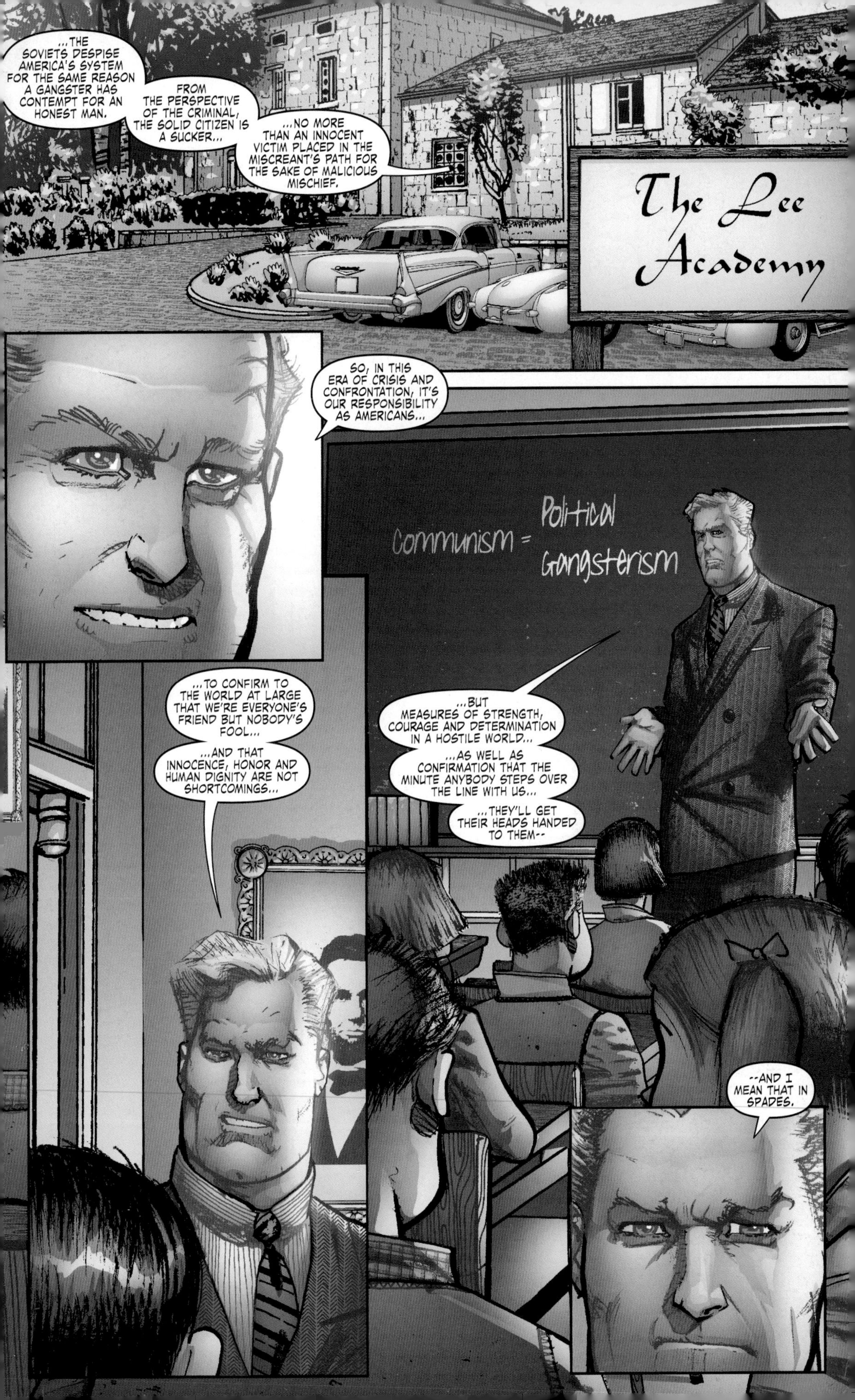
...THE SOVIETS DESPISE AMERICA'S SYSTEM FOR THE SAME REASON A GANGSTER HAS CONTEMPT FOR AN HONEST MAN.
FROM THE PERSPECTIVE OF THE CRIMINAL, THE SOLID CITIZEN IS A SUCKER...
...NO MORE THAN AN INNOCENT VICTIM PLACED IN THE MISCREANT'S PATH FOR THE SAKE OF MALICIOUS MISCHIEF.
The Lee Academy
SO, IN THIS ERA OF CRISIS AND CONFRONTATION, IT'S OUR RESPONSIBILITY AS AMERICANS...
Communism = Political Gangsterism
...TO CONFIRM TO THE WORLD AT LARGE THAT WE'RE EVERYONE'S FRIEND BUT NOBODY'S FOOL...
...AND THAT INNOCENCE, HONOR AND HUMAN DIGNITY ARE NOT SHORTCOMINGS...
...BUT MEASURES OF STRENGTH, COURAGE AND DETERMINATION IN A HOSTILE WORLD...
...AS WELL AS CONFIRMATION THAT THE MINUTE ANYBODY STEPS OVER THE LINE WITH US...
...THEY'LL GET THEIR HEADS HANDED TO THEM--
--AND I MEAN THAT IN SPADES.

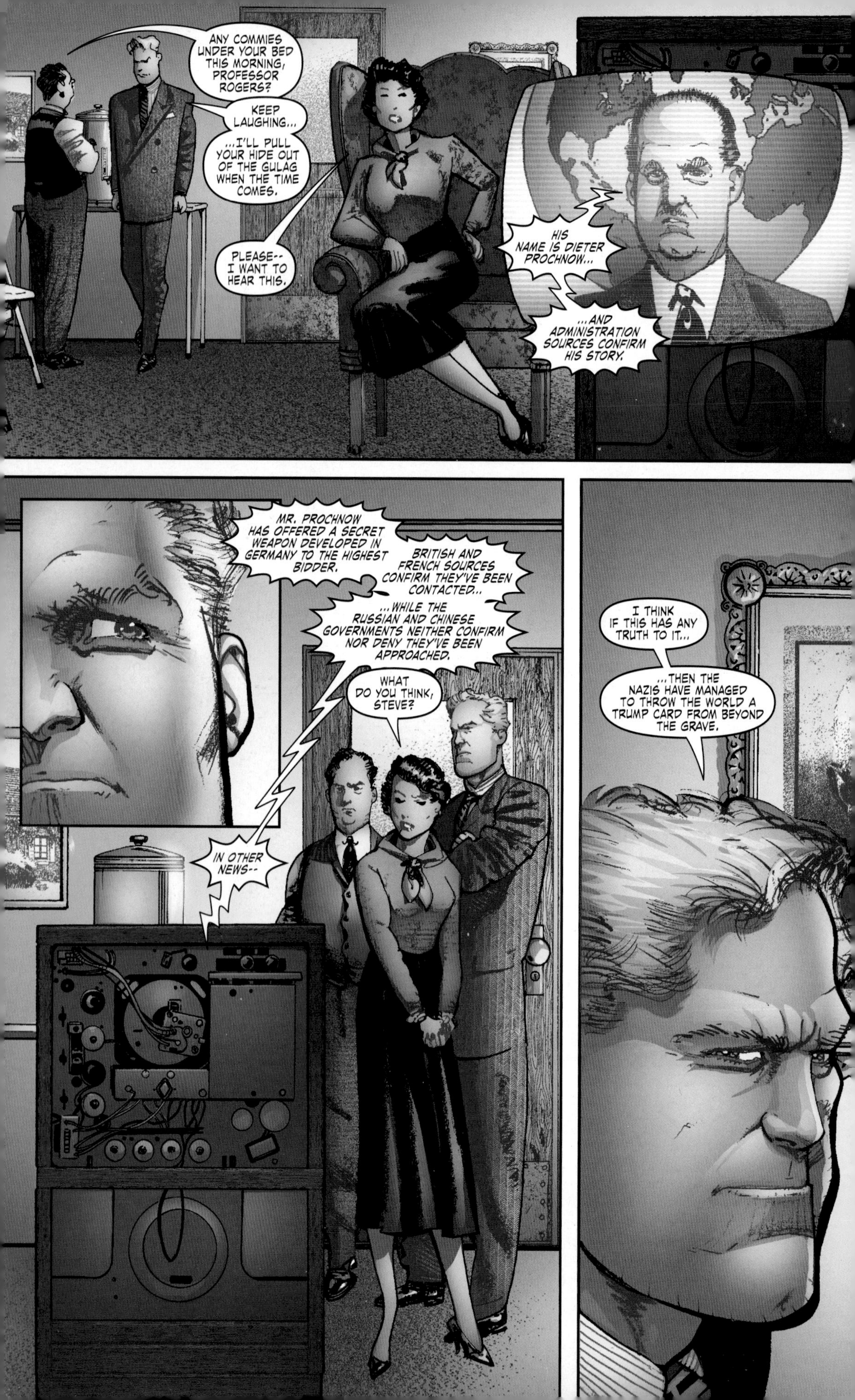
ANY COMMIES UNDER YOUR BED THIS MORNING, PROFESSOR ROGERS?
KEEP LAUGHING...
...I'LL PULL YOUR HIDE OUT OF THE GULAG WHEN THE TIME COMES.
PLEASE-- I WANT TO HEAR THIS.
HIS NAME IS DIETER PROCHNOW...
...AND ADMINISTRATION SOURCES CONFIRM HIS STORY.
MR. PROCHNOW HAS OFFERED A SECRET WEAPON DEVELOPED IN GERMANY TO THE HIGHEST BIDDER.
BRITISH AND FRENCH SOURCES CONFIRM THEY'VE BEEN CONTACTED...
...WHILE THE RUSSIAN AND CHINESE GOVERNMENTS NEITHER CONFIRM NOR DENY THEY'VE BEEN APPROACHED.
WHAT DO YOU THINK, STEVE?
IN OTHER NEWS--
I THINK IF THIS HAS ANY TRUTH TO IT...
...THEN THE NAZIS HAVE MANAGED TO THROW THE WORLD A TRUMP CARD FROM BEYOND THE GRAVE.

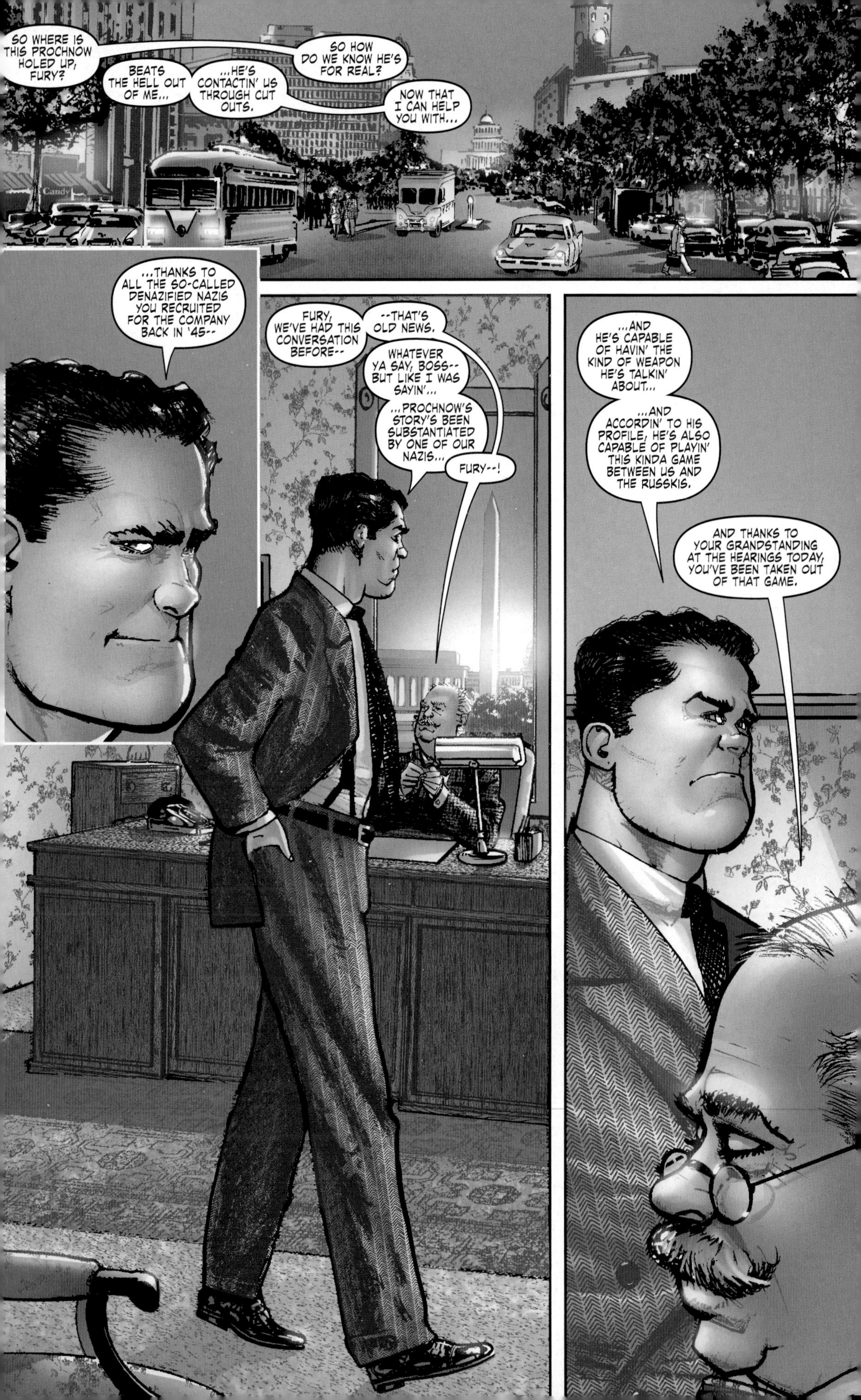
SO WHERE IS THIS PROCHNOW HOLED UP, FURY?
BEATS THE HELL OUT OF ME...
...HE'S CONTACTIN' US THROUGH CUT OUTS.
SO HOW DO WE KNOW HE'S FOR REAL?
NOW THAT I CAN HELP YOU WITH...
Candy
...THANKS TO ALL THE SO-CALLED DENAZIFIED NAZIS YOU RECRUITED FOR THE COMPANY BACK IN '45--
FURY, WE'VE HAD THIS CONVERSATION BEFORE--
--THAT'S OLD NEWS.
WHATEVER YA SAY, BOSS-- BUT LIKE I WAS SAYIN'...
...PROCHNOW'S STORY'S BEEN SUBSTANTIATED BY ONE OF OUR NAZIS...
FURY--!
...AND HE'S CAPABLE OF HAVIN' THE KIND OF WEAPON HE'S TALKIN' ABOUT...
...AND ACCORDIN' TO HIS PROFILE, HE'S ALSO CAPABLE OF PLAYIN' THIS KINDA GAME BETWEEN US AND THE RUSSKIS.
AND THANKS TO YOUR GRANDSTANDING AT THE HEARINGS TODAY, YOU'VE BEEN TAKEN OUT OF THAT GAME.

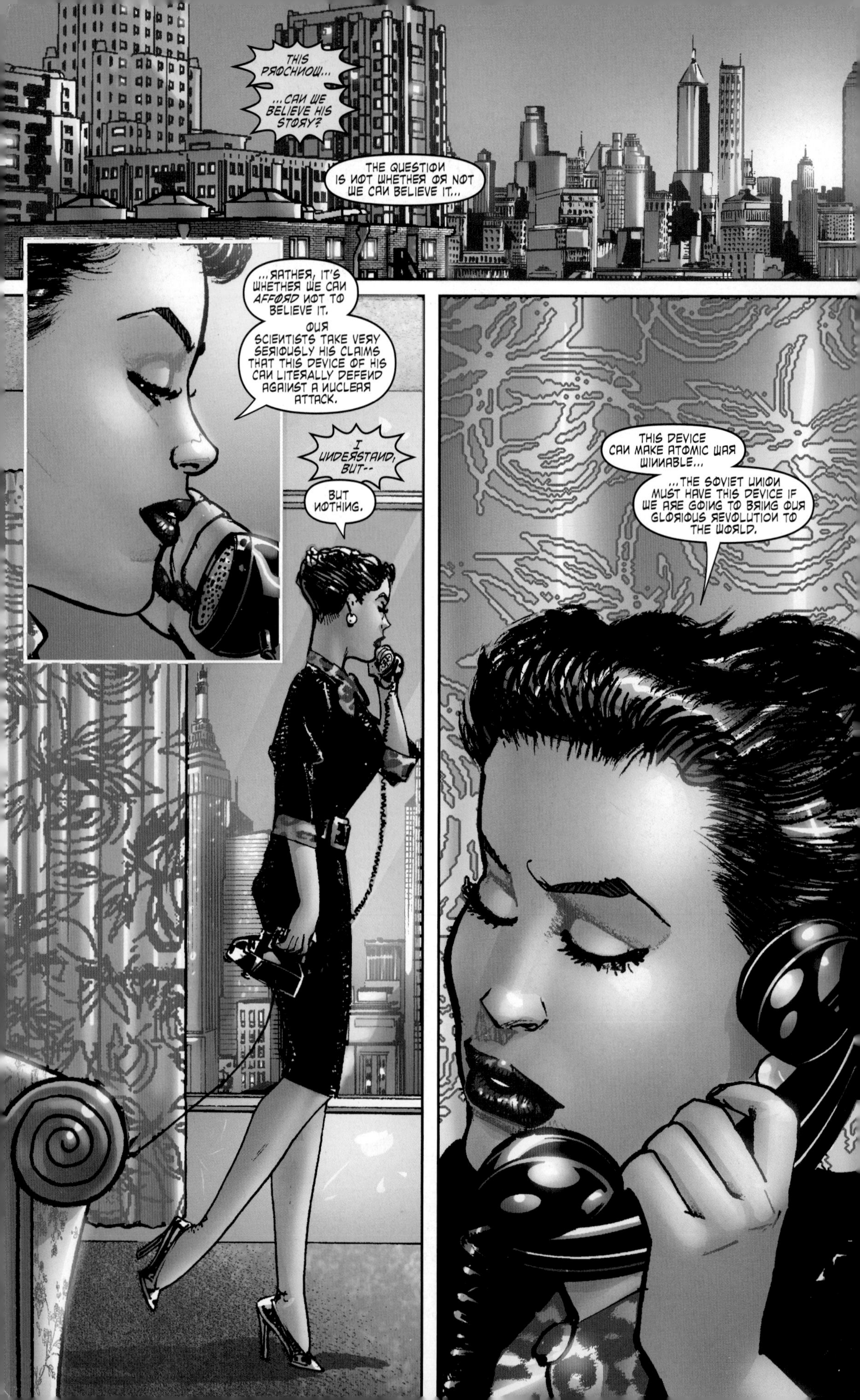
THIS PROCHNOW...
...CAN WE BELIEVE HIS STORY?
THE QUESTION IS NOT WHETHER OR NOT WE CAN BELIEVE IT...
...RATHER, IT'S WHETHER WE CAN AFFORD NOT TO BELIEVE IT.
OUR SCIENTISTS TAKE VERY SERIOUSLY HIS CLAIMS THAT THIS DEVICE OF HIS CAN LITERALLY DEFEND AGAINST A NUCLEAR ATTACK.
I UNDERSTAND, BUT--
BUT NOTHING.
THIS DEVICE CAN MAKE ATOMIC WAR WINNABLE...
...THE SOVIET UNION MUST HAVE THIS DEVICE IF WE ARE GOING TO BRING OUR GLORIOUS REVOLUTION TO THE WORLD.

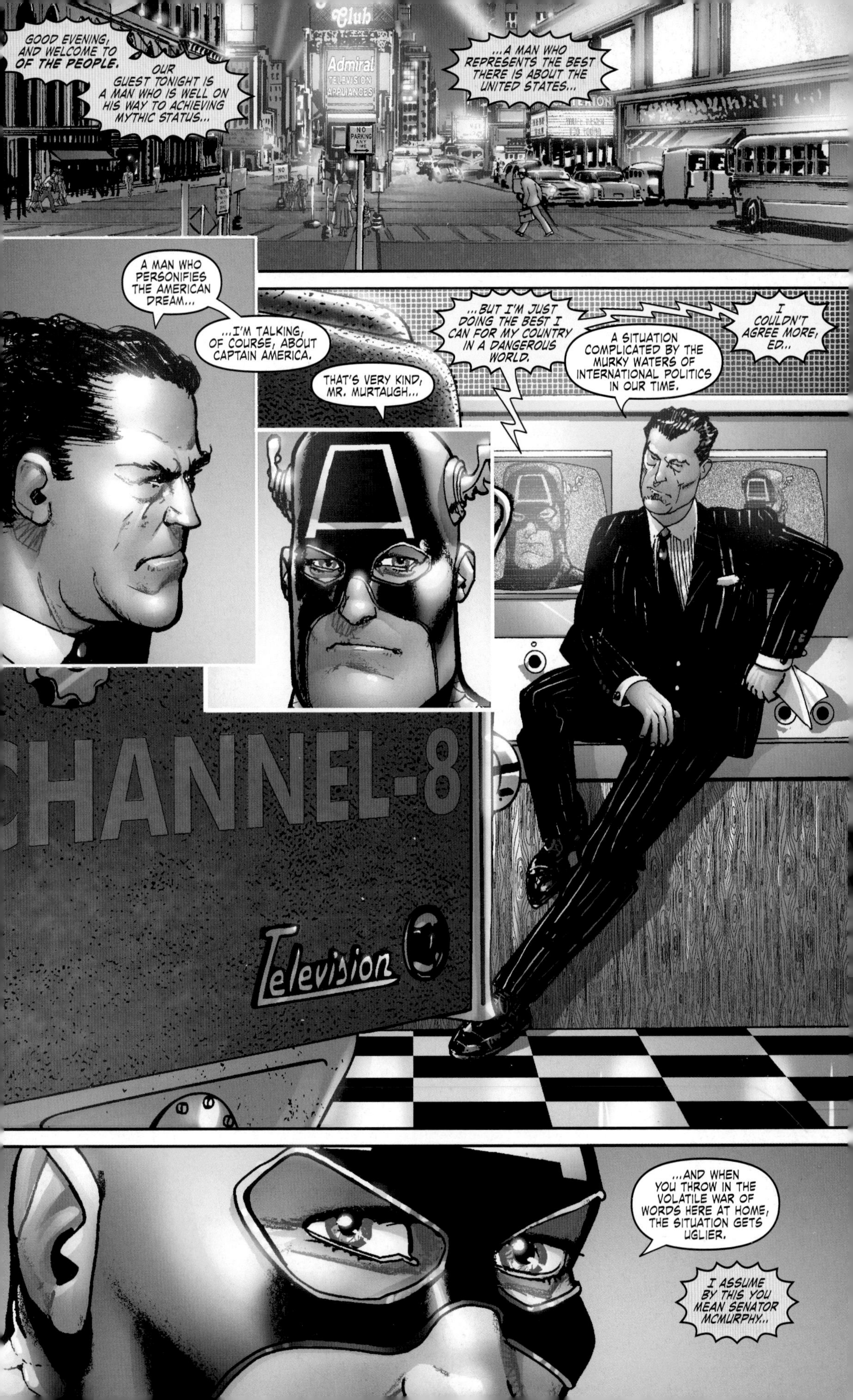
GOOD EVENING, AND WELCOME TO OF THE PEOPLE.
OUR GUEST TONIGHT IS A MAN WHO IS WELL ON HIS WAY TO ACHIEVING MYTHIC STATUS...
...A MAN WHO REPRESENTS THE BEST THERE IS ABOUT THE UNITED STATES...
Club
Admiral
TELEVISION APPLIANCES
NO PARKING ANY TIME
NO TURNS
A MAN WHO PERSONIFIES THE AMERICAN DREAM...
...I'M TALKING, OF COURSE, ABOUT CAPTAIN AMERICA.
THAT'S VERY KIND, MR. MURTAUGH...
...BUT I'M JUST DOING THE BEST I CAN FOR MY COUNTRY IN A DANGEROUS WORLD.
A SITUATION COMPLICATED BY THE MURKY WATERS OF INTERNATIONAL POLITICS IN OUR TIME.
I COULDN'T AGREE MORE, ED...
CHANNEL-8
Television
...AND WHEN YOU THROW IN THE VOLATILE WAR OF WORDS HERE AT HOME, THE SITUATION GETS UGLIER.
I ASSUME BY THIS YOU MEAN SENATOR MCMURPHY...

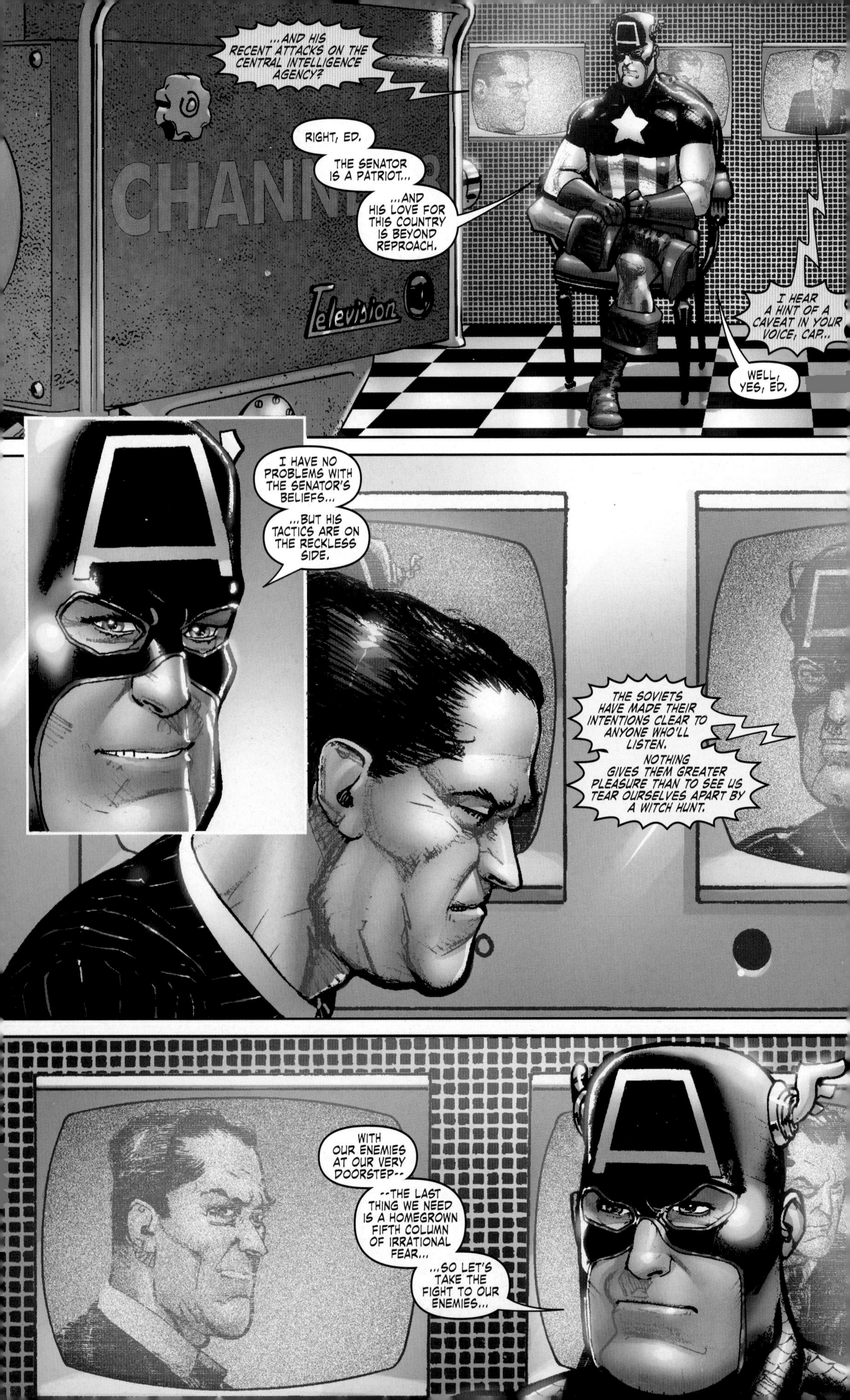
...AND HIS RECENT ATTACKS ON THE CENTRAL INTELLIGENCE AGENCY?
RIGHT, ED.
THE SENATOR IS A PATRIOT...
...AND HIS LOVE FOR THIS COUNTRY IS BEYOND REPROACH.
Television
I HEAR A HINT OF A CAVEAT IN YOUR VOICE, CAP...
WELL, YES, ED.
I HAVE NO PROBLEMS WITH THE SENATOR'S BELIEFS...
...BUT HIS TACTICS ARE ON THE RECKLESS SIDE.
THE SOVIETS HAVE MADE THEIR INTENTIONS CLEAR TO ANYONE WHO'LL LISTEN.
NOTHING GIVES THEM GREATER PLEASURE THAN TO SEE US TEAR OURSELVES APART BY A WITCH HUNT.
WITH OUR ENEMIES AT OUR VERY DOORSTEP--
--THE LAST THING WE NEED IS A HOMEGROWN FIFTH COLUMN OF IRRATIONAL FEAR...
...SO LET'S TAKE THE FIGHT TO OUR ENEMIES...

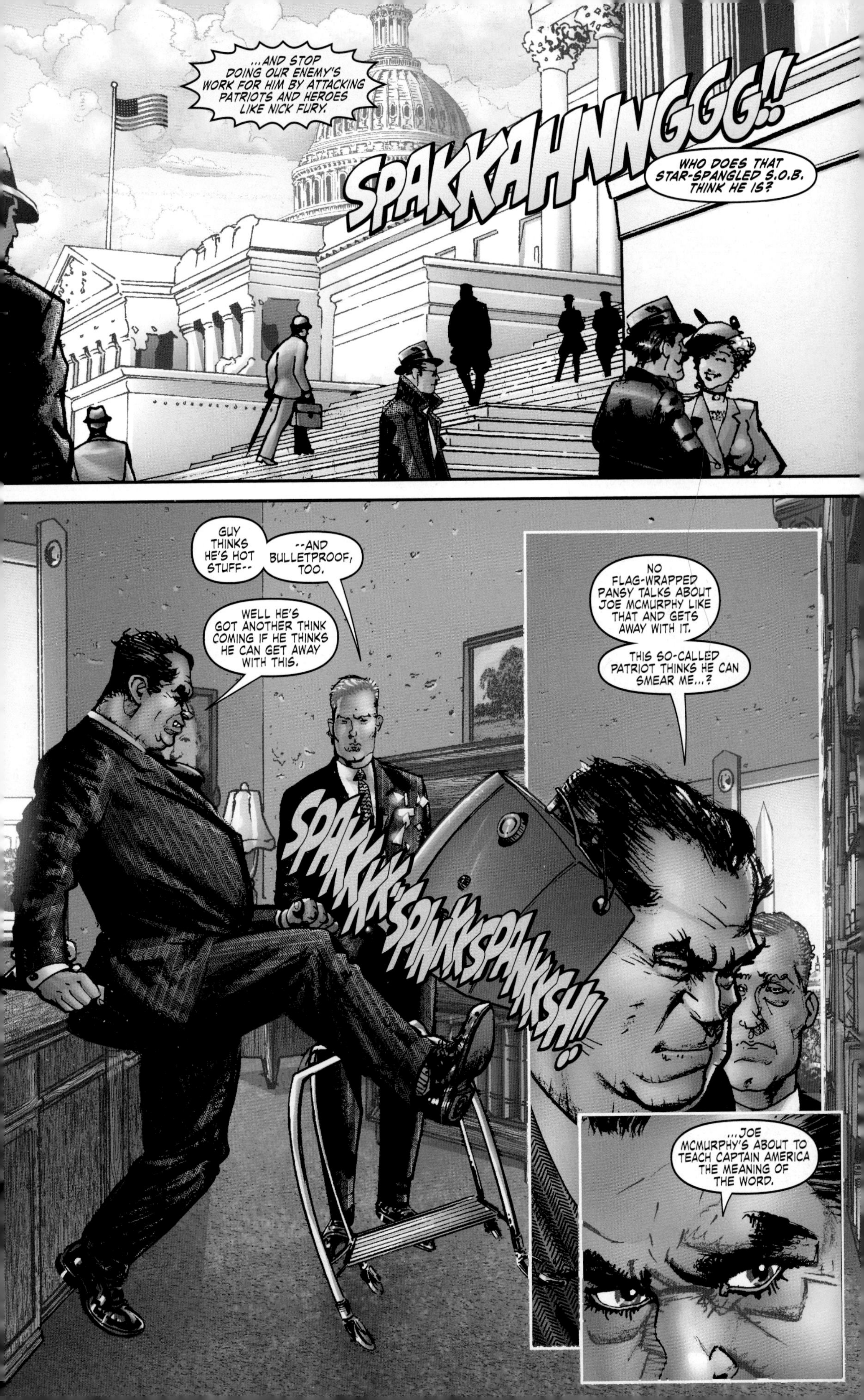
...AND STOP DOING OUR ENEMY'S WORK FOR HIM BY ATTACKING PATRIOTS AND HEROES LIKE NICK FURY.
SPAKKAHNNGGG!!
WHO DOES THAT STAR-SPANGLED S.O.B. THINK HE IS?
GUY THINKS HE'S HOT STUFF--
--AND BULLETPROOF, TOO.
WELL HE'S GOT ANOTHER THINK COMING IF HE THINKS HE CAN GET AWAY WITH THIS.
SPAKKK-SPINKKSPANKKSH!!
NO FLAG-WRAPPED PANSY TALKS ABOUT JOE MCMURPHY LIKE THAT AND GETS AWAY WITH IT.
THIS SO-CALLED PATRIOT THINKS HE CAN SMEAR ME...?
...JOE MCMURPHY'S ABOUT TO TEACH CAPTAIN AMERICA THE MEANING OF THE WORD.

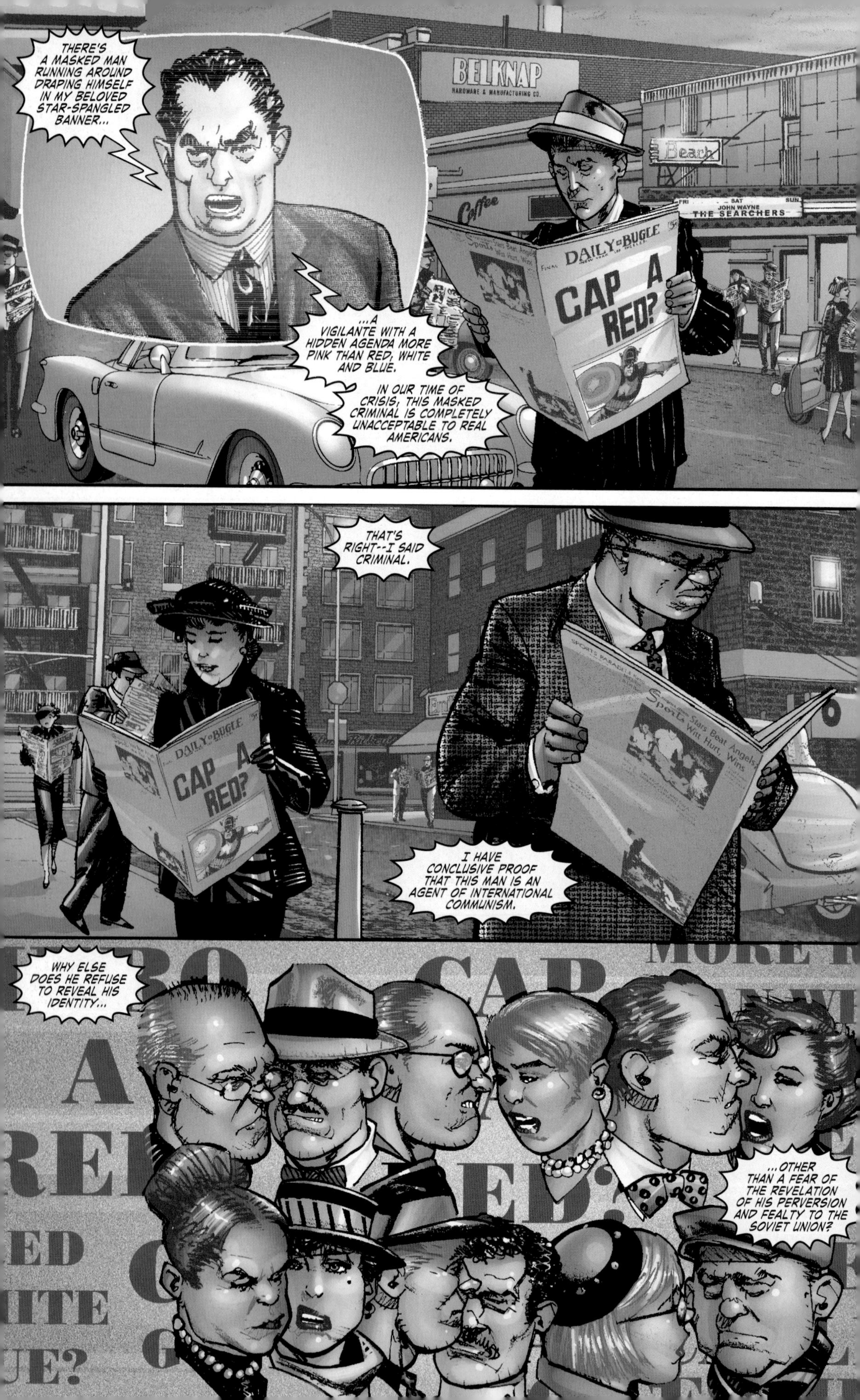

THERE'S A MASKED MAN RUNNING AROUND DRAPING HIMSELF IN MY BELOVED STAR-SPANGLED BANNER...
...A VIGILANTE WITH A HIDDEN AGENDA MORE PINK THAN RED, WHITE AND BLUE.
IN OUR TIME OF CRISIS, THIS MASKED CRIMINAL IS COMPLETELY UNACCEPTABLE TO REAL AMERICANS.
BELKNAP
HARDWARE & MANUFACTURING CO.
Beach
Coffee
FRI SAT SUN
JOHN WAYNE
THE SEARCHERS
DAILY BUGLE
CAP A RED?
THAT'S RIGHT--I SAID CRIMINAL.
DAILY BUGLE
CAP A RED?
Stars Beat Angels, Witt Hurt, Wins
I HAVE CONCLUSIVE PROOF THAT THIS MAN IS AN AGENT OF INTERNATIONAL COMMUNISM.
WHY ELSE DOES HE REFUSE TO REVEAL HIS IDENTITY...
...OTHER THAN A FEAR OF THE REVELATION OF HIS PERVERSION AND FEALTY TO THE SOVIET UNION?

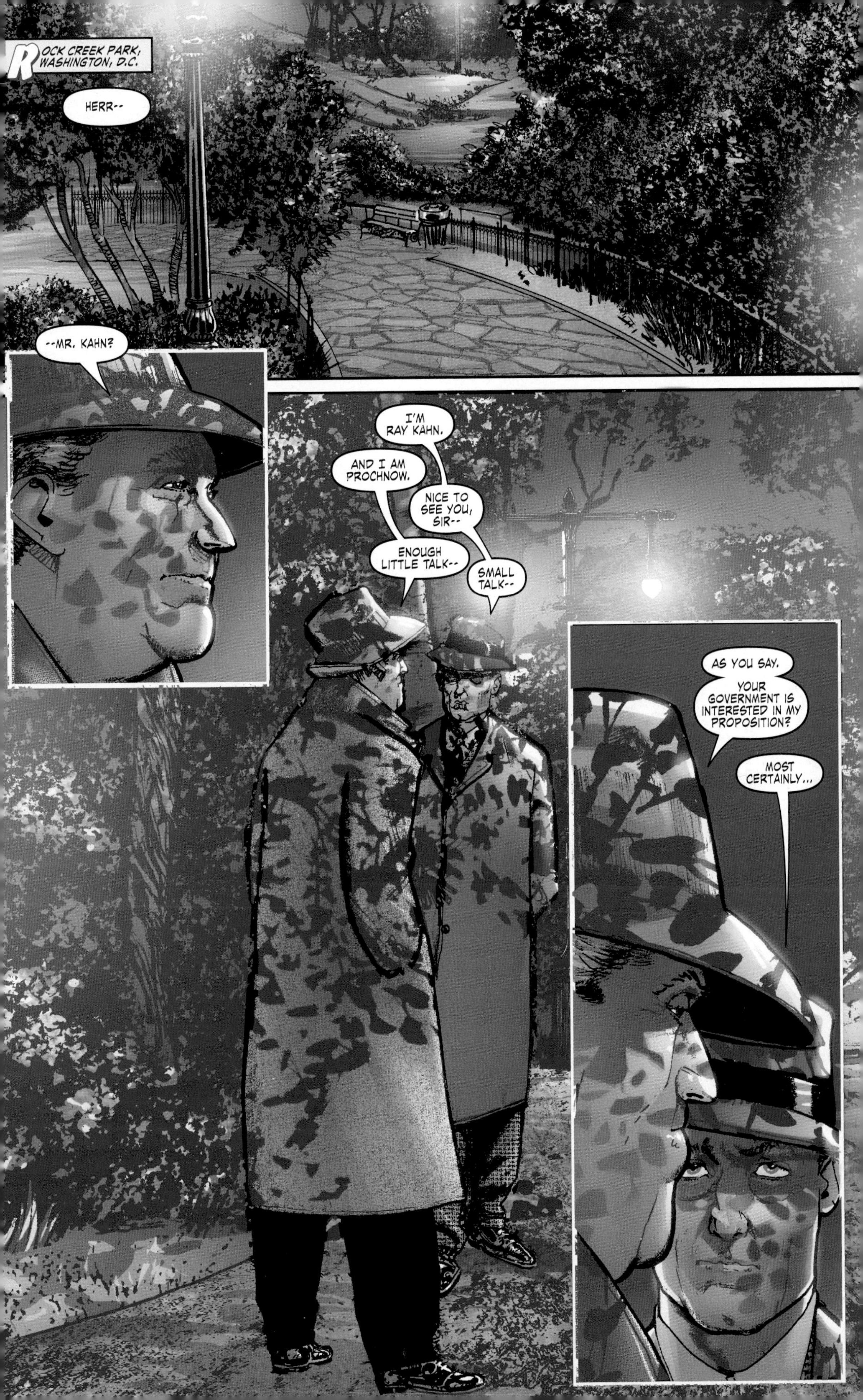
ROCK CREEK PARK, WASHINGTON, D.C.
HERR--
--MR. KAHN?
I'M RAY KAHN.
AND I AM PROCHNOW.
NICE TO SEE YOU, SIR--
ENOUGH LITTLE TALK--
SMALL TALK--
AS YOU SAY.
YOUR GOVERNMENT IS INTERESTED IN MY PROPOSITION?
MOST CERTAINLY...

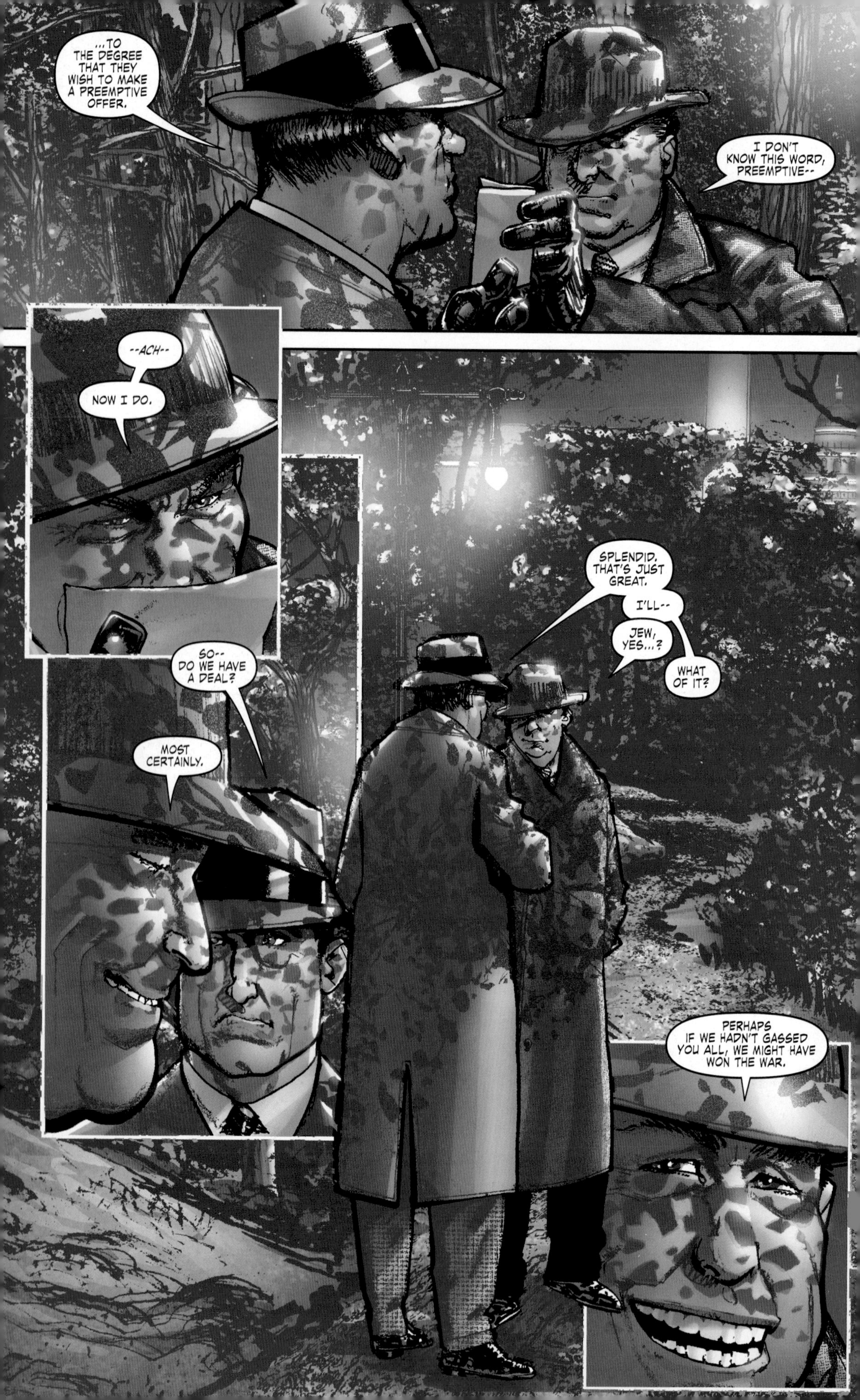
...TO THE DEGREE THAT THEY WISH TO MAKE A PREEMPTIVE OFFER.
I DON'T KNOW THIS WORD, PREEMPTIVE--
--ACH--
NOW I DO.
SO-- DO WE HAVE A DEAL?
MOST CERTAINLY.
SPLENDID. THAT'S JUST GREAT.
I'LL--
JEW, YES...?
WHAT OF IT?
PERHAPS IF WE HADN'T GASSED YOU ALL, WE MIGHT HAVE WON THE WAR.

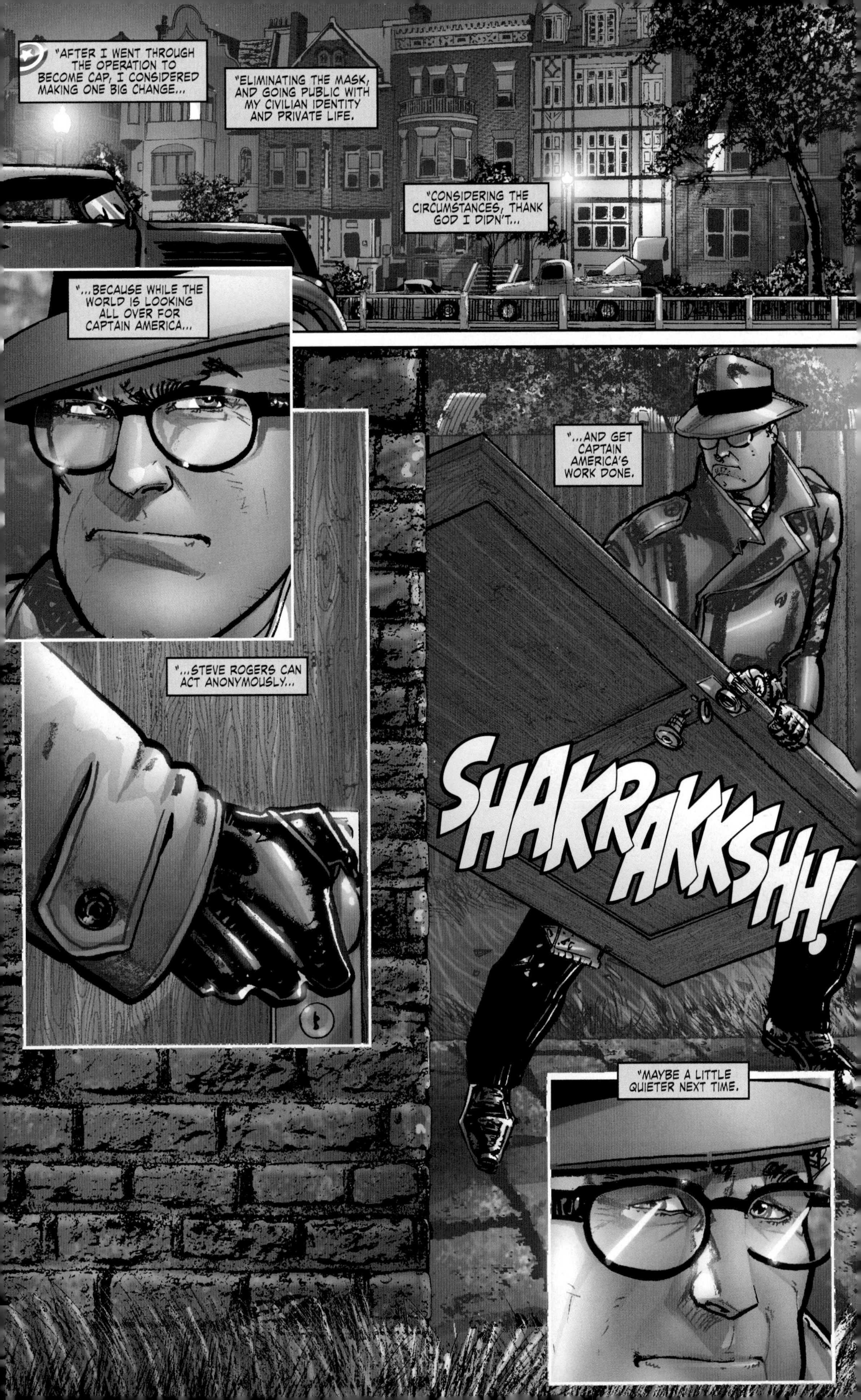
"AFTER I WENT THROUGH THE OPERATION TO BECOME CAP, I CONSIDERED MAKING ONE BIG CHANGE...
"ELIMINATING THE MASK, AND GOING PUBLIC WITH MY CIVILIAN IDENTITY AND PRIVATE LIFE.
"CONSIDERING THE CIRCUMSTANCES, THANK GOD I DIDN'T...
"...BECAUSE WHILE THE WORLD IS LOOKING ALL OVER FOR CAPTAIN AMERICA...
"...STEVE ROGERS CAN ACT ANONYMOUSLY...
"...AND GET CAPTAIN AMERICA'S WORK DONE.
SHAKRAKKSHH!
"MAYBE A LITTLE QUIETER NEXT TIME.

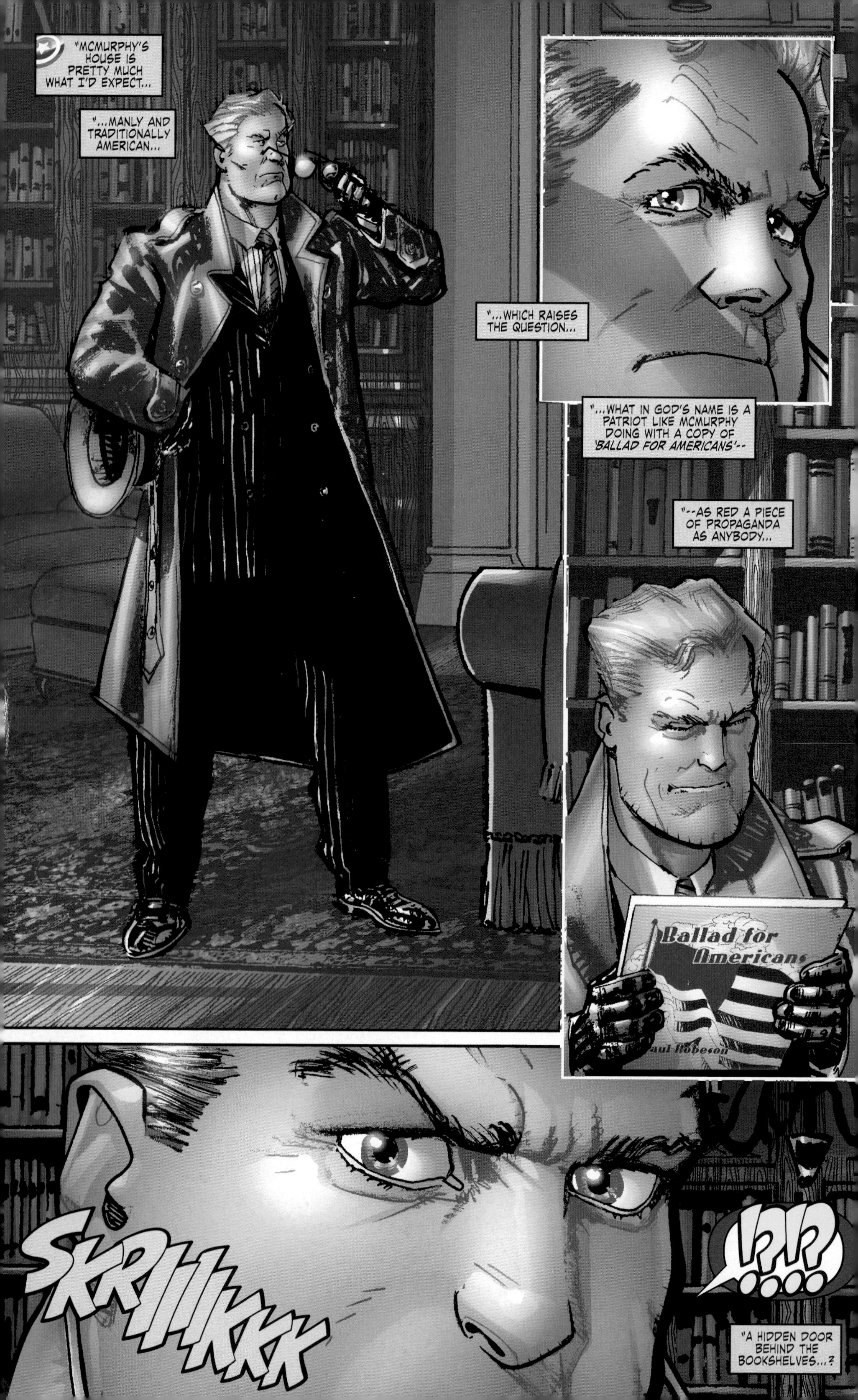
"McMURPHY'S HOUSE IS PRETTY MUCH WHAT I'D EXPECT...
"...MANLY AND TRADITIONALLY AMERICAN...
"...WHICH RAISES THE QUESTION...
"...WHAT IN GOD'S NAME IS A PATRIOT LIKE McMURPHY DOING WITH A COPY OF 'BALLAD FOR AMERICANS'--
"--AS RED A PIECE OF PROPAGANDA AS ANYBODY...
Ballad for Americans
SKRIIIKKK
!?!?
"A HIDDEN DOOR BEHIND THE BOOKSHELVES...?

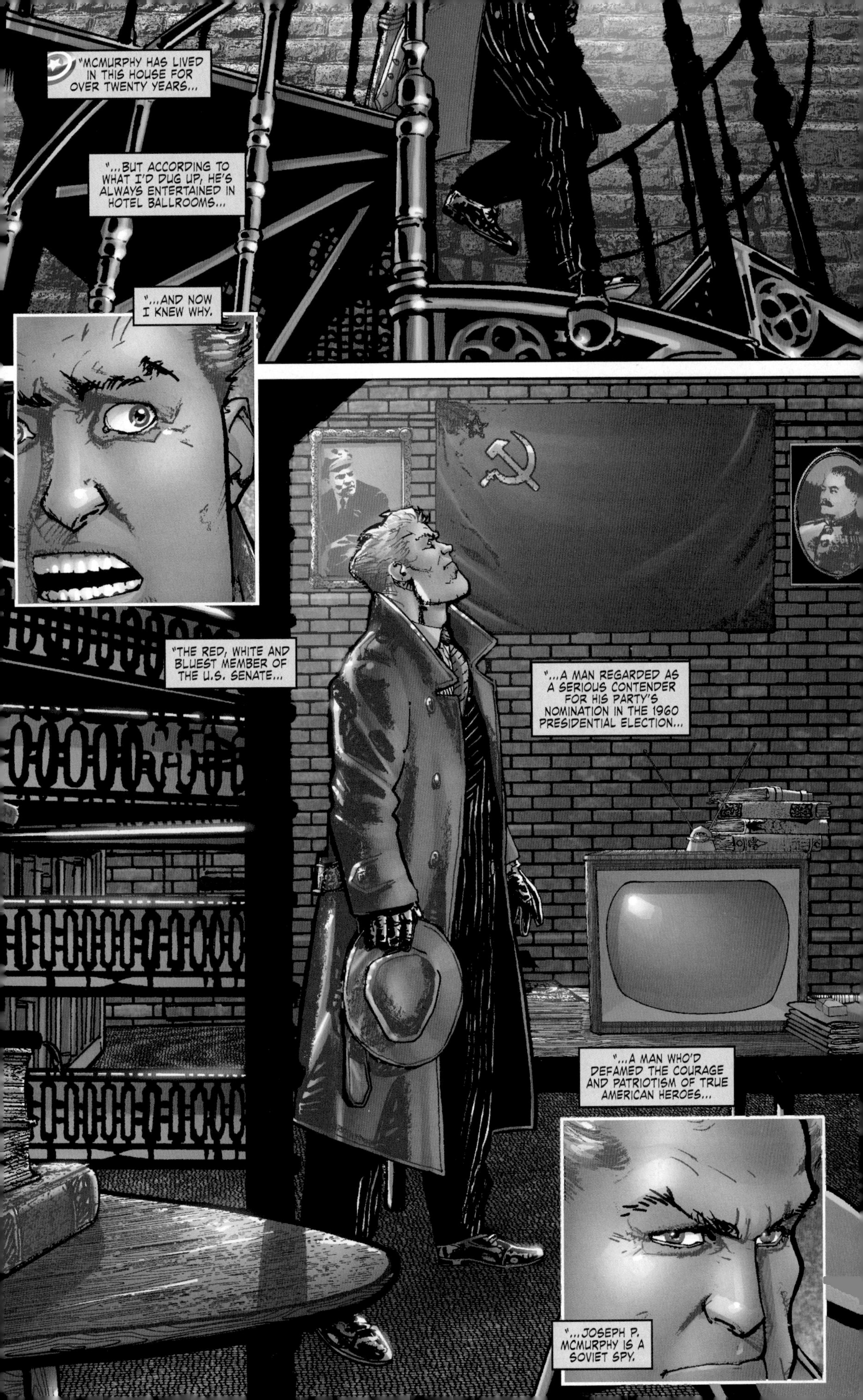
"MCMURPHY HAS LIVED IN THIS HOUSE FOR OVER TWENTY YEARS...
"...BUT ACCORDING TO WHAT I'D DUG UP, HE'S ALWAYS ENTERTAINED IN HOTEL BALLROOMS...
"...AND NOW I KNEW WHY.
"THE RED, WHITE AND BLUEST MEMBER OF THE U.S. SENATE...
"...A MAN REGARDED AS A SERIOUS CONTENDER FOR HIS PARTY'S NOMINATION IN THE 1960 PRESIDENTIAL ELECTION...
"...A MAN WHO'D DEFAMED THE COURAGE AND PATRIOTISM OF TRUE AMERICAN HEROES...
"...JOSEPH P. MCMURPHY IS A SOVIET SPY.

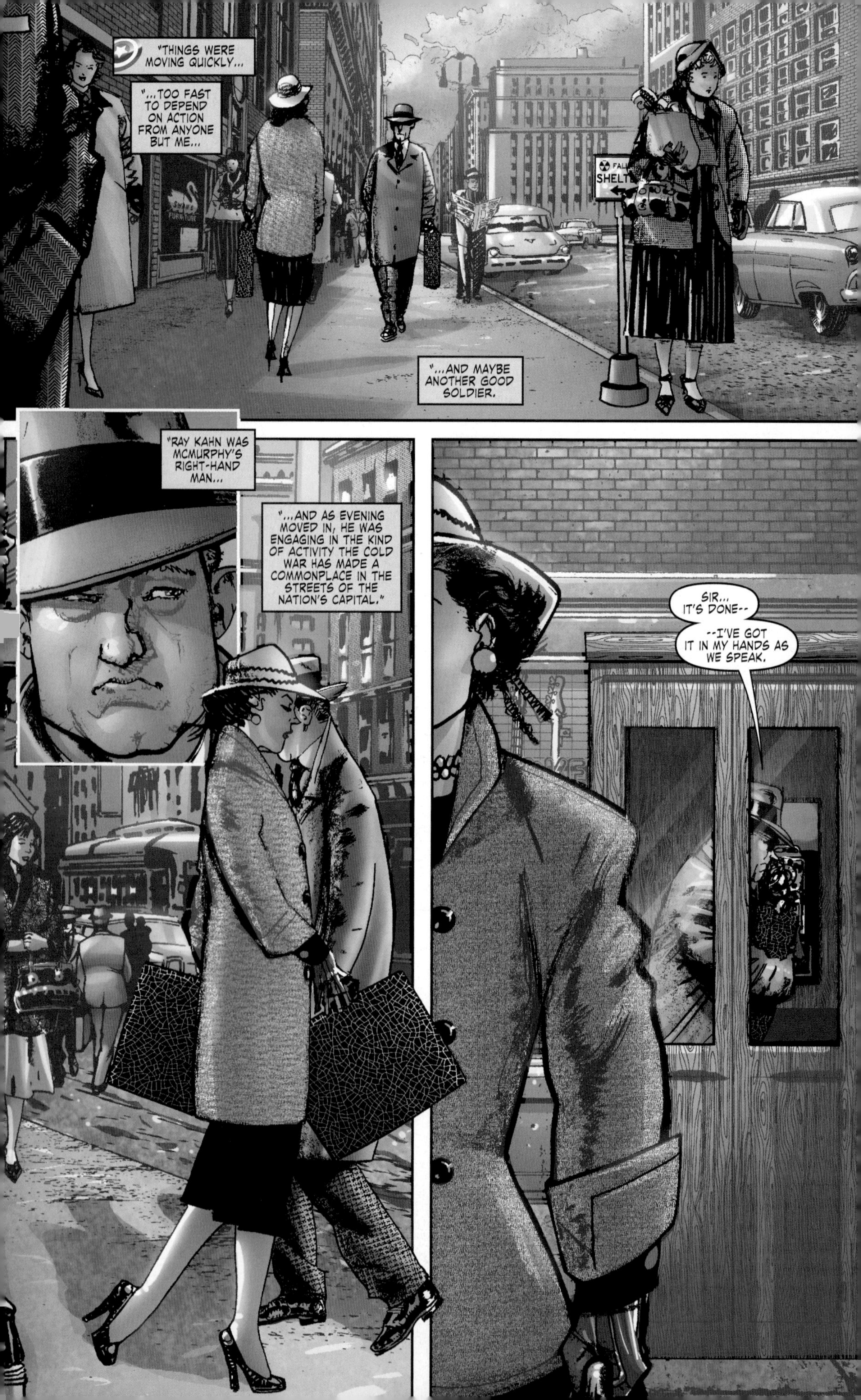
"THINGS WERE MOVING QUICKLY...
"...TOO FAST TO DEPEND ON ACTION FROM ANYONE BUT ME...
"...AND MAYBE ANOTHER GOOD SOLDIER.
"RAY KAHN WAS MCMURPHY'S RIGHT-HAND MAN...
"...AND AS EVENING MOVED IN, HE WAS ENGAGING IN THE KIND OF ACTIVITY THE COLD WAR HAS MADE A COMMONPLACE IN THE STREETS OF THE NATION'S CAPITAL."
SIR... IT'S DONE--
--I'VE GOT IT IN MY HANDS AS WE SPEAK.

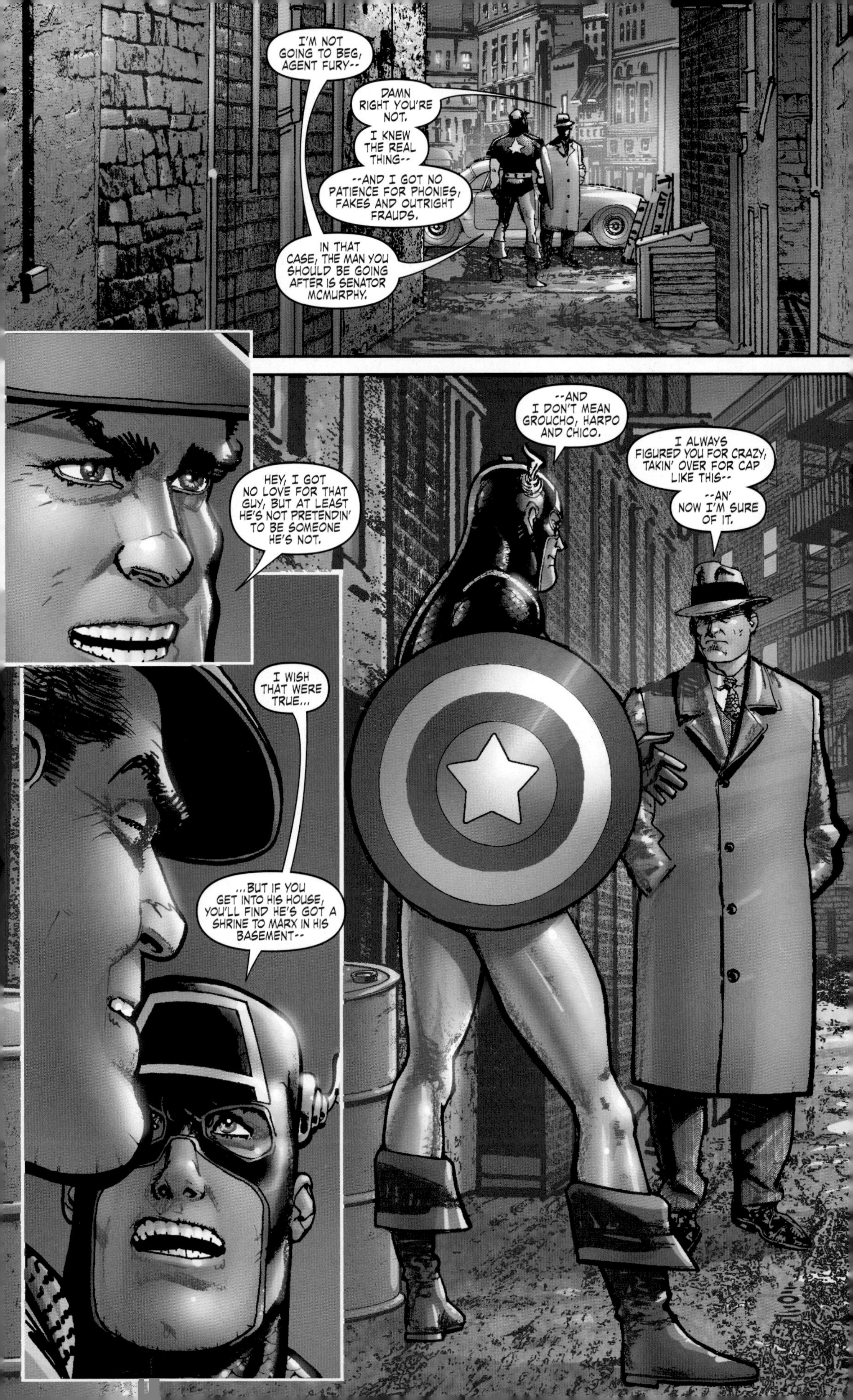

I'M NOT GOING TO BEG, AGENT FURY--
DAMN RIGHT YOU'RE NOT.
I KNEW THE REAL THING--
--AND I GOT NO PATIENCE FOR PHONIES, FAKES AND OUTRIGHT FRAUDS.
IN THAT CASE, THE MAN YOU SHOULD BE GOING AFTER IS SENATOR MCMURPHY.
HEY, I GOT NO LOVE FOR THAT GUY, BUT AT LEAST HE'S NOT PRETENDIN' TO BE SOMEONE HE'S NOT.
I WISH THAT WERE TRUE...
...BUT IF YOU GET INTO HIS HOUSE, YOU'LL FIND HE'S GOT A SHRINE TO MARX IN HIS BASEMENT--
--AND I DON'T MEAN GROUCHO, HARPO AND CHICO.
I ALWAYS FIGURED YOU FOR CRAZY, TAKIN' OVER FOR CAP LIKE THIS--
--AN' NOW I'M SURE OF IT.

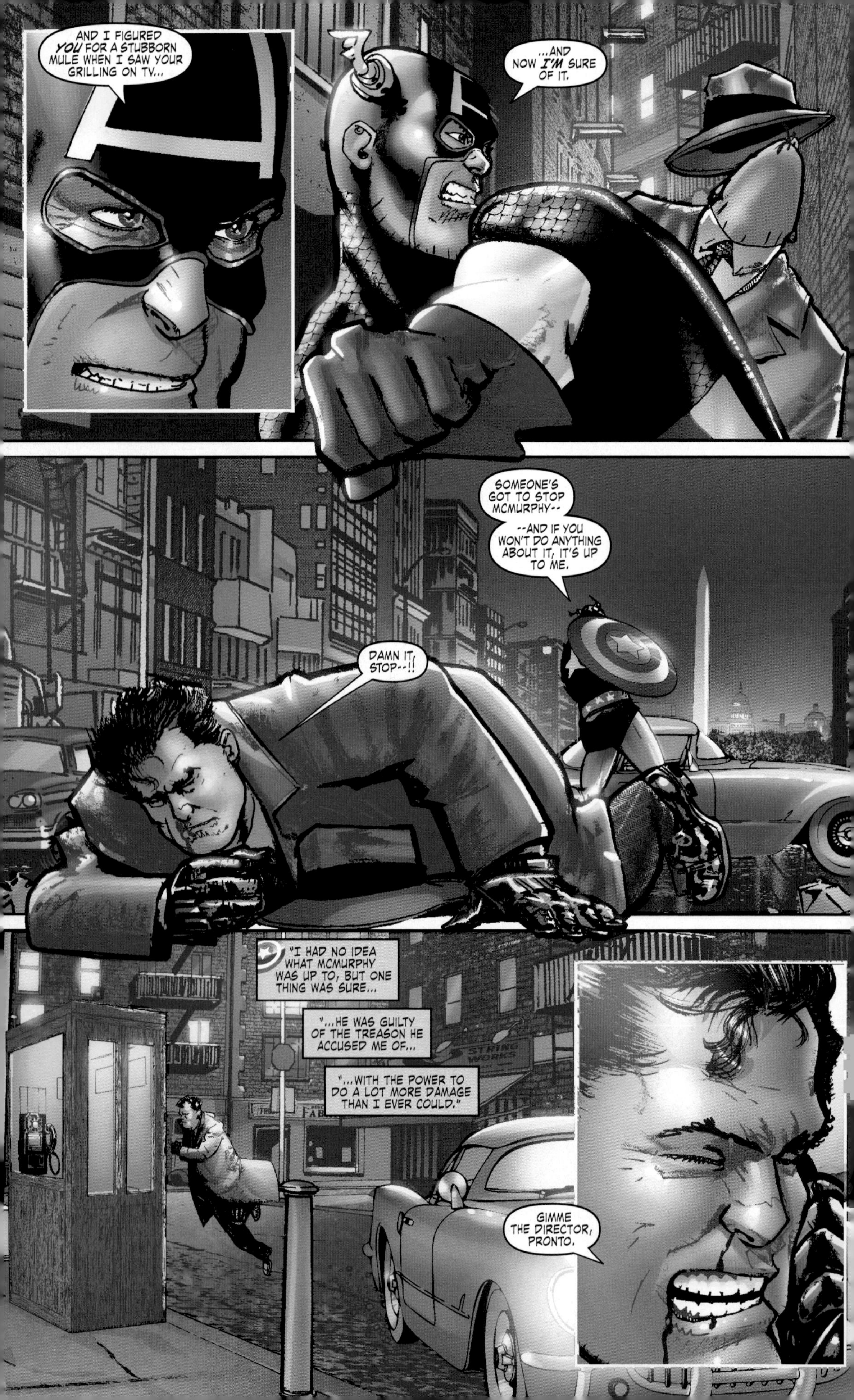
AND I FIGURED YOU FOR A STUBBORN MULE WHEN I SAW YOUR GRILLING ON TV...
...AND NOW I'M SURE OF IT.
SOMEONE'S GOT TO STOP MCMURPHY--
--AND IF YOU WON'T DO ANYTHING ABOUT IT, IT'S UP TO ME.
DAMN IT, STOP--!!
"I HAD NO IDEA WHAT MCMURPHY WAS UP TO, BUT ONE THING WAS SURE...
"...HE WAS GUILTY OF THE TREASON HE ACCUSED ME OF...
"...WITH THE POWER TO DO A LOT MORE DAMAGE THAN I EVER COULD."
GIMME THE DIRECTOR, PRONTO.

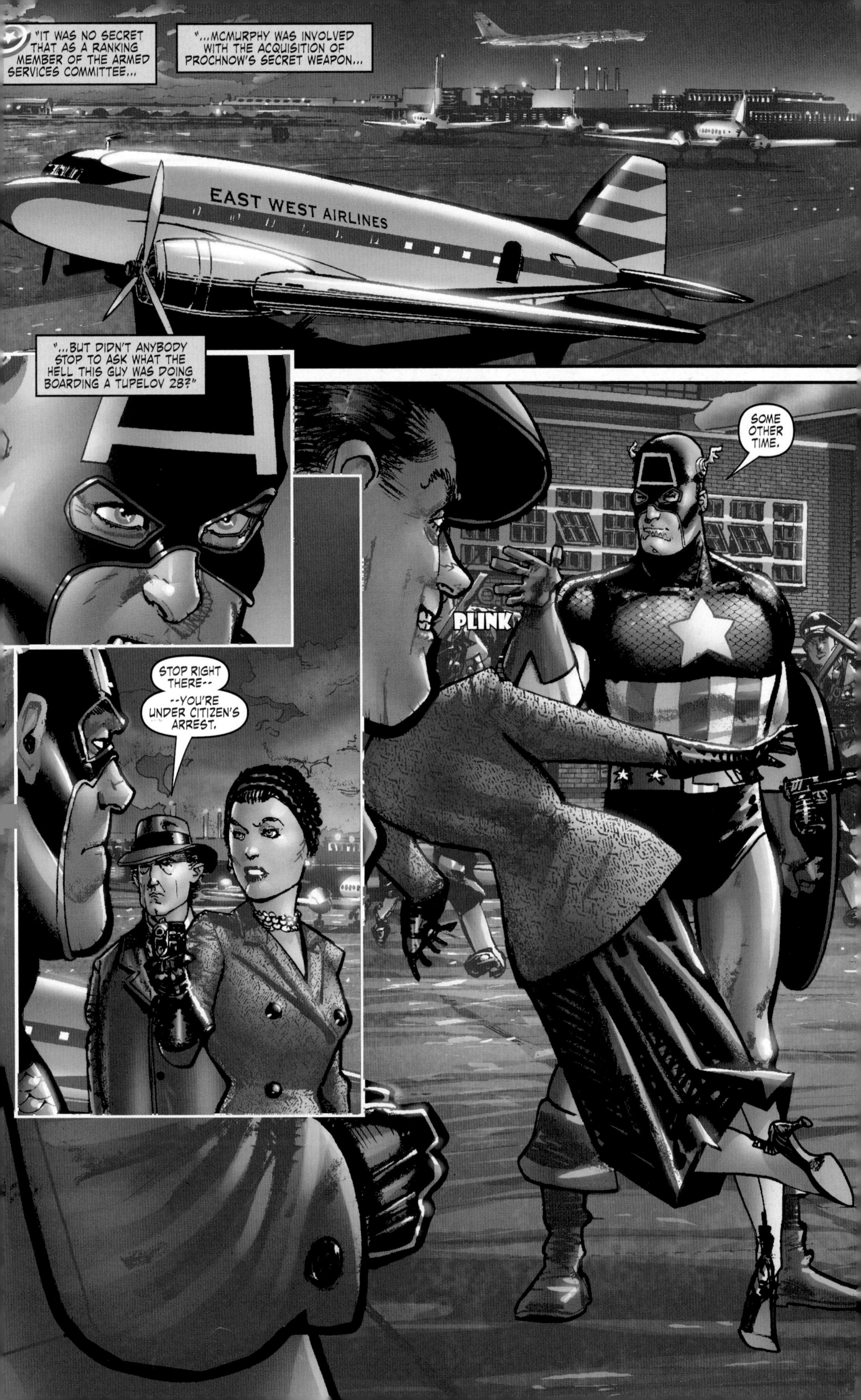
"IT WAS NO SECRET THAT AS A RANKING MEMBER OF THE ARMED SERVICES COMMITTEE...
"...MCMURPHY WAS INVOLVED WITH THE ACQUISITION OF PROCHNOW'S SECRET WEAPON...
EAST WEST AIRLINES
"...BUT DIDN'T ANYBODY STOP TO ASK WHAT THE HELL THIS GUY WAS DOING BOARDING A TUPELOV 28?"
SOME OTHER TIME.
PLINK
STOP RIGHT THERE--
--YOU'RE UNDER CITIZEN'S ARREST.

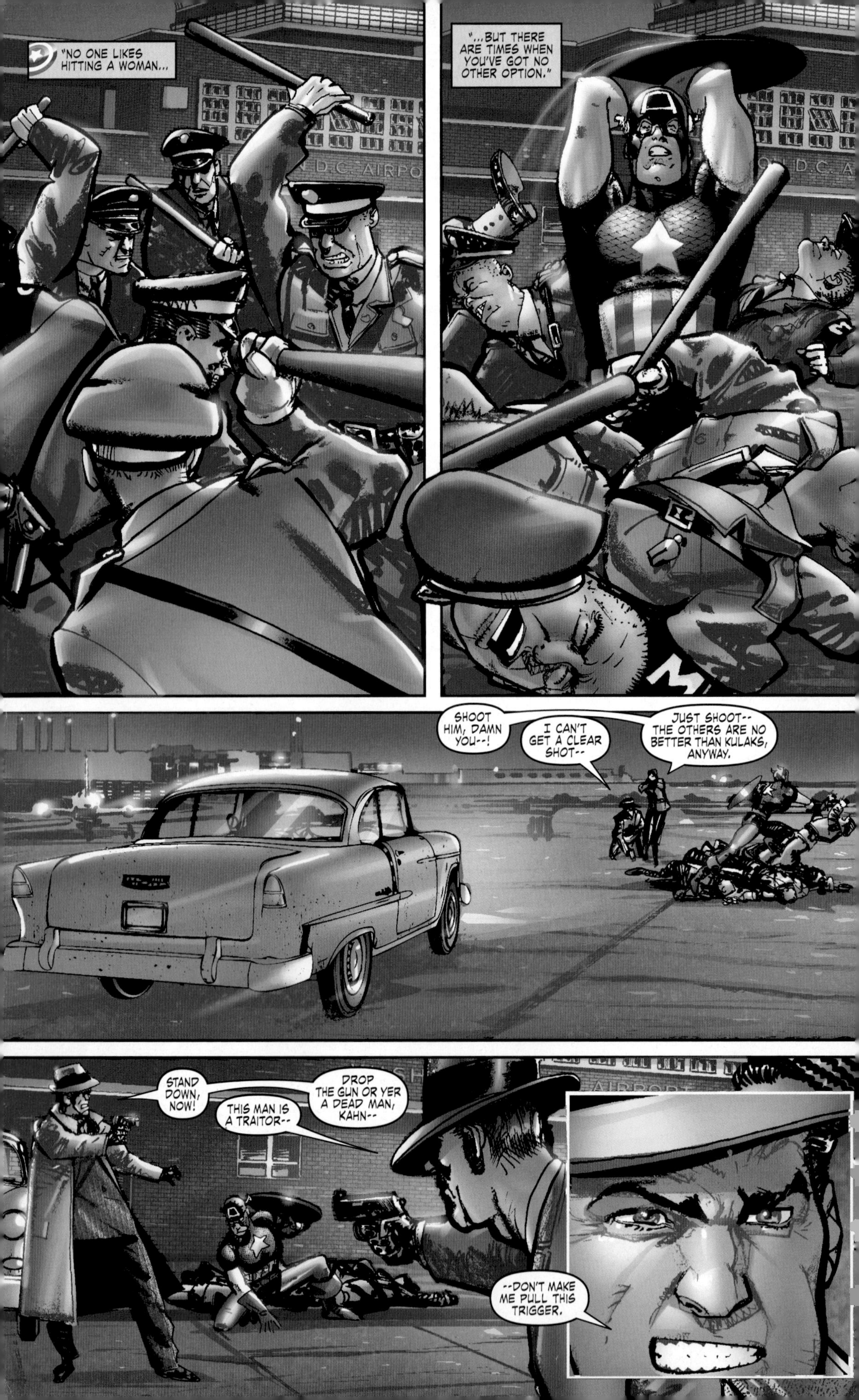
"NO ONE LIKES HITTING A WOMAN...
"...BUT THERE ARE TIMES WHEN YOU'VE GOT NO OTHER OPTION."
SHOOT HIM, DAMN YOU--!
I CAN'T GET A CLEAR SHOT--
JUST SHOOT-- THE OTHERS ARE NO BETTER THAN KULAKS, ANYWAY.
STAND DOWN, NOW!
THIS MAN IS A TRAITOR--
DROP THE GUN OR YER A DEAD MAN, KAHN--
--DON'T MAKE ME PULL THIS TRIGGER.

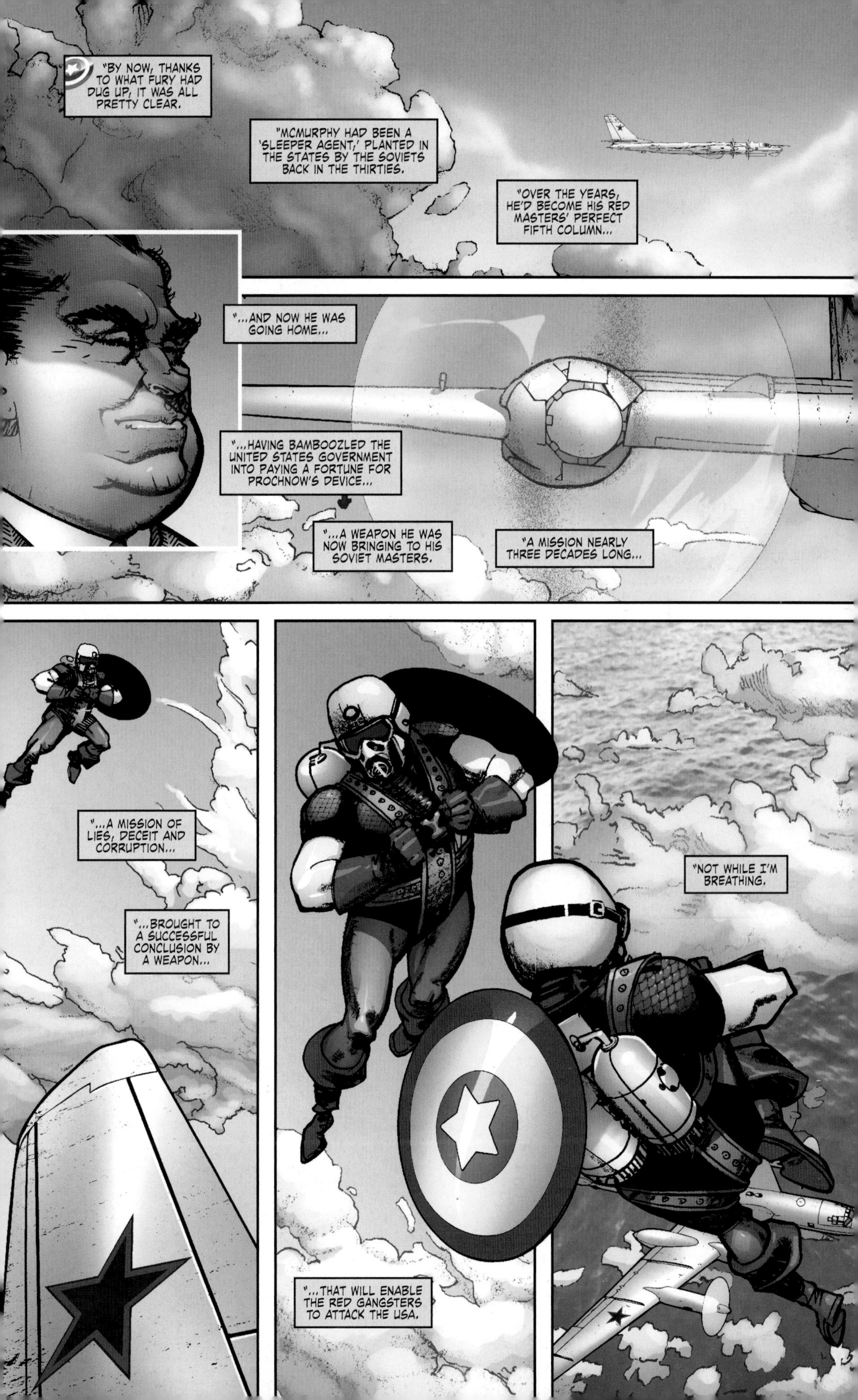
"BY NOW, THANKS TO WHAT FURY HAD DUG UP, IT WAS ALL PRETTY CLEAR.
"MCMURPHY HAD BEEN A 'SLEEPER AGENT,' PLANTED IN THE STATES BY THE SOVIETS BACK IN THE THIRTIES.
"OVER THE YEARS, HE'D BECOME HIS RED MASTERS' PERFECT FIFTH COLUMN...
"...AND NOW HE WAS GOING HOME...
"...HAVING BAMBOOZLED THE UNITED STATES GOVERNMENT INTO PAYING A FORTUNE FOR PROCHNOW'S DEVICE...
"...A WEAPON HE WAS NOW BRINGING TO HIS SOVIET MASTERS.
"A MISSION NEARLY THREE DECADES LONG...
"...A MISSION OF LIES, DECEIT AND CORRUPTION...
"...BROUGHT TO A SUCCESSFUL CONCLUSION BY A WEAPON...
"...THAT WILL ENABLE THE RED GANGSTERS TO ATTACK THE USA.
"NOT WHILE I'M BREATHING.

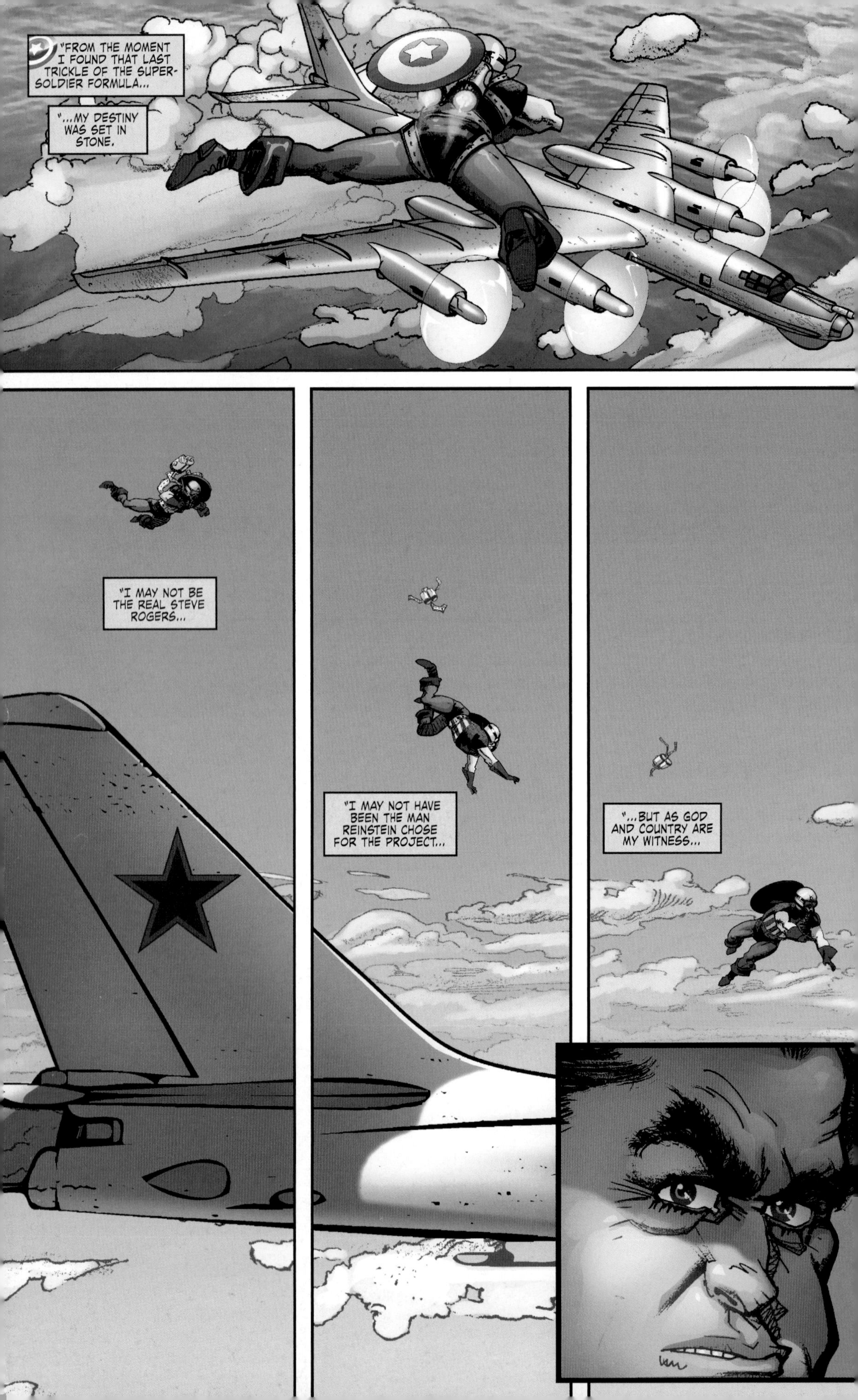
"FROM THE MOMENT I FOUND THAT LAST TRICKLE OF THE SUPER-SOLDIER FORMULA...
"...MY DESTINY WAS SET IN STONE.
"I MAY NOT BE THE REAL STEVE ROGERS...
"I MAY NOT HAVE BEEN THE MAN REINSTEIN CHOSE FOR THE PROJECT...
"...BUT AS GOD AND COUNTRY ARE MY WITNESS...

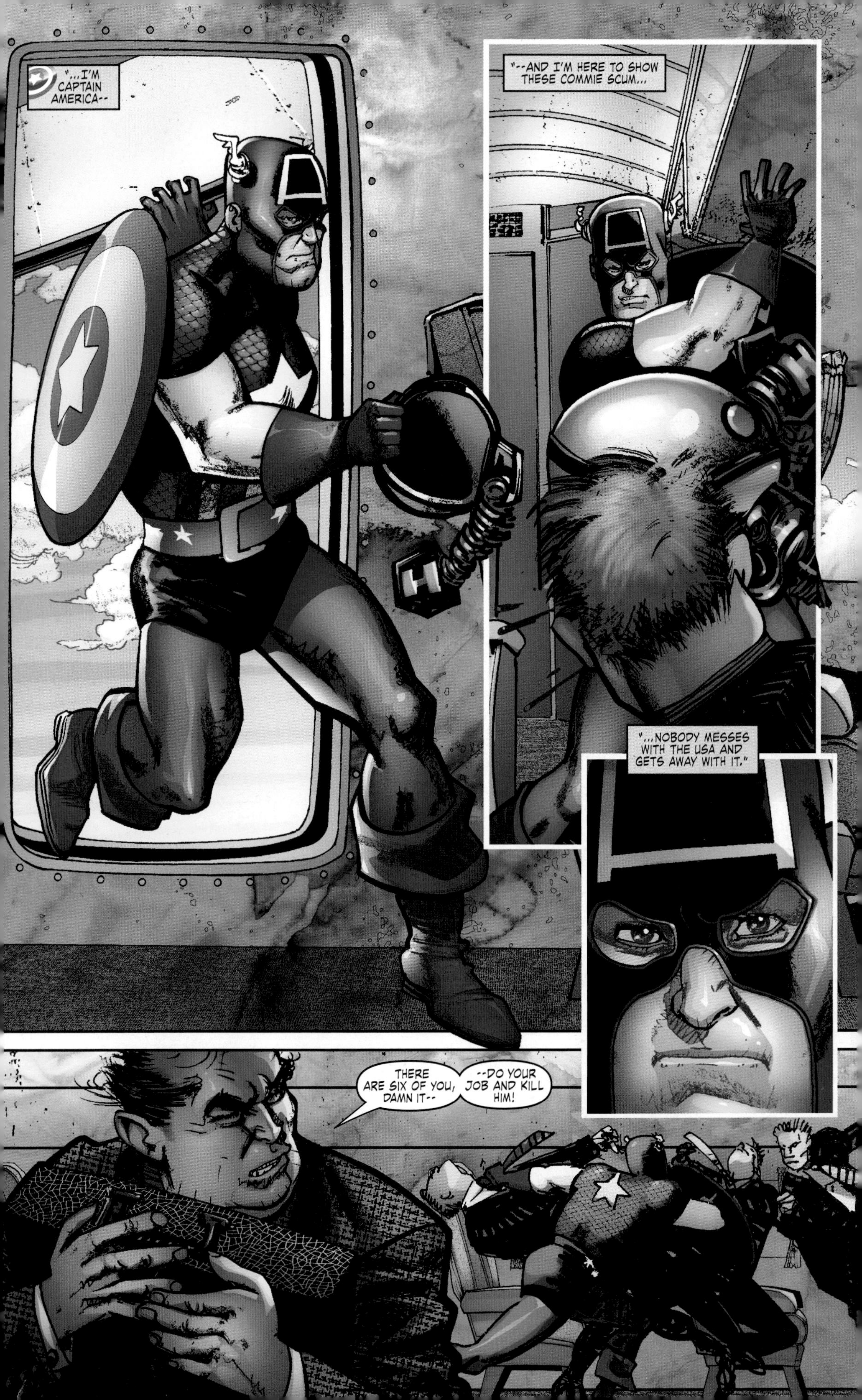
"...I'M CAPTAIN AMERICA--
"--AND I'M HERE TO SHOW THESE COMMIE SCUM...
"...NOBODY MESSES WITH THE USA AND GETS AWAY WITH IT."
THERE ARE SIX OF YOU, DAMN IT--
--DO YOUR JOB AND KILL HIM!

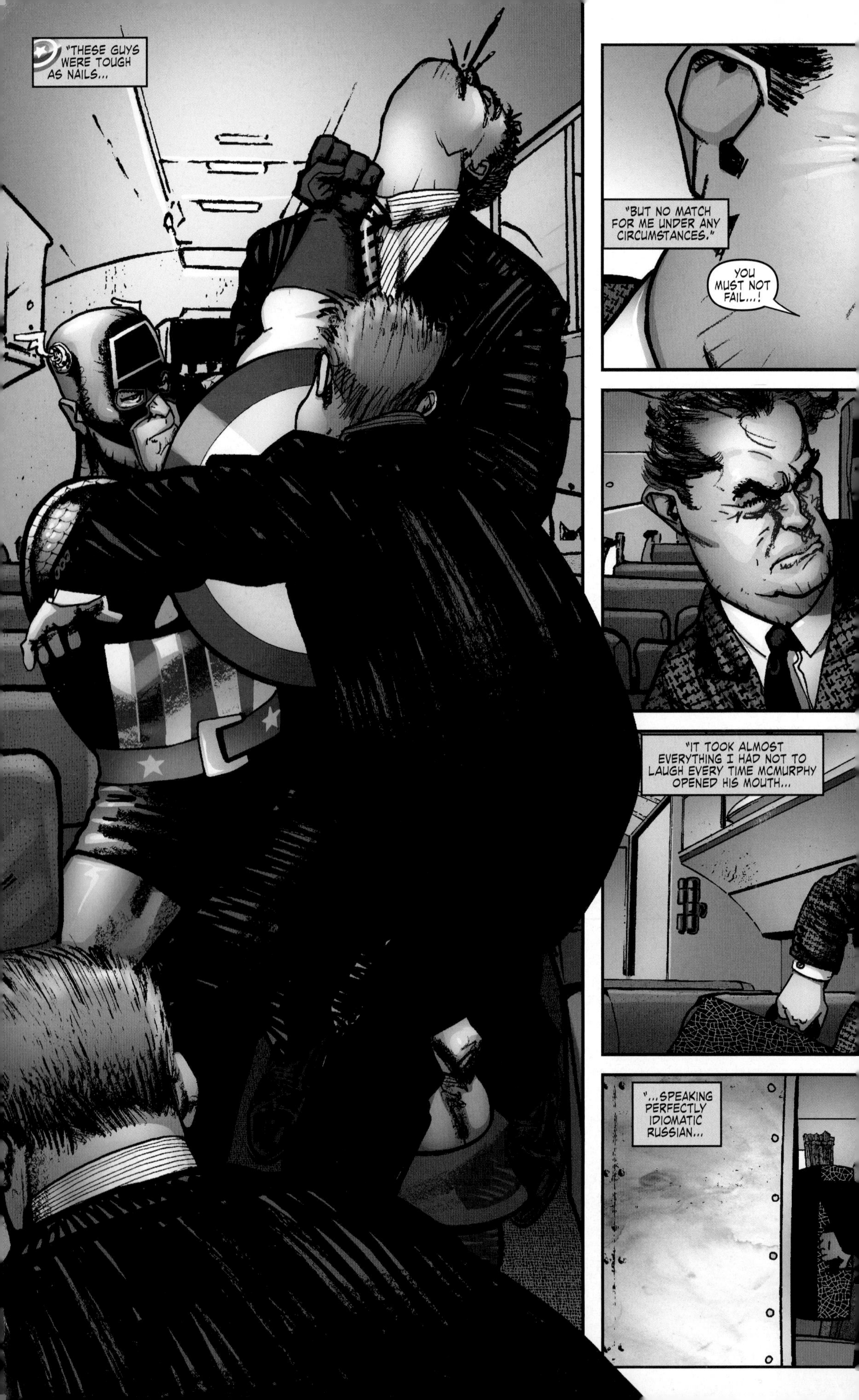
"THESE GUYS WERE TOUGH AS NAILS...
"BUT NO MATCH FOR ME UNDER ANY CIRCUMSTANCES."
YOU MUST NOT FAIL...!
"IT TOOK ALMOST EVERYTHING I HAD NOT TO LAUGH EVERY TIME MCMURPHY OPENED HIS MOUTH...
"...SPEAKING PERFECTLY IDIOMATIC RUSSIAN...

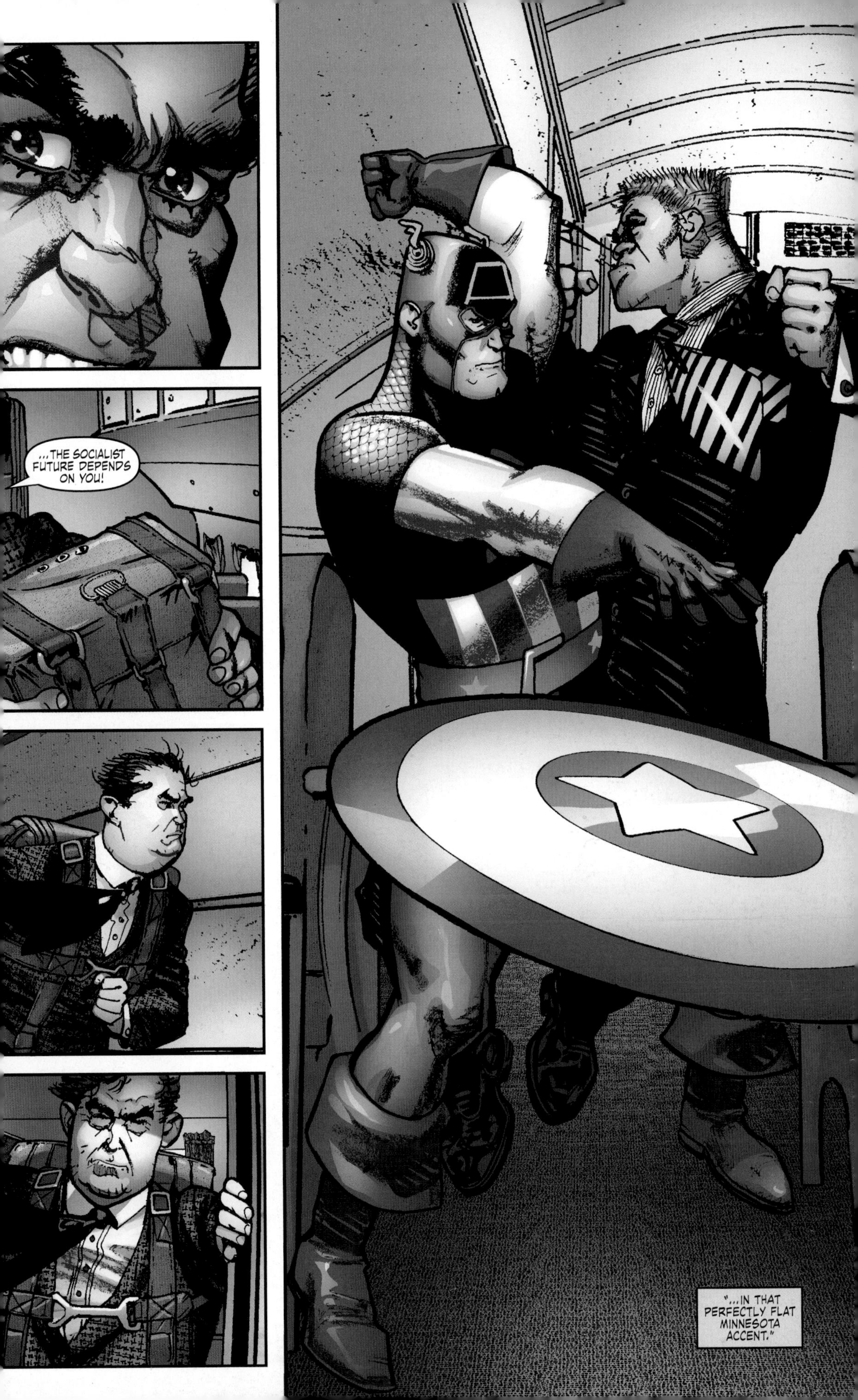
...THE SOCIALIST FUTURE DEPENDS ON YOU!
"...IN THAT PERFECTLY FLAT MINNESOTA ACCENT."

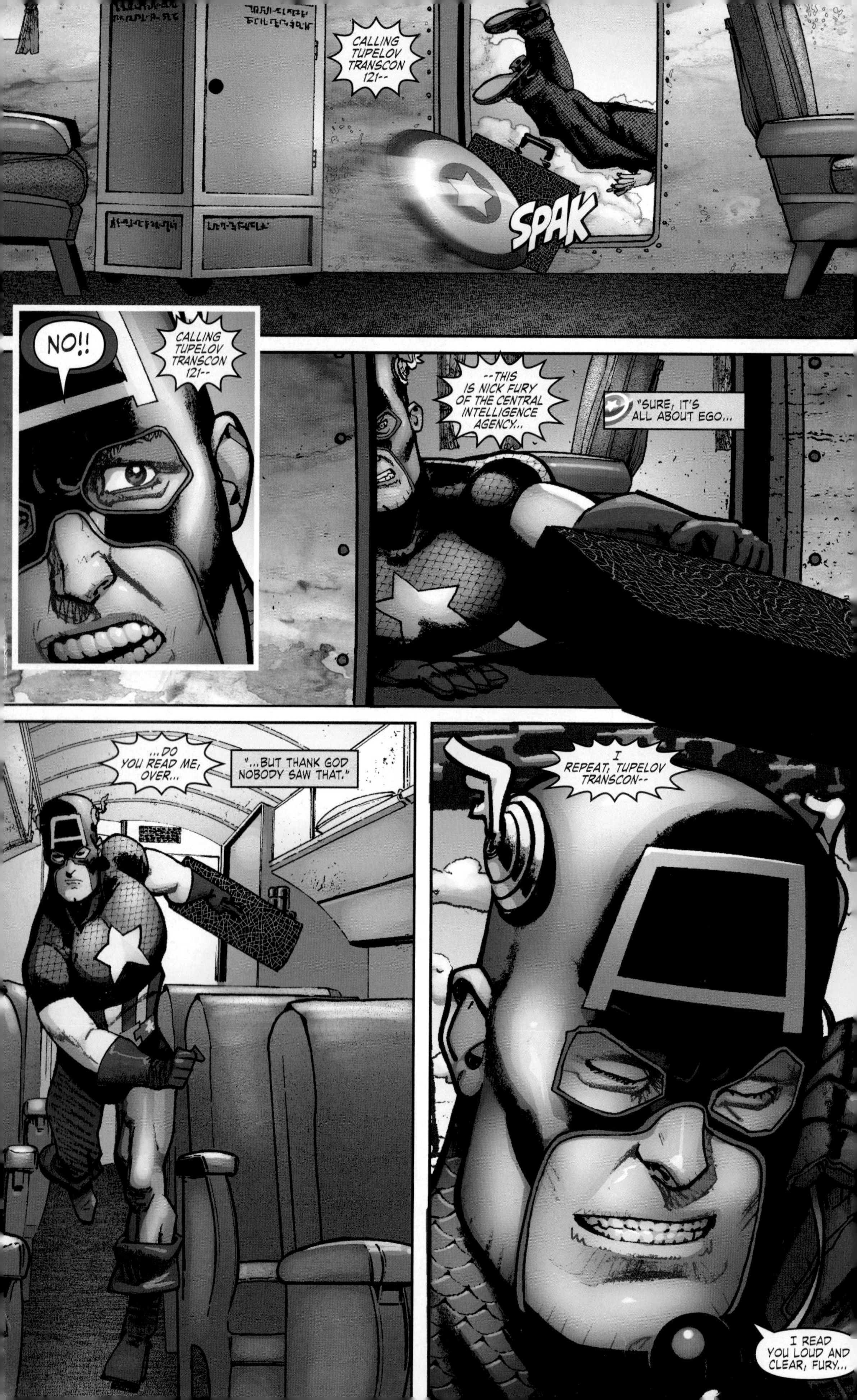
CALLING TUPELOV TRANSCON 121--
SPAK
NO!!
CALLING TUPELOV TRANSCON 121--
--THIS IS NICK FURY OF THE CENTRAL INTELLIGENCE AGENCY...
"SURE, IT'S ALL ABOUT EGO...
...DO YOU READ ME, OVER...
"...BUT THANK GOD NOBODY SAW THAT."
I REPEAT, TUPELOV TRANSCON--
I READ YOU LOUD AND CLEAR, FURY...

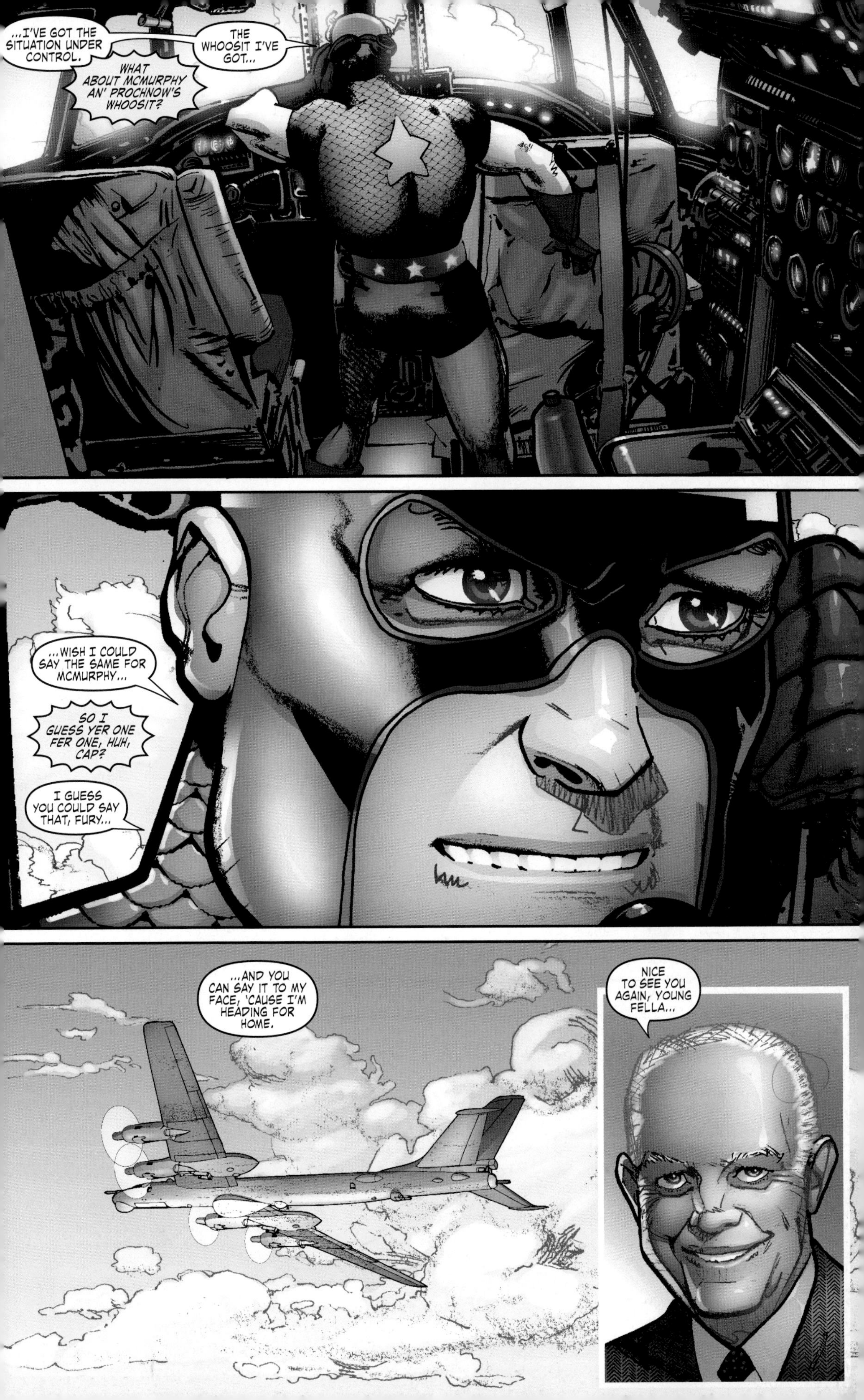
...I'VE GOT THE SITUATION UNDER CONTROL.
THE WHOOSIT I'VE GOT...
WHAT ABOUT MCMURPHY AN' PROCHNOW'S WHOOSIT?
...WISH I COULD SAY THE SAME FOR MCMURPHY...
SO I GUESS YER ONE FER ONE, HUH, CAP?
I GUESS YOU COULD SAY THAT, FURY...
...AND YOU CAN SAY IT TO MY FACE, 'CAUSE I'M HEADING FOR HOME.
NICE TO SEE YOU AGAIN, YOUNG FELLA...

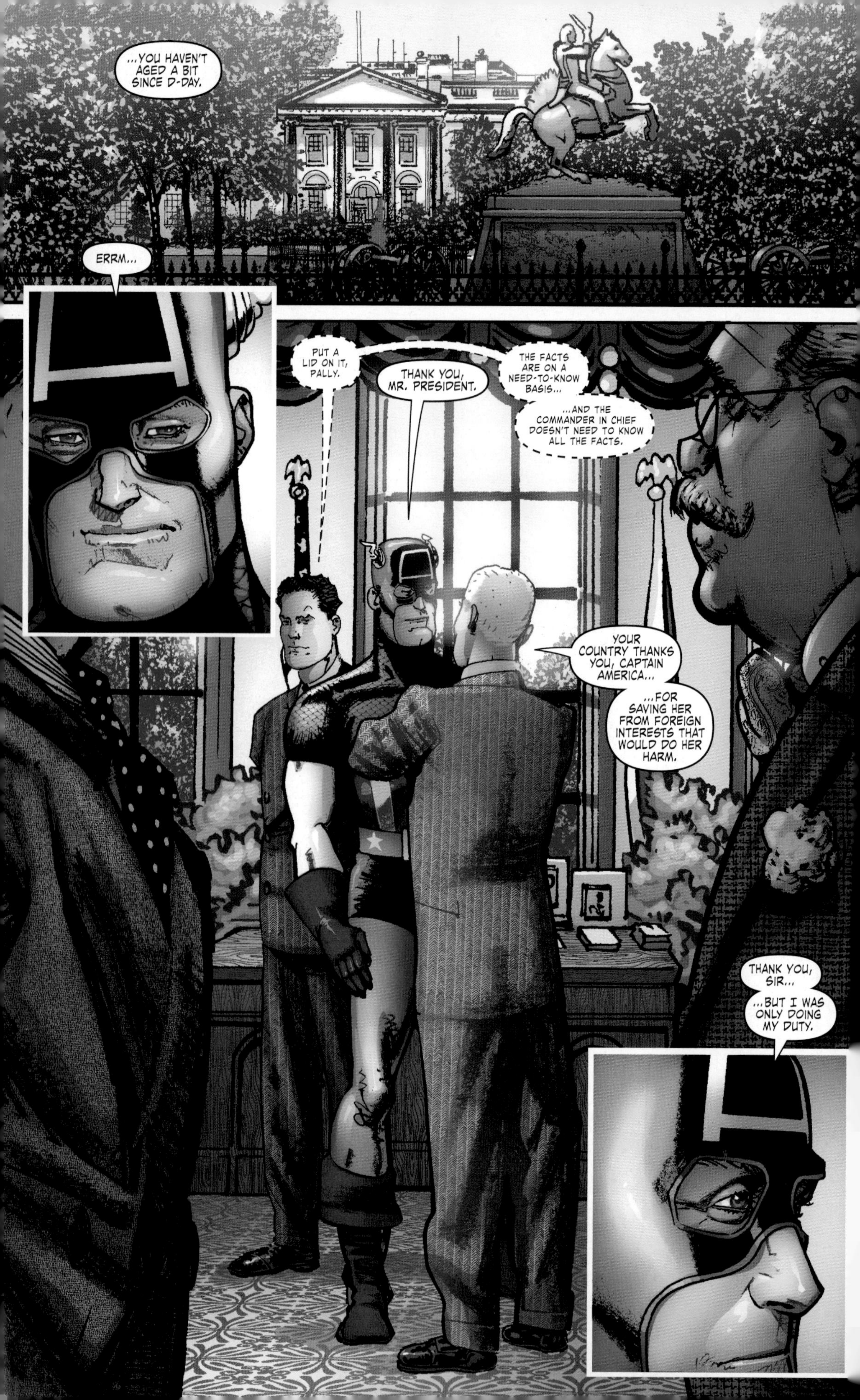
...YOU HAVEN'T AGED A BIT SINCE D-DAY.
ERRM...
PUT A LID ON IT, PALLY.
THANK YOU, MR. PRESIDENT.
THE FACTS ARE ON A NEED-TO-KNOW BASIS...
...AND THE COMMANDER IN CHIEF DOESN'T NEED TO KNOW ALL THE FACTS.
YOUR COUNTRY THANKS YOU, CAPTAIN AMERICA...
...FOR SAVING HER FROM FOREIGN INTERESTS THAT WOULD DO HER HARM.
THANK YOU, SIR...
...BUT I WAS ONLY DOING MY DUTY.

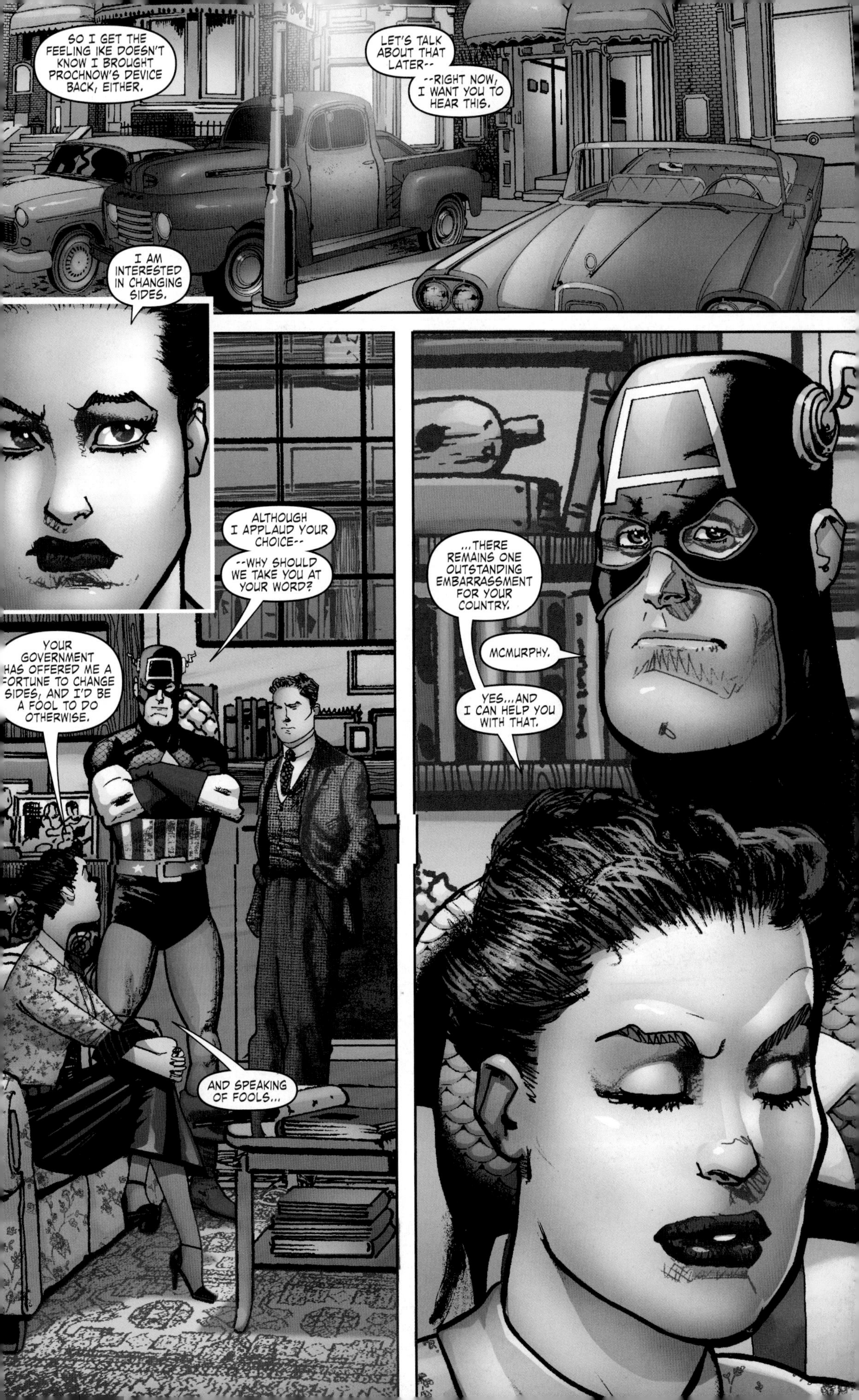
SO I GET THE FEELING IKE DOESN'T KNOW I BROUGHT PROCHNOW'S DEVICE BACK, EITHER.
LET'S TALK ABOUT THAT LATER--
--RIGHT NOW, I WANT YOU TO HEAR THIS.
I AM INTERESTED IN CHANGING SIDES.
ALTHOUGH I APPLAUD YOUR CHOICE--
--WHY SHOULD WE TAKE YOU AT YOUR WORD?
YOUR GOVERNMENT HAS OFFERED ME A FORTUNE TO CHANGE SIDES, AND I'D BE A FOOL TO DO OTHERWISE.
AND SPEAKING OF FOOLS...
...THERE REMAINS ONE OUTSTANDING EMBARRASSMENT FOR YOUR COUNTRY.
MCMURPHY.
YES...AND I CAN HELP YOU WITH THAT.

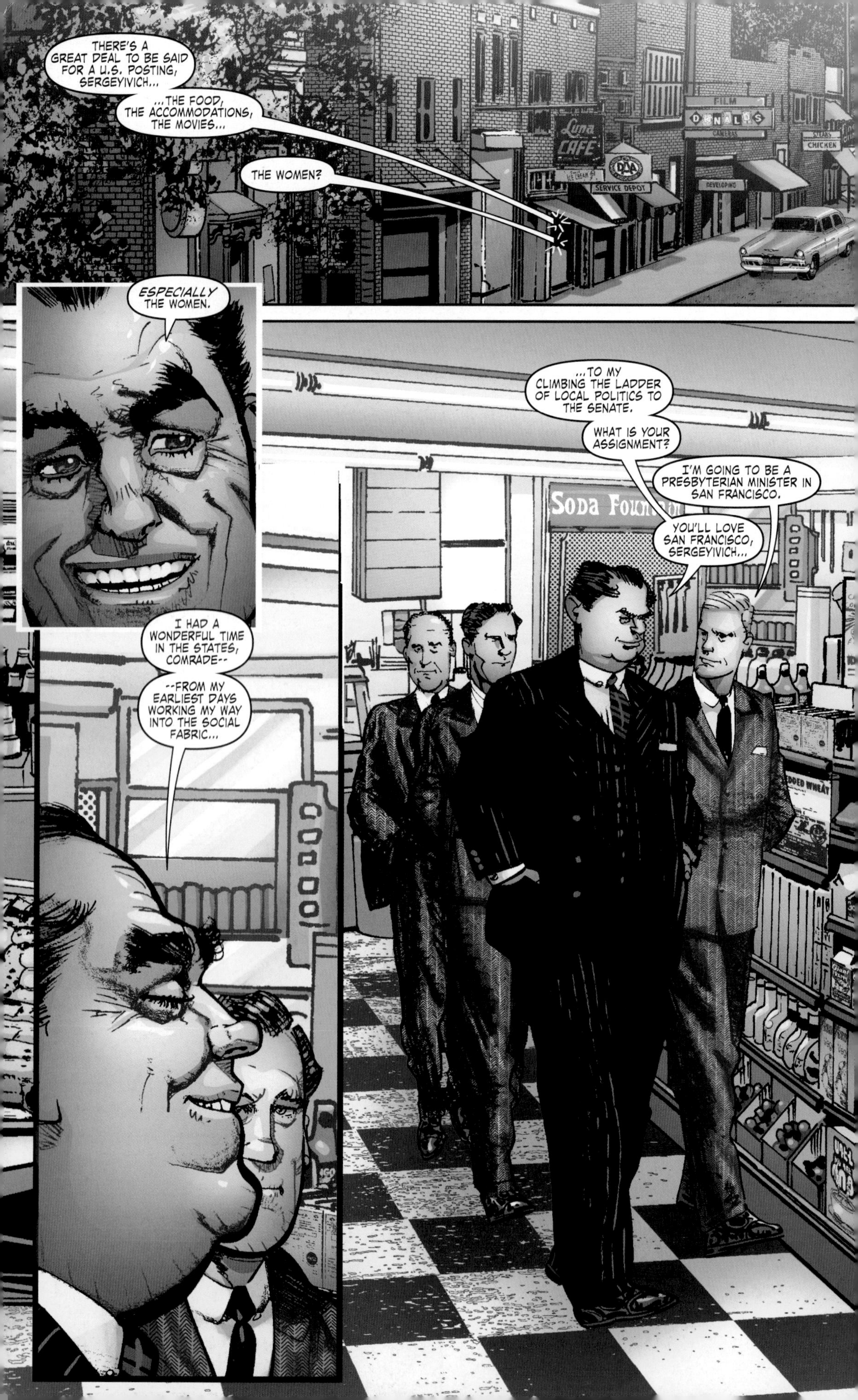
THERE'S A GREAT DEAL TO BE SAID FOR A U.S. POSTING, SERGEYIVICH...
...THE FOOD, THE ACCOMMODATIONS, THE MOVIES...
THE WOMEN?
Luna CAFE
SERVICE DEPOT
FILM
CAMERAS
DEVELOPING
CHICKEN
ESPECIALLY THE WOMEN.
I HAD A WONDERFUL TIME IN THE STATES, COMRADE--
--FROM MY EARLIEST DAYS WORKING MY WAY INTO THE SOCIAL FABRIC...
...TO MY CLIMBING THE LADDER OF LOCAL POLITICS TO THE SENATE.
WHAT IS YOUR ASSIGNMENT?
I'M GOING TO BE A PRESBYTERIAN MINISTER IN SAN FRANCISCO.
YOU'LL LOVE SAN FRANCISCO, SERGEYIVICH...

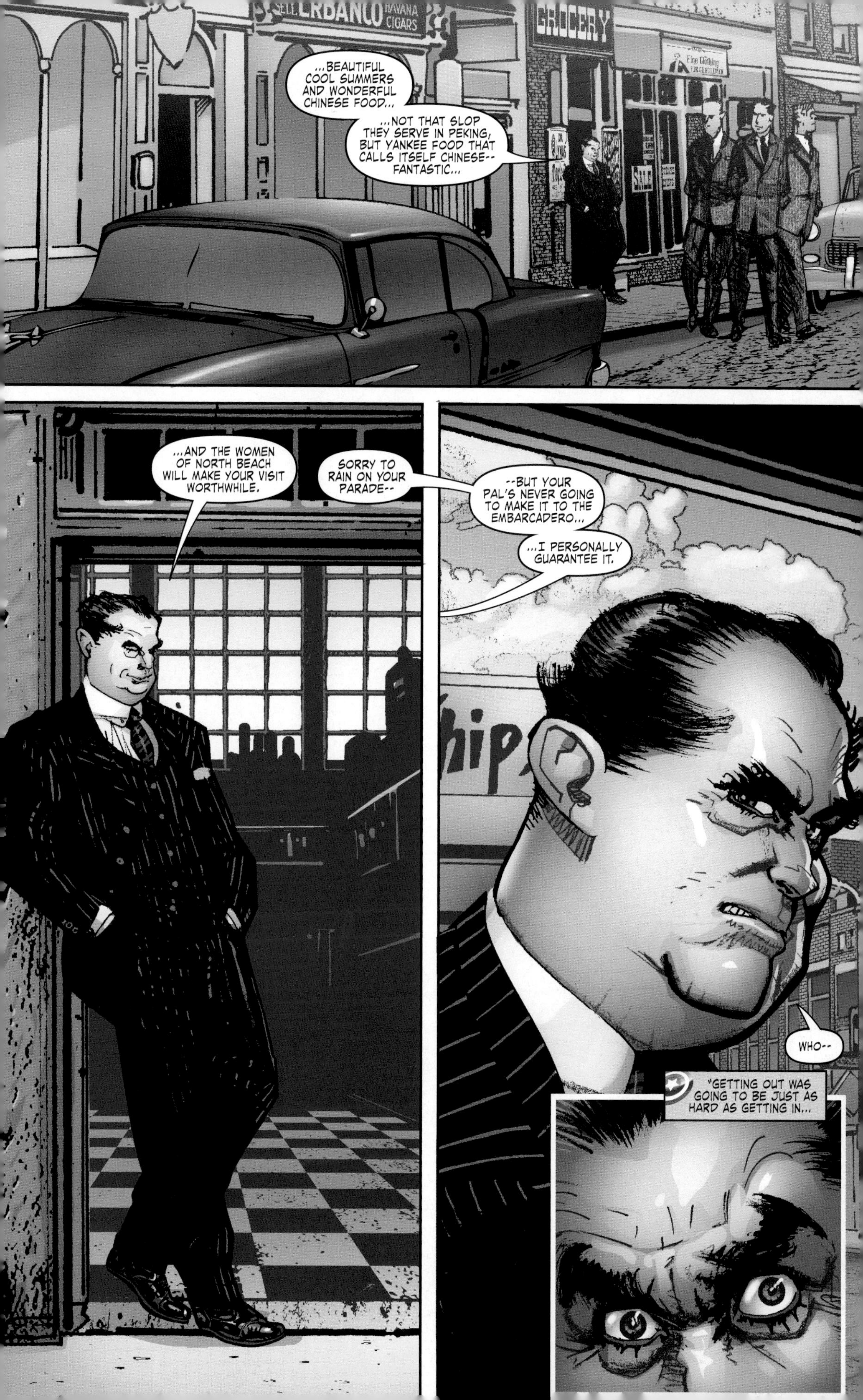
SELL ERBANCO HAVANA CIGARS
GROCERY
...BEAUTIFUL COOL SUMMERS AND WONDERFUL CHINESE FOOD...
...NOT THAT SLOP THEY SERVE IN PEKING, BUT YANKEE FOOD THAT CALLS ITSELF CHINESE-- FANTASTIC...
...AND THE WOMEN OF NORTH BEACH WILL MAKE YOUR VISIT WORTHWHILE.
SORRY TO RAIN ON YOUR PARADE--
--BUT YOUR PAL'S NEVER GOING TO MAKE IT TO THE EMBARCADERO...
...I PERSONALLY GUARANTEE IT.
WHO--
"GETTING OUT WAS GOING TO BE JUST AS HARD AS GETTING IN...

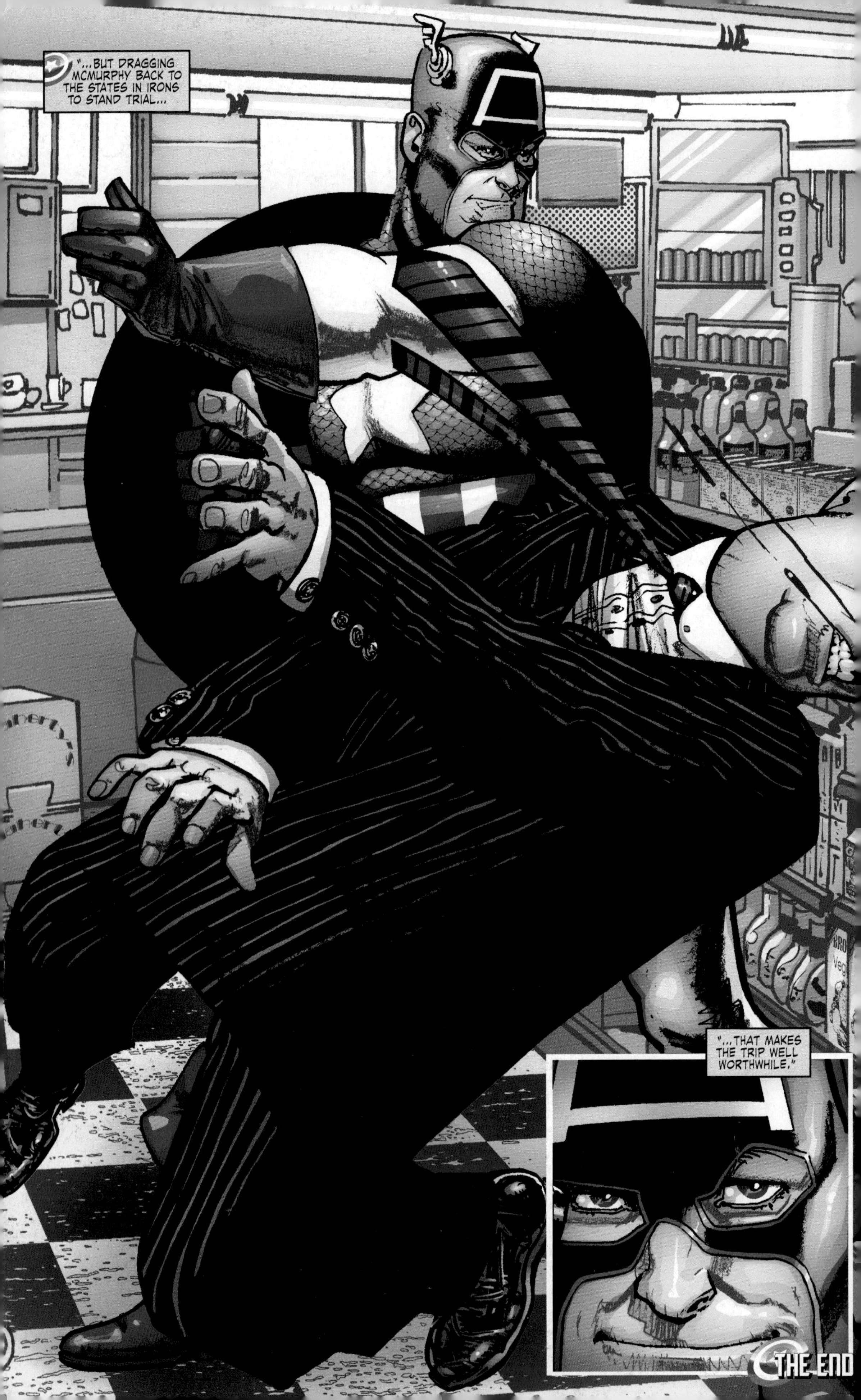
"...BUT DRAGGING MCMURPHY BACK TO THE STATES IN IRONS TO STAND TRIAL...
"...THAT MAKES THE TRIP WELL WORTHWHILE."
THE END

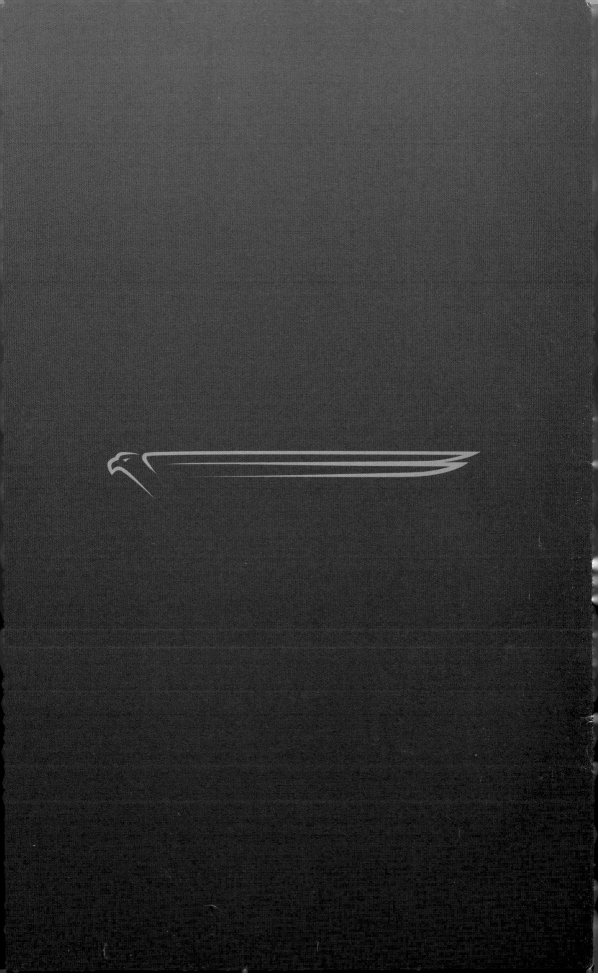

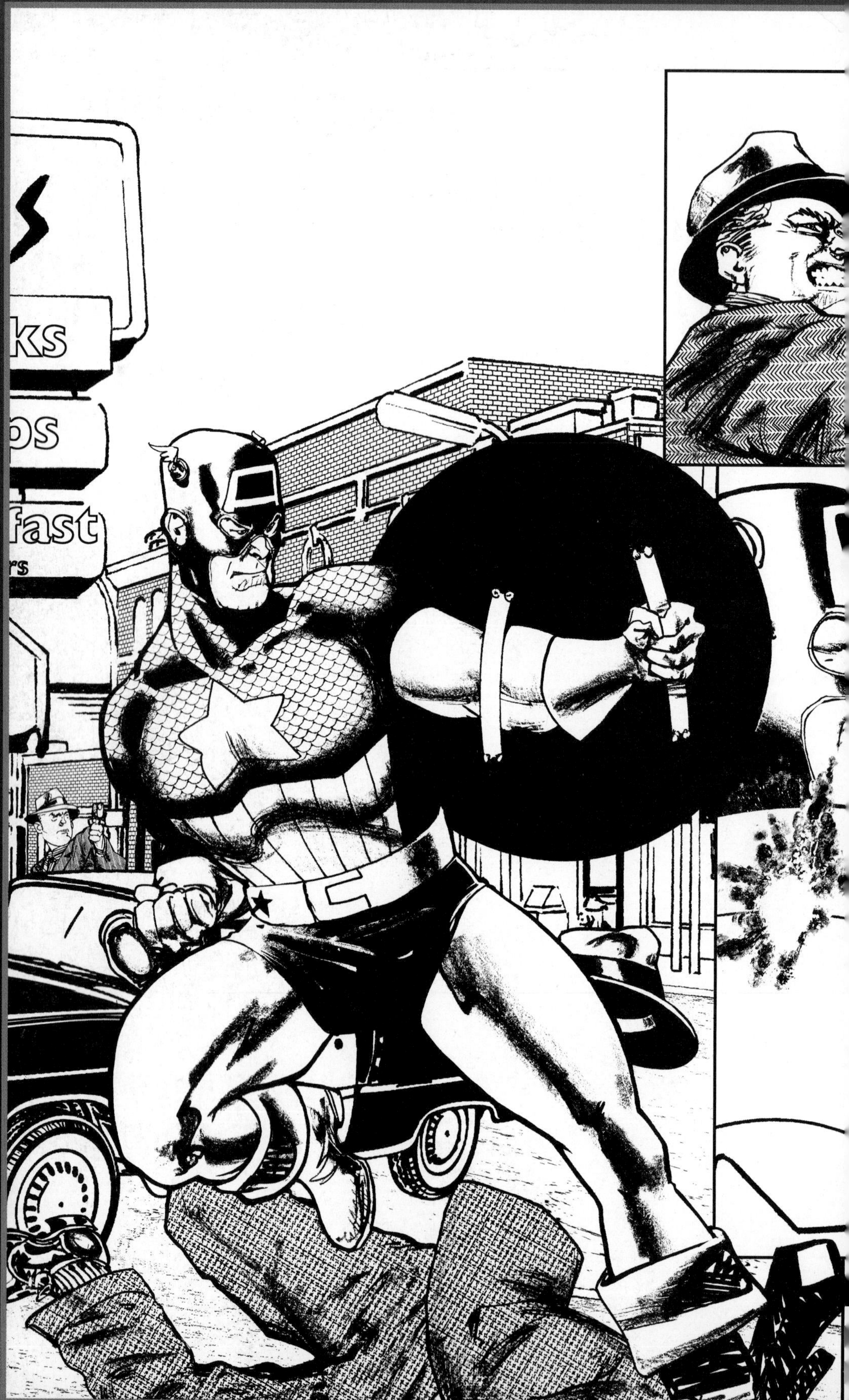

AMERICA FIRST!, PGS. 2-3

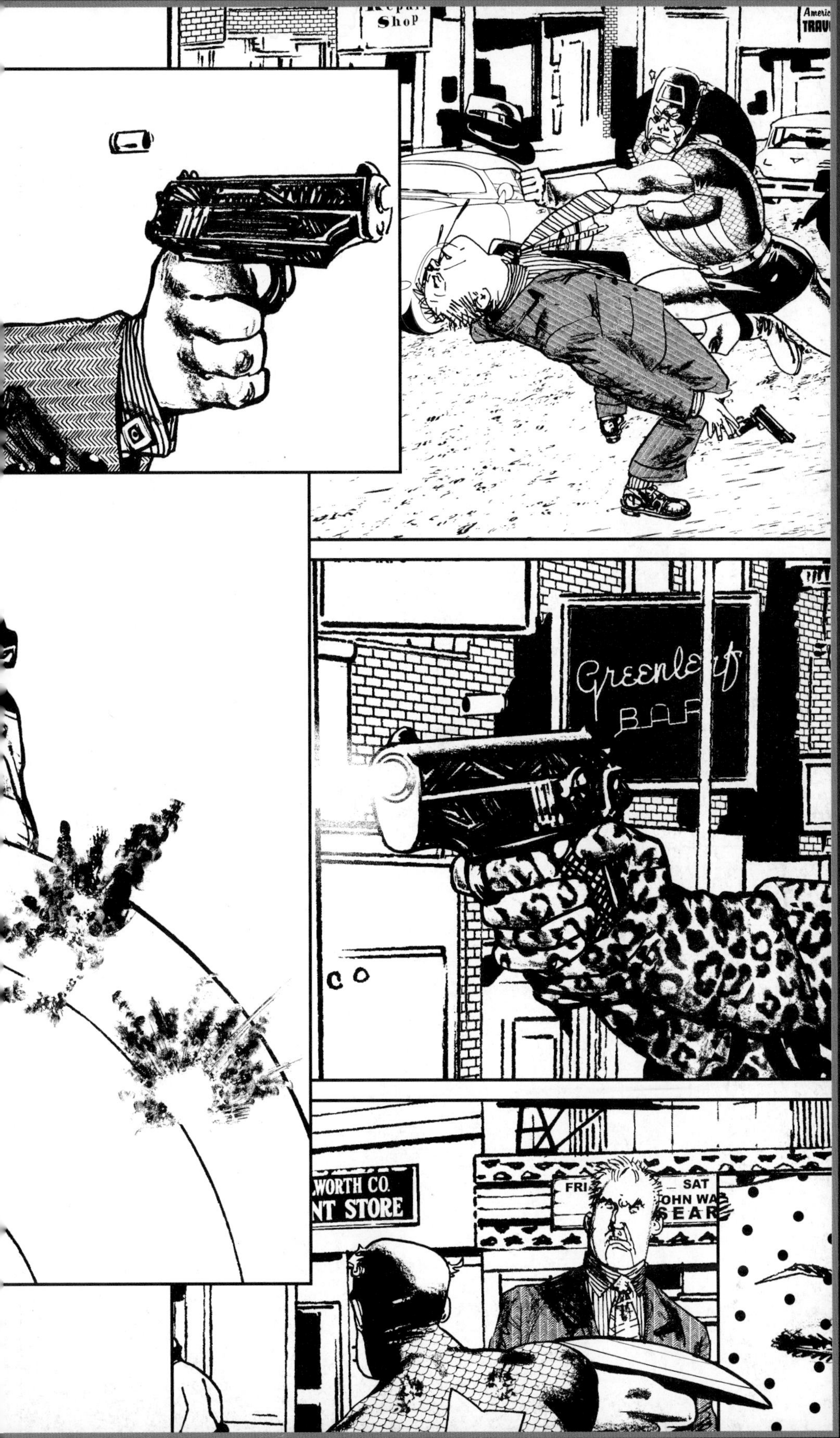
Shop
Greenleaf
BAR
WORTH CO.
NT STORE
FRI
SAT
JOHN WA
SEAR

ART BY HOWARD CHAYKIN

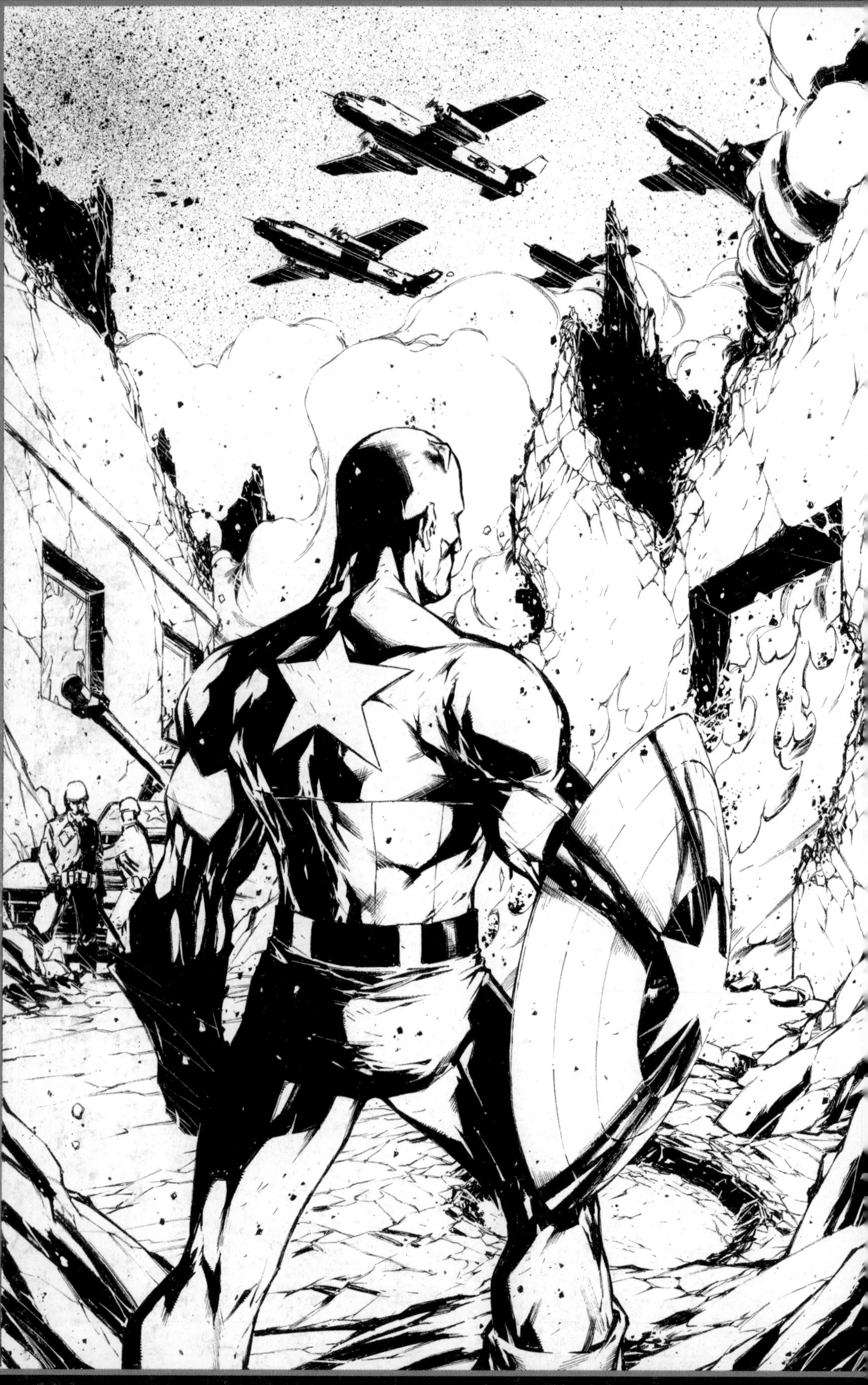

PRISONERS OF DUTY, PG. 32
ART BY AGUSTIN PADILLA